minding the
body

doubleday
new york london
toronto sydney auckland

women writers on body and soul

minding the body

edited by patricia foster

PUBLISHED BY DOUBLEDAY
a division of Bantam Doubleday Dell Publishing Group, Inc.
1540 Broadway, New York, NY 10036

DOUBLEDAY and the portrayal of an anchor with a dolphin are
trademarks of Doubleday, a division of Bantam Doubleday Dell
Publishing Group, Inc.

Additional copyright information can be found on pages 319–21.

Book design by Claire Naylon Vaccaro

Library of Congress Cataloging-in-Publication Data

Minding the body / edited by Patricia Foster.
     p.   cm.
    1. Body, Human, in literature.   2. Soul in literature.
    3. Literature—Women author—History and criticism.   4. Women and
literature.   I. Foster, Patricia.
    PN56.B62M46 1994
    809′.93356—dc20   93-36385
                                            CIP

ISBN 0-385-47022-3

Printed in the United States of America

May 1994

First Edition

10 9 8 7 6 5 4 3 2 1

To my parents, John and Bebe Foster, who encouraged me to question the ways of the world, and in memory of my grandmother, Mary Baxter, who lived in a time and place where women's voices were silenced

acknowledgments

My deepest thanks to the contributors in this book whose stories have added to my insight and wisdom. I am grateful to my agent, Kimberly Witherspoon, and to my editor, Deb Futter, for their enthusiastic support of this book, and to colleagues Jerome Stern, Sheila Taylor, and S. E. Gontarski for their willingness to listen. Special thanks to my husband, David Wilder, for his computer expertise, and to women all over the world who take seriously their own experience of bodily knowing.

contents

contents

minding the
body

patricia   foster

"reading" the body:

an introduction

In the 1930s when my grandmother Mary Baxter, a miner's wife, asked Dr. Elkin for some form of birth control after the exhaustion of twelve pregnancies, he said impatiently, "You're a woman, Mrs. Baxter. That's what women are made for." I imagine my grandmother walking home through the thick heat of a summer afternoon, a slow, defeated walk, dirt clouds rising in eddies from the shuffle of her feet on the dry shale road. Her mind is a small bruised plum, her thoughts flattened, bent, and trampled underfoot. Behind her the mountains are stark, fierce, as gutted as she is, slag heaps of bleak, gray rock. How much she must have wanted relief from pregnancy to have asked the remote Dr. Elkin, a dedicated man, but one not given to intimacy. Although there were abortionists in the community, they were considered bad women, the kind a Christian woman wouldn't consult without acknowledgment of sin. Even the word abortion was taboo. Women used the euphemism "miscarriage" instead and believed that such acts had consequences after death. "At least I won't have any of those little children flying around my head when I die," my grandmother told one of her daughters much later in life while they washed clothes together on her cluttered back porch. I don't know if my grandmother ever considered abortion, but I do know that she survived three more pregnancies despite the high blood pressure that made each pregnancy a risk. Altogether, she was pregnant twelve years and nine months of her life until, like the mines, her body was finally bled dry.

By the time I knew her she looked like an old woman—fat, wrinkled, with ill-fitting false teeth—although she couldn't have been over fifty-four. Her bloated ankles spilled over the tops of her shoes. Her face, no longer oval as it had been in her youth, was as round as the biscuits she made each morning. She'd lost all of her teeth at forty without even an afternoon to mourn the damage. Perhaps she treated herself to ice cream, something soft to cushion the newly bruised gums. Odd, but I don't remember her smile. What I remember are her eyes, their faded blue gaze full of pain and humor, each emotion unresolved to the existence of the other. Her eyes laughed as I toddled up her wooden steps, then quickly turned dull and thick as marbles, incapable of emotion. "Come on in," she said wearily. "Come in now." And yet I wonder what thoughts lived behind those eyes, in the humming coils of her brain. Did she yearn in her thirties to be beautiful, to go dancing, to have men flirt with her? Did she long to have sex free of pregnancy, to quicken to the pulse of passion without the encumbrance of fear? Did she wish for a female physician, someone she could talk to about matters of her body, who would understand the emotional and physical need to restrict pregnancy? Or did she dream about more superfluous things: a beauty parlor with a beautician whose strong, sure fingers could massage her scalp, give her a permanent, a manicure, a facial? What about the longing for a moment alone uninterrupted in the bath, the body submerged, all demands forgotten except the need to breathe? Did she ever have an afternoon free to read? Money to buy a department store dress?

I don't know the answers to such questions. I only knew my grandmother as a large, silent, country woman—a dish towel tucked in her belt—who picked me up and placed me in the warm water of her claw-footed tub. To my child's eyes she seemed plodding and slow, her body a metaphor for exhaustion. Yet when I think of her now I'm always saddened at the anguish she must have suffered in a culture that defined women as breeders, mothers, and subordinate members of families and communities. Like the mountains she lived in, she was worn out by cultural imperatives for service and duty.

In contrast to my grandmother's life in rural Alabama, my own control of my body seems privileged, liberated. Whereas her body was restricted by the prohibitions of her culture and class, I grew up in Middle Class America in an age of optimism—the late 1950s—just before the challenge of the Women's Movement. By the time I was eighteen in 1966, the birth control pill was freely marketed. Women were encouraged to explore their sexuality, to aspire to intellectual independence, to enter professions, even to question the traditional medical authority regarding the female body. When I turned twenty-five, abortion became legal. More and more women rushed to graduate school and forged ahead in their careers. The future was gold-threaded, luminous. The world seemed ours for the taking. And yet just beneath the surface of this surge of freedom, there existed side pockets of perversion, ways of restricting the self that were subtly encouraged within culture. While the majority of women around the country burst out of the old restricting stereotypes, some of us made a U-turn, finding a unique way to subvert ourselves. At age twenty-four, I became anorexic, sliding smoothly into that abyss of illusionary control where thinness is the speedometer of the mind. Like other anorexics I've read about, I gained self-confidence as I lost physical presence in the world, as if self-sacrifice was the heart of self-esteem.

Yet when I look back at my life I see that the seeds of this disease were planted much earlier, fertilized in the narcissism about and fear of the female body I learned growing up. Remembering that time, I write the color of it, the way it's been tattooed in my memory:

I am thirteen. I stand with my sister in profile before our full-length mirror, pants pulled down to our crotches, blouses hiked up, tucked under our bras. This is the posture of our most girlish agenda: comparing ourselves. At first we laugh at each other, making eye contact in the mirror, feeling foolish and silly in this weekly ritual. I see her belly button, a weird outie and the mole just below her flat training brassiere. Then, quickly, we become serious, zooming in, fixating on our own individual bodies, that expanse of white flesh gleaming in the glass.

"Who in the kingdom has the flattest stomach of them all," we chant together in exaggerated heat. We believe we are princesses, martyrs, mistresses of our fate.

"Okay, now go," my sister says, the signal for us to squeeze in our stomachs.

I hold my breath, place both hands flat against my stomach on either side of my navel, pressing into the flesh. The pressure is erotic, a secretive violation, the body sublime as it readjusts itself

to force. My ribs jut forward as my stomach sinks inward, letting
out air until it's almost concave, a hollowed-out sphere. I don't
know where my intestines go, where my liver flees, what can be
left between skin and spine. It's so spare I believe I can push right
through, touching bones, muscles, my structural essence.

"Jesus, that's sick," my sister says, breaking the spell. Her
eyes capture mine in the mirror. It's one of the few contests she
loses, and she's not a good loser. "Really sick," she says.
"You're not normal."

But oddly I feel as if I've been cleansed. She has released her
breath; with her stomach now relaxed, soft and slightly distended,
she seems bloated with life. But I keep holding in, distorting my
body. I'm good at this. Better than Kafka's Hunger Artist, better
than any of my friends. I wonder idly if sacrifice is at the heart of
my life; if so, my body has the proper penitential look.

"You're not normal," she repeats, staring at me with a
frightened, fixated gaze.

My sister was right. I wasn't normal. But I began to see
my abnormality, my obsession with the erasure of my body
as my salvation, the only goal I could achieve in life. It was
as if I were trying to equate the "nothing" I believed existed
on the inside with its outside cover. I wanted literally to
escape into air, to hide in the loneliness of my fear. My
efforts might be described as a criticism of society with the
criticism displaced, walled off from the mind, interned in
the body.

Although the choices in my life seem too peculiar to my
age, education, and class to compare them to those of my
grandmother, we have both felt weighted by the imprint of
culture. Whereas my grandmother's performance required
submission to procreation, my own performance was a sub-

version of that fact. I did not want to be female. I was terrified of the demands on my sex for perfection and conformity. And I chose a typically modern way to subvert them. It seems significant that I grew up saturated with a peculiar strain of the Calvinist tradition, conscious of the mind/body split with a southern bias. Unlike many East Coast women who were told to discount the body in favor of the mind—"pretty is as pretty does"—my community suggested the opposite: Rather than deny the body, it was elevated to the status of a sexual bargaining chip. I understood very early that without the right face and body certain doors remained closed. A woman who didn't strut her stuff merely faded into the background, a wallflower, a dud. She'd better perfect her peach cobbler, make a mean pecan pie; she'd better learn to lie still in the middle of the road and not mind the tramp of feet over her belly.

When I look back at my grandmother's life I become easily upset as if someone has punched a fist in my stomach; the rules of the game were so directly oppressive to women. I can see that she had no way out, no chance to live large, to put on her hat and *go*. Yet it has taken me years to understand how my own culture has constructed myths that have denied women power over and respect for our bodies and have repressed the urge to speak. For a long time I couldn't see this. I thought my failure was simply personal.

Recently I taught a class in Women's Literature at a state university and was amazed at the dissatisfaction young women felt about their bodies. They perceived the imperfections of their physical selves—overweight thighs, small breasts, curved stomachs, sagging buttocks—as a personal rejection and punished themselves accordingly. "I'd rather have five pounds off my thighs than an A in this class," one woman confessed. Others agreed. When given the choice between mental stimulus or physical perfection, most said they would choose physical perfection. Listening to them, I felt as if I'd entered a time warp, had been thrust back into the fifties with only the advantage of women's career goals as a significant difference. How and why have women returned to such a fragile status?

Although I can't answer such questions, I wonder now if the cultural acceptance/rejection of the female body will always be a cyclical drama, women advancing economically only to be restricted psychologically by the cult of physical perfection. When I meet young women today I long to tell them about my grandmother, about myself, to show them how much they have gained. I want to explain how control of one's body cannot be isolated from having a voice in the world. I want to suggest that a muted woman with a perfect body is really no one at all. But I know that most of them will not listen; they're too busy scheduling the next aerobics class, too worried about calories consumed in last night's binge. Like me, it may take them years to realize that the body is not only a sexual statement, but a social one as well, an ongoing story with multiple plots that women individually and collectively must speak.

It was with these thoughts that I began this anthology, a curiosity about the experiences a woman might have with her body. The impulse to do a book was at first a mere grain of sand, a question: If I have struggled all of my life (or so it has seemed to me) to make peace with my body, to achieve some equilibrium between cultural expectation and reality, am I alone, or are there other women who have felt imprisoned by culture, who have found no other way to speak except through the body? I realized that only after much reading and thinking have I been able to let go of my earlier mythology, to open myself to new perceptions. And here was the kernel for this book: Why not ask women writers to explore their relationship to their bodies and the mythologies that have fueled their response so that others might read and reflect?

When I wrote to contributors, I asked that they probe what seemed disturbing or exhilarating in their personal lives, what had snagged, invalidated, buoyed, or surprised them about their bodies. I wanted stories that moved me, narratives in which something in the writer's life was at stake, narratives that questioned our society's mandates about the female body. Obviously, such narratives are revealing, troublesome, complex, not easily written. And yet the essays I read for this book were like touching litmus paper. They reflected much of what I had felt but had been unable to voice.

I knew that I wanted diversity in issues, ethnicity, age, geographical influence, and literary exposure. As a result, the topics my contributors have explored include a wide range of personal experience: infertility, reconstructive surgery, the beauty myth, anorexia, menopause, aging, dieting, the erotics of ethnicity, breast cancer, multiple sclerosis, and the politics of femininity. And yet to label the narratives in such restrictive categories is simplistic, for all of the narratives transcend a single topic as all of the writers transcend a single philosophy, a single self. Joyce Winer's essay "The Floating Lightbulb" is as much about the nature of desire as it is about infertility and the process of in vitro fertilization. Judith Hooper's exploration of the psychological and physical aspects of breast cancer in "Beauty Tips for the Dead" speaks not only about strategies of self-preservation, but also questions the way this disease has been perceived by medical publicists and counselors whose job it is to educate and guide women through recovery. Margaret Atwood's tour de force, "The Female Body," re-creates the body's multiple incarnations through wardrobe accessories, decorator objects, Barbie dolls, and advertisements for beer, cars, shaving lotion, cigarettes, you-name-it, but, in doing so, suggests the body's psychological force. Nancy Mairs in "Carnal Acts" eloquently describes the discovery of her writing voice as she discusses the eccentric progression of her multiple sclerosis.

To reveal our fears about the body—aging, eroticism, infertility, beauty—has been difficult for women in our culture because these very fears have often been used against us to deny our rights to visibility. And yet perhaps more unusual for women is the act of celebration and enjoyment of the body in its multiplicitous shapes and conditions, for acceptance of imperfection has been a cultural taboo. Women have been taught to worry about physical perfection and to consider such concerns a necessary stimulus to improvement. "Letting yourself go" for a woman is tantamount to betrayal of a legacy of femininity concerned primarily with pleasing the male gaze. In "A Weight that Women Carry,"

Sallie Tisdale suggests that the "first feeling of liking my body—not being resigned to it or despairing of change, but actually *liking* it—was tentative and guilty and frightening. It was alarming because it was the way I'd felt as a child before the world had interfered."

Pam Houston says, "My legs are strong and beautiful; dancer's legs, my mother's legs: She spent a lifetime developing sinewy, shapely leg muscles, and then gave them, like a promise, to me."

In a reflective moment, Doris Grumbach considers the flaws of her body on her seventieth birthday: "There is nothing lovely about the sight of me. I have been taught that firm and unlined is beautiful. Shall I try to learn to love what I am left with? I wonder. It would be easier to resolve never again to look in a full-length mirror." Yet by her next birthday, she has come to new insights about physical aging: "No longer am I burdened by the weight of my years. I seem to have grown older in the year but more content with whatever age it is I am."

I think this celebration of *what is* rather than *what's desired* is a tribute to women's emerging self-acceptance and respect in the world. Rather than asking "How do I look?" as a question of identity, many of the women in this collection are asking "How have I been taught to see myself?" as a way of critiquing cultural assumptions.

It's true that social interpretations of the female body have often suggested that the body *is* the self. One of my aunts reminded me that in my grandmother's culture, "You got married and you disappeared. You gave up your mind." My grandmother never had a chance to experience equality between the sexes but lived in an era when young women were defined by the purity of their bodies. "Girls were always under scrutiny," my aunt says, "but coincidentally, our morals were suspect." It saddens me that my grandmother never told her daughters that they might be loved and respected by the men they dated, but only that "men will take advantage of you." Perhaps even their own brothers and uncles. Such victim status suggests the battleground of the body for women in earlier times.

Yet in my own life I've seen quite different but equally negative responses to the idea that *body equals self* in the increase in anorexia and bulimia, in unsafe medical practices such as breast implants and crash diets. As Lucy Grealy movingly reflects about the prospect of reconstructive facial surgery after childhood cancer: "I didn't feel I could pass up yet another chance to 'fix' my face, which I confusedly thought concurrent with 'fixing' my self, my soul, my life." Reading this, I can only say "me too, me too." Growing up I thought that enhancing and improving the body was synonymous with elevating the self.

Recently while helping to chaperone a pool party of eight-year-olds, I watched an enthusiastic little boy leap out of the swimming pool and run shrieking around its perimeter, shouting "Boys rule, girls drool!" He was triumphant with the magnificence of his chant, the ultimate cry of the conqueror. I couldn't help but laugh—and worry—about the intent of his quest: to dominate the girls and take over the pool. Yet I noticed that the girls ignored him and his chant died after two consecutive laps. I'm aware that power—the quest for power, the critique of power, even the loss of power

—is very much a part of this book. Judith Ortiz Cofer speaks about the conflict of power in the assimilation of the Puerto Rican girl in America: "The hierarchy for popularity (in my high school) was as follows: pretty white girl, pretty Jewish girl, pretty Puerto Rican girl, pretty black girl. Drop the last two categories." In response to a different but equally oppressive hierarchy—the promotion of beauty over health for women—Naomi Wolf speaks against such condescension: "The unquestioned glamorization of breast implants is about women's role in society, just as the unquestioned removal of women's ovaries in the nineteenth century and the unquestioned clitoral excising of women in Muslim countries are examples of medicine serving ideology." Connie Porter in "Beauty and the Beast" questions the perpetuation of destructive stereotypes about black women in comic characters such as Wanda and Sha-Na-Na (played by black men), portraits of dark-skinned, sexually aggressive, ugly women whose desperation is meant to be repulsive. Such characters, Porter says, "feed into a warped internalized view" many black women have of themselves: "What makes us unique is also what makes us ugly, laughable even—lips and noses, hair and butts."

In reflecting on the power structure that often separates mind from body, spirit from matter, and wilderness from domesticity, Native American writer Linda Hogan suggests the need to restore power and integrity to the inner world, to make friends with what is wild: "The body, made of earth's mud and breathed into, is the temple, and we need to learn to worship it as such, to move slowly within it, respecting it, loving it, treating ourselves and all our loved ones with tenderness. And the love for the body and for the earth are the same love."

As feminist theorists said almost two decades ago: We must revision not only our lives but the texts that speak about our lives. Today, hearing our collective voices, voices that are jubilant, critical, inquiring, regretful, I wish I could speak to my grandmother, that I could say "Mary, wake up, listen to the stories we women have to tell." But of course, it's too late. My grandmother will never read this book. What she will do is remain a ticking bomb inside my head, reminding me of all that women in history have been obliged by culture to give up. Yet I'm thankful her memory has inspired me to inquire of myself and others how we women are engendered in culture, how we can better learn to "read" and care for our bodies.

Patricia Foster
Tallahassee, Florida
July 1993

sallie   tisdale

a weight that women carry

the compulsion to diet in a starved culture

I don't know how much I weigh these days, though I can make a good guess. For years I'd known that number, some-times within a quarter pound, known how it changed from day to day and hour to hour. I want to weigh myself now; I lean toward the scale in the next room, imagine standing there, lining up the balance. But I don't do it. Going this long, starting to break the scale's spell—it's like waking up suddenly sober.

By the time I was sixteen years old I had reached my adult height of five feet six inches and weighed 164 pounds. I weighed 164 pounds before and after a healthy pregnancy. I assume I weigh about the same now; nothing significant seems to have happened to my body, this same old body I've had all these years. I usually wear a size 14, a common cloth-ing size for American women. On bad days I think my body looks lumpy and misshapen. On my good days, which are more frequent lately, I think I look plush and strong; I think I look like a lot of women whose bodies and lives I admire.

I'm not sure when the word "fat" first sounded pejorative to me, or when I first applied it to myself. My grandmother was a petite woman, the only one in my family. She stole food from other people's plates, and hid the debris of her own meals so that no one would know how much she ate. My mother was a size 14, like me, all her adult life; we shared clothes. She fretted endlessly over food scales, calorie counters, and diet books. She didn't want to quit smoking because she was afraid she would gain weight, and she worried about her weight until she died of cancer five years ago. Dieting was always in my mother's way, always there in the conversations above my head, the dialogue of stocky women. But I was strong and healthy and didn't pay too much attention to my weight until I was grown.

It probably wouldn't have been possible for me to escape forever. It doesn't matter that whole human epochs have celebrated big men and women, because the brief period in which I live does not; since I was born, even the voluptuous calendar girl has gone. Today's models, the women whose pictures I see constantly, unavoidably, grow more minimal by the day. When I berate myself for not looking like— whomever I think I should look like that day, I don't really care that no one looks like that. I don't care that Michelle Pfeiffer doesn't look like the photographs I see of Michelle Pfeiffer. I want to look—think I should look—like the photographs. I want her little miracles: the makeup artists, photographers, and computer imagers who can add a mole, remove a scar, lift the breasts, widen the eyes, narrow the hips, flatten the curves. The final product is what I see, have seen my whole adult life. And I've seen this: Even when big people become celebrities, their weight is constantly remarked upon and scrutinized; their successes seem always to be *in spite of* their weight. I thought my successes must be too.

I feel myself expand and diminish from day to day, sometimes from hour to hour. If I tell someone my weight, I change in their eyes: I become bigger or smaller, better or worse, depending on what that number, my weight, means to them. I know many men and women, young and old, gay and straight, who look fine, whom I love to see and whose faces and forms I cherish, who despise themselves for their weight. For their ordinary, human bodies. They and I are simply bigger than we think we should be. We always talk about weight in terms of gains and losses, and don't wonder at the strangeness of the words. In trying always to lose weight, we've lost hope of simply being seen for ourselves.

My weight has never actually affected anything—it's never seemed to mean anything one way or the other to how I lived. Yet for the last ten years I've felt quite bad about it. After a time, the number on the scale became my totem, more important than my experience—it was layered, metaphorical, *metaphysical*, and it had bewitching power. I thought if I could change that number I could change my life.

In my mid-twenties I started secretly taking diet pills. They made me feel strange, half crazed, vaguely nauseated. I lost about twenty-five pounds, dropped two sizes, and bought new clothes. I developed rituals and taboos around food, ate very little, and continued to lose weight. For a long time afterward I thought it only coincidental that with every passing week I also grew more depressed and irritable.

I could recite the details, but they're remarkable only for

being so common. I lost more weight until I was rather thin, and then I gained it all back. It came back slowly, pound by pound, in spite of erratic and melancholy and sometimes frantic dieting, dieting I clung to even though being thin had changed nothing, had meant nothing to my life except that I was thin. Looking back, I remember blinding moments of shame and lightning-bright moments of clear-headedness, which inevitably gave way to rage at the time I'd wasted—rage that eventually would become, once again, self-disgust and the urge to lose weight. So it went, until I weighed exactly what I'd weighed when I began.

I used to be attracted to the sharp angles of the chronic dieter—the caffeine-wild, chain-smoking, skinny women I see sometimes. I considered them a pinnacle not of beauty but of will. Even after I gained back my weight, I wanted to be like that, controlled and persevering, live that underfed life so unlike my own rather sensual and disorderly existence. I felt I should always be dieting, for the dieting of it; dieting had become a rule, a given, a constant. Every ordinary value is distorted in this lens. I felt guilty for not being completely absorbed in my diet, for getting distracted, for not caring enough all the time. The fat person's character flaw is a lack of narcissism. She's let herself go.

So I would begin again—and at first it would all seem so . . . easy. Simple arithmetic. After all, 3,500 calories equal one pound of fat—so the books and articles by the thousands say. I would calculate how long it would take to achieve the magic number on the scale, to succeed, to win.

All past failures were suppressed. If 3,500 calories equal one pound, all I needed to do was cut 3,500 calories out of my intake every week. The first few days of a new diet would be colored with a sense of control—organization and planning, power over the self. Then the basic futile misery took over.

I would weigh myself with foreboding, and my weight would determine how went the rest of my day, my week, my life. When 3,500 calories didn't equal one pound lost after all, I figured it was my body that was flawed, not the theory. One friend, who had tried for years to lose weight following prescribed diets, made what she called "an amazing discovery." The real secret to a diet, she said, was that you had to be willing to be hungry *all the time*. You had to eat even less than the diet allowed.

I believed that being thin would make me happy. Such a pernicious, enduring belief. I lost weight and wasn't happy and saw that elusive happiness disappear in a vanishing point, requiring more—more self-disgust, more of the misery of dieting. Knowing all that I know now about the biology and anthropology of weight, knowing that people naturally come in many shapes and sizes, knowing that diets are bad for me and won't make me thin—sometimes none of this matters. I look in the mirror and think: Who am I kidding? *I've got to do something about myself.* Only then will this vague discontent disappear. Then I'll be loved.

For ages humans believed that the body helped create the personality, from the humors of Galen to W. H. Sheldon's somatotypes. Sheldon distinguished among three templates—endomorph, mesomorph, and ectomorph—and combined them into hundreds of variations with physical, emotional, and psychological characteristics. When I read about weight now, I see the potent shift in the last few decades: The modern culture of dieting is based on the idea that the personality creates the body. Our size must be in some way voluntary, or else it wouldn't be subject to change. A lot of my misery over my weight wasn't about how I looked at all. I was miserable because I believed *I* was bad, not my body. I felt truly reduced then, reduced to being just a body and nothing more.

Fat is perceived as an *act* rather than a thing. It is antisocial, and curable through the application of social controls. Even the feminist revisions of dieting, so powerful in themselves, pick up the theme: the hungry, empty heart; the woman seeking release from sexual assault, or the man from the loss of the mother, through food and fat. Fat is now a symbol not of the personality but of the soul—the cluttered, neurotic, immature soul.

Fat people eat for "mere gratification," I read, as though no one else does. Their weight is *intentioned*, they simply eat "too much," their flesh is lazy flesh. Whenever I went on a diet, eating became cheating. One pretzel was cheating. Two apples instead of one was cheating—a large potato instead of a small, carrots instead of broccoli. It didn't matter which diet I was on; diets have failure built in, failure is in the definition. Every substitution—even carrots for broccoli— was a triumph of desire over will. When I dieted, I didn't feel pious just for sticking to the rules. I felt condemned for the act of eating itself, as though my hunger were never normal. My penance was to not eat at all.

My attitude toward food became quite corrupt. I came, in fact, to subconsciously believe food itself was corrupt. Diet books often distinguish between "real" and "unreal" hunger, so that *correct* eating is hollowed out, unemotional. A friend of mine who thinks of herself as a compulsive eater says she feels bad only when she eats for pleasure. "Why?" I ask, and she says, "Because I'm eating food I don't need." A few years ago I might have admired that. Now I try to imagine a world where we eat only food we need, and it seems inhuman. I imagine a world devoid of holidays and wedding feasts, wakes and reunions, a unique shared joy. "What's wrong with eating a cookie because you like cookies?" I ask her, and she hasn't got an answer. These aren't rational beliefs, any more than the unnecessary pleasure of ice cream is rational. Dieting presumes pleasure to be an insignificant, or at least malleable, human motive.

I felt no joy in being thin—it was just work, something I had to do. But when I began to gain back the weight, I felt despair. I started reading about the "recidivism" of dieting. I wondered if I had myself to blame not only for needing to diet in the first place but for dieting itself, the weight inevitably regained. I joined organized weight-loss programs, spent a lot of money, listened to lectures I didn't believe on quack nutrition, ate awful, processed diet foods. I sat in groups and applauded people who'd lost a half pound, feeling smug because I'd lost a pound and a half. I felt ill much of the time, found exercise increasingly difficult, cried often. And I thought that if I could only lose a little weight, everything would be all right.

When I say to someone "I'm fat," I hear, "Oh, no! You're not *fat!* You're just—" What? Plump? Big-boned?

Rubenesque? I'm just *not thin*. That's crime enough. I began this story by stating my weight. I said it all at once, trying to forget it and take away its power; I said it to be done being scared. Doing so, saying it out loud like that, felt like confessing a mortal sin. I have to bite my tongue not to seek reassurance, not to defend myself, not to plead. I see an old friend for the first time in years, and she comments on how much my fourteen-year-old son looks like me—"except, of course, he's not chubby." "Look who's talking," I reply, through clenched teeth. This pettiness is never far away; concern with my weight evokes the smallest, meanest parts of me. I look at another woman passing on the street and think, At least I'm not *that* fat.

Recently I was talking with a friend who is naturally slender about a mutual acquaintance who is quite large. To my surprise my friend reproached this woman because she had seen her eating a cookie at lunchtime. "How is she going to lose weight that way?" my friend wondered. When you are as fat as our acquaintance is, you are primarily, fundamentally, seen as fat. It is your essential characteristic. There are so many presumptions in my friend's casual, cruel remark. She assumes that this woman should diet all the time—and that she *can*. She pronounces whole categories of food to be denied her. She sees her unwillingness to behave in this externally prescribed way, even for a moment, as an act of rebellion. In his story "A Hunger Artist," Kafka writes that the guards of the fasting man were "usually butchers, strangely enough." Not so strange, I think.

I know that the world, even if it views me as overweight (and I'm not sure it really does), clearly makes a distinction

between me and this very big woman. I would rather stand
with her and not against her, see her for all she is besides fat.
But I know our experiences aren't the same. My thin friend
assumes my fat friend is unhappy because she is fat: Therefore, if she loses weight she will be happy. My fat friend has
a happy marriage and family and a good career, but insofar
as her weight is a source of misery, I think she would be
much happier if she could eat her cookie in peace, if people
would shut up and leave her weight alone. But the world
never lets up when you are her size; she cannot walk to the
bank without risking insult. Her fat is seen as perverse bad
manners. I have no doubt she would be rid of the fat if she
could be. If my left-handedness invited the criticism her
weight does, I would want to cut that hand off.

In these last several years I seem to have had an infinite
number of conversations about dieting. They are really all
the same conversation—weight is lost, then weight is gained
back. This repetition finally began to sink in. Why did everyone sooner or later have the same experience? (My friend
who had learned to be hungry all the time gained back all
the weight she had lost and more, just like the rest of us.)
Was it really our bodies that were flawed? I began reading
the biology of weight more carefully, reading the fine print
in the endless studies. There is, in fact, a preponderance of
evidence disputing our commonly held assumptions about
weight.

The predominant biological myth of weight is that thin
people live longer than fat people. The truth is far more

complicated. (Some deaths of fat people attributed to heart disease seem actually to have been the result of radical dieting.) If health were our real concern, it would be dieting we questioned, not weight. The current ideal of thinness has never been held before, except as a religious ideal; the underfed body is the martyr's body. Even if people can lose weight, maintaining an artificially low weight for any period of time requires a kind of starvation. Lots of people are naturally thin, but for those who are not, dieting is an unnatural act; biology rebels. The metabolism of the hungry body can change inalterably, making it ever harder and harder to stay thin. I think chronic dieting made me gain weight—not only pounds, but fat. This equation seemed so strange at first that I couldn't believe it. But the weight I put back on after losing was much more stubborn than the original weight. I had lost it by taking diet pills and not eating much of anything at all for quite a long time. I haven't touched the pills again, but not eating much of anything no longer works.

When Oprah Winfrey first revealed her lost weight, I didn't envy her. I thought, She's in trouble now. I knew, I was certain, she would gain it back; I believed she was biologically destined to do so. The tabloid headlines blamed it on a cheeseburger or mashed potatoes; they screamed OPRAH PASSES 200 POUNDS, and I cringed at her misery and how the world wouldn't let up, wouldn't leave her alone, wouldn't let her be anything else. How dare the world do this to anyone? I thought, and then realized I did it to myself.

The "Ideal Weight" charts my mother used were at their lowest acceptable-weight ranges in the 1950s, when I was a child. They were based on sketchy and often inaccurate actuarial evidence, using, for the most part, data on northern Europeans and allowing for the most minimal differences in size for a population of less than half a billion people. I never fit those weight charts, I was always just outside the pale. As an adult, when I would join an organized diet program, I accepted their version of my Weight Goal as gospel, knowing it would be virtually impossible to reach. But reach I tried; that's what one does with gospel. Only in the last few years have the weight tables begun to climb back into the world of the average human. The newest ones distinguish by gender, frame, and age. And suddenly I'm not off the charts anymore. I have a place.

A man who is attracted to fat women says, "I actually have less specific physical criteria than most men. I'm attracted to women who weigh 170 or 270 or 370. Most men are only attracted to women who weigh between 100 and 135. So who's got more of a fetish?" We look at fat as a problem of the fat person. Rarely do the tables get turned, rarely do we imagine that it might be the viewer, not the viewed, who is limited. What the hell is wrong with *them*, anyway? Do they believe everything they see on television?

My friend Phil, who is chronically and almost painfully thin, admitted that in his search for a partner he finds himself prejudiced against fat women. He seemed genuinely bewildered by this. I didn't jump to reassure him that such prejudice is hard to resist. What I did was bite my tongue at my urge to be reassured by him, to be told that I, at least, wasn't fat. That over the centuries humans have been inclined to prefer extra flesh rather than the other way around seems unimportant. All we see now tells us otherwise. Why

does my kindhearted friend criticize another woman for eating a cookie when she would never dream of commenting in
such a way on another person's race or sexual orientation or
disability? Deprivation is the dystopian ideal.

My mother called her endless diets "reducing plans."
Reduction, the diminution of women, is the opposite of feminism, as Kim Chernin points out in *The Obsession*. Smallness is what feminism strives against, the smallness that
women confront everywhere. All of women's spaces are
smaller than those of men, often inadequate, without privacy. Furniture designers distinguish between a man's and a
woman's chair, because women don't spread out like men.
(A sprawling woman means only one thing.) Even our
voices are kept down. By embracing dieting I was rejecting a
lot I held dear, and the emotional dissonance that created
just seemed like one more necessary evil.

A fashion magazine recently celebrated the return of the
"well-fed" body; a particular model was said to be "the ar-
chetype of the new womanly woman . . . stately, powerful." She is a size 8. The images of women presented to us,
images claiming so maliciously to be the images of women's
whole lives, are not merely social fictions. They are *absolute*
fictions; they can't exist. How would it feel, I began to wonder, to cultivate my own real womanliness rather than despise it? Because it was my fleshy curves I wanted to be rid
of, after all. I dreamed of having a boy's body, smooth,
hipless, lean. A body rapt with possibility, a receptive body
suspended before the storms of maturity. A dear friend of
mine, nursing her second child, weeps at her newly voluptuous body. She loves her children and hates her own moth-

erliness, wanting to be unripened again, to be a bud and not a flower.

Recently I've started shopping occasionally at stores for "large women," where the smallest size is a 14. In department stores the size 12 and 14 and 16 clothes are kept in a ghetto called the Women's Department. (And who would want that, to be the size of a woman? We all dream of being "juniors" instead.) In the specialty stores the clerks are usually big women and the customers are big too, big like a lot of women in my life—friends, my sister, my mother and aunts. Not long ago I bought a pair of jeans at Lane Bryant and then walked through the mall to the Gap, with its shelves of generic clothing. I flicked through the clearance rack and suddenly remembered the Lane Bryant shopping bag in my hand and its enormous weight, the sheer heaviness of that brand name shouting to the world. The shout is that I've let myself go. I still feel like crying out sometimes: Can't I feel *satisfied?* But I am not supposed to be satisfied, not allowed to be satisfied. My discontent fuels the market; I need to be afraid in order to fully participate.

American culture, which has produced our dieting mania, does more than reward privation and acquisition at the same time: It actually associates them with each other. Read the ads: The virtuous runner's reward is a new pair of $180 running shoes. The fat person is thought to be impulsive, indulgent, but insufficiently or incorrectly greedy, greedy for the wrong thing. The fat person lacks ambition. The young executive is complimented for being "hungry";

he is "starved for success." We are teased with what we will *have* if we are willing to *have not* for a time. A dieting friend, avoiding the food on my table, says, "I'm just dying for a bite of that."

Dieters are the perfect consumers: They never get enough. The dieter wistfully imagines food without substance, food that is not food, that begs the definition of food, because food is the problem. Even the ways we *don't eat* are based in class. The middle class don't eat in support groups. The poor can't afford not to eat at all. The rich hire someone to not eat with them in private. Dieting is an emblem of capitalism. It has a venal heart.

The possibility of living another way, living without dieting, began to take root in my mind a few years ago, and finally my second trip through Weight Watchers ended dieting for me. This last time I just couldn't stand the details, the same kind of details I'd seen and despised in other programs, on other diets: the scent of resignation, the weighing-in by the quarter pound, the before-and-after photographs of group leaders prominently displayed. Jean Nidetch, the founder of Weight Watchers, says, "Most fat people need to be hurt badly before they do something about themselves." She mocks every aspect of our need for food, of a person's sense of entitlement to food, of daring to *eat what we want.* Weight Watchers refuses to release its own weight charts except to say they make no distinction for frame size; neither has the organization ever released statistics on how many people who lose weight on the program eventually gain it back. I hated the endlessness of it, the turning of food into portions and exchanges, everything measured out, permitted, denied. I hated the very idea of "maintenance." Finally I realized I didn't just hate the diet. I was sick of the way I acted on a diet, the way I whined, my niggardly, penny-pinching behavior. What I liked in myself seemed to shrivel and disappear when I dieted. Slowly, slowly I saw these things. I saw that my pain was cut from whole cloth, imaginary, my own invention. I saw how much time I'd spent on something ephemeral, something that simply wasn't important, didn't matter. I saw that the real point of dieting is dieting—to not be done with it, ever.

I looked in the mirror and saw a woman, with flesh, curves, muscles, a few stretch marks, the beginnings of wrinkles, with strength and softness in equal measure. My body is the one part of me that is always, undeniably, here. To like myself means to be, literally, shameless, to be wanton in the pleasures of being inside a body. I feel *loose* this way, a little abandoned, a little dangerous. That first feeling of liking my body—not being resigned to it or despairing of change, but actually *liking* it—was tentative and guilty and frightening. It was alarming, because it was the way I'd felt as a child, before the world had interfered. Because surely I was wrong; I knew, I'd known for so long, that my body wasn't all right this way. I was afraid even to act as though I were all right: I was afraid that by doing so I'd be acting a fool.

For a time I was thin. I remember—and what I remember is nothing special—strain, a kind of hollowness, the same troubles and fears, and no magic. So I imagine losing weight again. If the world applauded, would this comfort me? Or would it only compromise whatever approval the world gives me now? What else will be required of me besides thinness? What will happen to me if I get sick, or lose the use of a limb, or, God forbid, grow old?

By fussing endlessly over my body, I've ceased to inhabit it. I'm trying to reverse this equation now, to trust my body and enter it again with a whole heart. I know more now than I used to about what constitutes "happy" and "unhappy," what the depths and textures of contentment are like. By letting go of dieting, I free up mental and emotional room. I have more space, I can move. The pursuit of another, elusive body, the body someone else says I should have, is a terrible distraction, a sidetracking that might have lasted my whole life long. By letting myself go, I go places.

Each of us in this culture, this twisted, inchoate culture, has to choose between battles: One battle is against the cultural ideal, and the other is against ourselves. I've chosen to stop fighting myself. Maybe I'm tilting at windmills; the cultural ideal is ever-changing, out of my control. It's not a cerebral journey, except insofar as I have to remind myself to stop counting, to stop thinking in terms of numbers. I know, even now that I've quit dieting and eat what I want, how many calories I take in every day. If I eat as I please, I eat a lot one day and very little the next; I skip meals and snack at odd times. My nourishment is good—as far as nutrition is concerned, I'm in much better shape than when I was dieting. I know that the small losses and gains in my weight over a period of time aren't simply related to the number of calories I eat. Someone asked me not long ago how I could possibly know my calorie intake if I'm not dieting (the implication being, perhaps, that I'm dieting secretly). I know because calorie counts and grams of fat and fiber are embedded in me. I have to work to *not* think of them, and I have to learn to not think of them in order to really live without fear.

When I look, *really* look, at the people I see every day on the street, I see a jungle of bodies, a community of women and men growing every which way like lush plants, growing tall and short and slender and round, hairy and hairless, dark and pale and soft and hard and glorious. Do I look around at the multitudes and think all these people— all these people who are like me and not like me, who are various and different—are not loved or lovable? Lately, everyone's body interests me, every body is desirable in some way. I see how muscles and skin shift with movement; I sense a cornucopia of flesh in the world. In the midst of it I am a little capacious and unruly.

I repeat with Walt Whitman, "I dote on myself . . . there is that lot of me, and all so luscious." I'm eating better, exercising more, feeling fine—and then I catch myself thinking *Maybe I'll lose some weight.* But my mood changes or my attention is caught by something else, something deeper, more lingering. Then I can catch a glimpse of myself by accident and think only: That's me. My face, my hips, my hands. Myself.

joyce winer

the floating lightbulb

We want in order to remind ourselves that we are alive. We might want, say, the beaded gypsy skirt pictured in the catalog that came in yesterday's mail. We can imagine ourselves barefoot and tan in this skirt, its shimmering folds clinging to our thighs as we stride along the beach at dusk. We can imagine a life in that skirt. Or we might want the blue suede platform shoes with ankle ties the salesman just set in the window as we passed by. (It's 1970, and the shoes cost $39.) We couldn't articulate exactly why we want those shoes, but the idea of them and the knowledge that we can't afford them are enough to send us home in tears to our new husband. He is a nice enough guy. He wants us happy. He wants us to buy the damn shoes, and we do. A few years later, for reasons that may or may not have to do with the shoes, we want a divorce. We consider ourselves lucky to get out of that marriage with no children, no ties. We grab the shoes on the way out.

Time passes and we want other, more important things. We pursue work that can bring to light some essential part of us. And of course, we want love. Over the years we seek these things outside our bodies and bring them in. If some-one were to ask us, "Do you want children?" we would answer, "Of course, someday." But unlike anything else we want, we know children come from within our bodies. We believe we can trust our bodies to deliver them when we want them. Our very bodies entitle us to them. If a person told us we would never have children, that person would be denying us our entitlement. And we would consider that person a fool. If a doctor told us we were infertile, we would want a child like we want nothing else.

It's 1991 and I'm remarried. Today my husband stays home while I attend the annual birthday party for my friend Sharon's four-year-old twins. The living and dining rooms are overrun with a dozen children galloping, toddling, or crawling through a tangle of toys, streamers, and torn wrapping paper. There are fresh crayon marks and spots of grape juice on the wood floor, and someone has knocked over the spider plant by the window. But none of the adults—including the birthday parents—seem to notice this. In fact, they seem totally unscathed by the chaos as they sit around the table, talking and finishing off the remnants of a half-melted Baskin Robbins ice cream cake while a Bob Dylan tape drones in the background.

As the only nonparent here, I sit and eat cake with them, trying to connect with the conversation. It is normal conversation about jobs, vacations, news of mutual acquaintances. About how the kids have grown. It should be easy enough for me to find an opening, a place where I can slip through this invisible membrane I feel separating me from the rest of them. But I can't.

There is no wanting like infertility. No getting through, around, away from it. It defines me. On any given day I'm an infertile woman who writes, an infertile woman who picks up the dry cleaning, an infertile woman who meets her husband at a restaurant. Today I'm an infertile woman in the midst of all these mothers, and I feel rotten. Not just moodwise. Rotten physically. Rotten as in decayed. Rotten as in "to the core." Somehow I think that if I open my mouth all my rottenness will spew forth like the little girl in *The Exorcist*. So I keep quiet and occupy myself by stealing glances at these other women's bodies as though I might discover some common feature they share and that I lack—a certain curve of the hip, a high instep, a mole—to answer my perpetual question: *Why not me?* But the only feature they seem to have in common with each other is their softly slumped posture, their sweet resignation to the dishevelment of motherhood.

I should have listened when my husband warned me not to accept Sharon's invitation, but this year there was a new twist.

Jesse and Seth have themselves requested my presence. Or at least this is what Sharon told me with a sense of great pride, the subtext of which was that I was to be honored by their emerging recognition that I am as important and constant in their lives as I am in hers. Somehow I doubt this is true. But I couldn't bring myself to disappoint her or the twins or whosever idea it was. Couldn't say no, I hate these parties, hate these people with their kids who make me feel like a dying species. Can't bring myself to answer the woman who finally turns to me, smiles, and asks, "Which one is yours?"

I've sometimes thought my infertility is the price I'm

paying for the failure of my first marriage, or punishment for any number of small and almost-forgotten sins. Like the time in junior high school when my friends and I took turns calling total strangers in the middle of the night, pretending we were alone and in labor, abandoned by our husbands. Then, when our victims offered to call an ambulance or come help us, we'd hang up in a spasm of giggling. Or later in high school when my best friend and I shoplifted barrettes and lipsticks from Woolworth's. As an individual, I wonder: Have I really been so bad? Do I even believe in sin? Is that the problem? As an individual woman, I eventually come slamming up against the cold truth that my infertility is no more and no less than a trade-off. It's simply the price my body is paying for delaying my need for children throughout my most fertile years out of deference to another undeniable need. For the need to have made a life of my own, rather than accept the one prescribed for me by my culture. For my choice to be a writer, and all the time it takes. In other words, the very definition of woman, for me, contains the concept of sacrifice. In an attempt to be helpful, my brother once asked me, "Why are you fighting so hard?" after I'd tried to explain my delayed and sometimes agonized route to the life I knew was right for me. As though I had a choice. As though he himself hadn't needed to struggle for years to attain his life, his career.

Now, sticking out from the debris of wrapping paper, I spot a neck and a tail of the dinosaur pals I bought for the boys. I get down on the floor to rescue them. Even though the dinosaur pals did not go over so well (the boys are much more interested in G.I. Joe and Teenage Mutant Ninja Turtles), I don't want my gifts to be accidentally swept up with the trash. I set the dinosaurs face to face and place their pals, Grok and Urg, on the creatures' backs. As I'm doing this, it occurs to me that perhaps there's something monstrous or defective or absurdly out-of-whack about me that God or Nature has determined to weed from the human race. I'm scheduled for extinction. It's not a comforting thought, but at least it relieves me of some blame.

While I'm thinking about this, one baby boy crawls over and fixes me with his big brown-eyed stare. He's the only child here not walking yet, and I wonder whether he's sad or angry about this. Perhaps he's drawn to me out of his own sense of inadequacy, of separateness from the others. My heart goes out to him. To assure him that I understand, that we are two of a kind and he is not alone, I smile and offer him one of the dinosaur pals. He hesitates a moment before he breaks into a full wail.

Later, driving home, I can still hear his wailing in my ears. I roll up the window, open my mouth, and scream till my throat is raw.

Like many women born after 1945, I remained in charge of my body through my twenties and thirties. Which means that during that time I was either on the pill, or the coil, or the diaphragm. Though I can remember many episodes of depression relating to some failure in my career or my love life or both, my body, in its ability to give, receive, and function sexually, seemed unassailable. I got my period regularly. I never got cramps or *mittelschmertz* or PMS.

As a single woman throughout most of these years, I made good use of the time, body-wise. I had great orgasms, with or without lovers. I kept copies of Anaïs Nin's *Little Birds* and *Erotica* by my bedside. Between lovers, I would lie naked and read late into the night until my eyes burned. With my head full of ripe word images and the juice already puddled at the opening of my vagina, I would dip my fingers into it and up inside. Then I'd draw my fingers out and make myself slick with the wetness until I was conscious of only my clitoris and vagina—of *becoming* only my clitoris and vagina and everything that lived farther inside me that I couldn't see, couldn't touch, but that I could feel as far up as the insides of my nipples and the top of my brain. It was like I'd turned me inside out to reveal—no, to become—my most essential self. And after I came, I would drift into sleep luxuriant in the feeling not of mere sexual release, but of being my most essential female self.

I mention this because, at that time, I used my sexuality with lovers and with myself as rock-bottom proof that my body was okay. It was there to support me and, I expected, would continue to do so when I was ready to charge it with its ultimate task of pregnancy and childbirth. I believe this was based on more than mere vanity and presumptuousness. It was rooted in some female imperative, a sense of entitlement that females are born to. Call it the right to use what you've got. From the time she was three and old enough to differentiate herself as a girl, I observed that my niece was obsessed with having "a baby in her tummy." I understood her feeling exactly. Even though I'm sure I never expressed it with such simple charm as she did, even though I spent years denying its ultimate importance (it's not the right time, he's not the right man), it was there, ticking away.

So was my biological clock.

Some people want a thing so badly, they'll do just about anything for it. I'm told that in California, in order to achieve enlightenment, they'll work themselves into an ecstatic trance and walk barefoot across beds of hot coals. I bring this up because of two coincidences. First, the doctor my husband and I chose to help us get pregnant practiced in California.

Unlike other doctors we'd seen, he was not at all deterred by my forty-three years. We made four trips totaling sixteen thousand miles to be treated by him.

The second coincidence occurred at our initial visit. The doctor was explaining to us that women who become pregnant through his treatment are given intramuscular injections of the hormone progesterone to support the pregnancy for the first hundred days. I took a sharp breath as though I could already feel the pain. He nodded, then shrugged his shoulders apologetically. "I know," he said, "but we do what works." He glanced down at my entire medical history on the desk in front of him. Then he looked back at us. "I think you women would sit on hot coals if you had to," he said.

There is an old saying: You can't be a little bit pregnant. This is not true. Pregnancy is something that happens by degrees. I know because I've seen it with my own eyes.

My husband and I are in the procedure room next to the gamete lab. The doctor has just walked in and knocked on the small window adjoining the two rooms. A moment later the *in vitro* technologist, the "keeper of gametes" who presided over our conception, opens the window. Ironically, her name is Mary. Mary turns on a TV monitor. We stare at the monitor as she adjusts the focus on the globular translucent mass. "There's one of them," the doctor says. "Two cells here, two behind."

We are staring at the beginning of life. Mary smiles.

"Four cells, that's good," she says. She refocuses the microscope and the two cells in front seem to dissolve. We are moving through them and into the two cells attached behind. Mary tells us that every day the number of cells will double, that a week from now this embryo will consist of a hundred cells, will send out a snaillike foot, and—if conditions are hospitable—will anchor itself to my uterus. She focuses again and we go back and forth, back and forth like space travelers through the transparent membranes of the embryo. I hold my breath. I am both thrilled and terrified. Already I imagine hundreds, thousands, billions of cells marshaled together in the forms of arms, legs, a face. I want to do something to help it, to protect it. But now Mary moves the microscope to show us the other five embryos that will also be transferred to my uterus, maximizing the odds of success. Also maximizing the odds of twins. Triplets. More? Crazed by our successful fertilization, I allow myself to visualize a whole family delivered at once.

But *whoa,* I'm getting ahead of myself. Even with all these gorgeous embryos inside me, the likelihood of just one of them implanting is low—about one chance in four. This is what the doctor tells us as I lie on the table, my feet in the stirrups, a sheet draped across my knees. His attitude is hopeful, but realistic. All I can see of him is the top of his head as he goes on to talk about one of his patients who is a former country music singer. He likes country music. It doesn't seem at all odd that while my husband sits beside me, I'm feeling the doctor's hands between my legs, feeling the speculum slide in, widening me. Maybe the reason it doesn't seem odd is that I'm too preoccupied with worry that the doctor isn't concentrating on what he's doing. He might drop the petri dish. (Contrary to the common vernacular, "test tube" babies would be more accurately labeled "petri dish" babies.) Or maybe the embryos will get stuck on their way through the slim catheter I feel moving up inside me now.

When the procedure is done, I can't help asking "Are they really in there?" The doctor looks slightly amused and tells me he understands my question. He says he's pleased, everything's gone well, and now all we have to do is keep our fingers crossed. A hopeful but realistic answer. While I remain on my back with my knees raised and my fingers crossed (where I'll be for the next three hours), he gives us instructions. No sex, no alcohol, no aspirin, no strenuous exercise. In two weeks we'll know if I'm pregnant. In four weeks, if we're lucky, we'll see the heart flutter on the ultrasound screen. His last bit of medical advice is to wish us luck. I watch him and my husband shake hands like men who have just struck a deal. Then the doctor leaves. As the door closes behind him, I shiver. I have six embryos inside

me. I am more pregnant than I've ever been. And yet I'm
still just a little bit pregnant.

My husband believes in magic, but I don't. He argues it's
the illusion that makes good magic, while I counter that if
any illusion is involved, it can't really be magic. Give me
the ten plagues on Egypt or the parting of the Red Sea.
Something that's so grand it's beyond human capability to
figure out or explain. Something that's close to God—that's
my kind of magic.

But when my husband reads that Blackstone the magician is in town, he buys tickets. Blackstone is the creator of
the famous "Floating Lightbulb" trick. On the night before
my pregnancy test, we go. My husband squeezes my hand as
we watch the lightbulb rise from Blackstone's palm and
hover in the semidarkness above his head. Suddenly it lights
up. I have to admit I'm kind of impressed, even though I
reason that so far the trick is probably more a feat of engineering than real magic in my book. I lean over and whisper
to my husband that there must be wires supporting the bulb,
a battery in its base. "That's the whole point," he whispers
back. "You think that's what it is. But can you ever be sure?"
I gaze upward into the light grids above the stage, straining
to glimpse the slender filaments, the point of attachment.
But then something strange happens. The bulb begins to
move away from Blackstone, toward the audience. It floats
slowly through the air in our direction and stops almost
above our heads.

In the week or so since we returned from California I've

been trying not to think about embryos. But watching *them* hover in the dark atmosphere of the theater, my mind is suddenly flooded by the memory of our embryos suspended as if by magic on the monitor screen. I envision them now, their own timeless light pulsing through the darkness of my body's vast universe. They are the oldest travelers on the oldest journey, bearing their own lives inexorably forward, unmoored, seeking home. And now I remember that yesterday morning as I showered, I felt an odd sensation in my breasts—a charge, an urgency I've never felt before. Looking up, I'm breathless, beyond explanation, amazed at the brilliance of Blackstone's lightbulb. No longer floating free, it seems fixed, burning brightly in the darkness. It's enough to hope.

Two days later when the nurse calls to tell me I'm pregnant, I have to call her back twice to ask whether she's sure there isn't some mix-up. Has she got the right patient? The right test results? The first time she is amused; the second, annoyed. *I'm pregnant.* I repeat the words to myself like a mantra at least a dozen times a day as though the words themselves are the secret to keeping this pregnancy going. As though I must repent for my lack of belief. I believe. I don't believe. It's a miracle. It's a trick.

The magician's assistant keeps smiling as the magician cuts her body in two. Though I know it's all illusion, I still marvel that she does not visibly shrink from the sword. That she seems to feel no pain. I think about her twice a day when my husband gives me an injection to trick my body into staying pregnant. The needle is one and a half inches of 22 gauge steel, attached to the head of a 30 cc syringe. What this means is that it is long enough to pierce through the fat layer of my hip into my gluteal muscle, where it deposits a dose of progesterone suspended in sesame oil.

My husband makes the magic sign with his fingers down my back to the bottom of my spine, then traces a triangle outward toward my hip. He does this to calm both of us, as well as to outline from memory the area the nurse showed him. Often I can feel the tension through his fingers; he wants to do this right, but he doesn't want to hurt me. He's nervous about hitting an artery, a major nerve. I try to guide him by finding a spot that isn't already bruised or sore. I show him where it hurts less, farther out on my hip. But he says there's more blood there when he withdraws the needle. And sometimes—before he has a chance to press down with the alcohol pad, a bead of progesterone leaks out too. He can't stand to see the blood and the medicine coming out of me. Finally we agree on a site. I feel the prick of the needle, then the dull burning of the thick medicine forcing its way slowly down the muscle toward my thigh. It doesn't hurt, I tell myself. I'm the magician's assistant.

A few weeks later I go to the bookstore. But I don't head for literature, as I've always done before. I go straight for the pregnancy and childbirth section. I feel proud, temporarily reentitled. I take a book from the shelf and scan the table of contents, hoping that the salesgirl behind the counter will notice and think, *She is pregnant.* I can almost hear her thinking this. I need to hear her think it. It is not enough that the results of two blood tests have confirmed my pregnancy. I need her affirmation. I'm wondering whether women who get pregnant by screwing ever feel this way, when it suddenly occurs to me that nothing about me has really changed. Today I'm an infertile woman in a bookstore trying to purchase belief in my own power from a girl young enough to be my daughter. It's pathetic how I want her to envy me. Envy what? She's daydreaming, secure in her fantasies, in her chosen method of birth control.

If she even noticed me, what would she see? A petite green-eyed woman with short, pixie-ish hair, blessed by the seeming agelessness (sorry, my view, not hers) of my generation. But of course she would instantly recognize what sets us apart and what I can deny as long as I don't bring my face too close to the mirror—the slightly coarse quality of my skin, not yet lined, I think, but somehow bordered, delineated by my forty-four years—as opposed to her own untextured complexion. If she knew what I'd been through in order to conceive, she would probably be disgusted. I'm too old for this, an intruder on her sexual territory. A woman around my age whom I recently met has two sons: one twenty-three, the other barely five. She told me that when at the age of seventeen her older son found out his mother was pregnant, he was embarrassed to the point of outrage. He wouldn't look her in the eye. He refused to bring his friends over. "He couldn't deal with my sexuality," the woman explained. He drove his car through her garden.

At best, the salesgirl would pity me. I force myself to look through the book in my hands. Maybe I'll buy it. It contains lots of illustrations. Here's one of the penis piercing the vagina. The sperm piercing the ovum. The chorionic root of the embryo piercing the endometrium. Finally, gloriously, the pregnant woman, pierced by her man, enjoys sex. I stare longest at this illustration. The woman is kneeling astride her "partner" (the term *husband* is far too presumptive for this author). The man's hands rest on the woman's enormous belly. The caption describes this as one of the preferred positions for pregnant sex. As if to confirm the truth of this, both "partners" have ecstatic expressions on their faces. Briefly, absurdly, I wonder what Jesse Helms would think about the illustration. But it's drawn with such delicate strokes. It exudes tender love.

Suddenly I know what the salesgirl is daydreaming about. She is in love. Not the polite, careful make-room-for-baby love depicted in the book, but the kind that made Marlon Brando roar his lungs out as the Metro roared above him in *The Last Tango in Paris*. On her break, the salesgirl will leave the bookstore, meet her boyfriend and lift her skirt for him in some bare walkup apartment. She won't give a thought to getting pregnant as she wiggles on the floor beneath his tongue, his fingers, his prick. She'll throw herself into it and she will feel loved to the bone.

I feel my face go hot. I want to fuck. We haven't done it for a month, and in this moment I want it more than anything—want it wild, want it almost more than I want this baby. But we're following doctor's orders. We can't do it until after we have seen the heart flutter on the ultrasound scheduled two days from now. Don't ask why. The reasons given to us seemed to be based more on caution and superstition than on medical fact. But I can respect that, even from a doctor. Especially from a doctor. I like a doctor who admits that biology is as much witchcraft as it is science. *Wrap an onion in a wet rag and bury it six inches belowground on a night when the moon is full.* That was what one of my college roommates told me she was going to do to bring on a miscarriage, when she thought she was pregnant. I don't know where she got this idea. This was in the days before abortion was legal, when women were likely to believe in anything. Though I never saw her bury the onion, I believe she did it. Three days later, she miscarried.

The heat that's started low in my belly spreads to my thighs, moves like fingers beneath my skin upward to my breasts. *Two more days.* I close the book and put it back on the shelf. Then I walk out without a glance in the direction of the salesgirl. On the way home I console myself by remembering a quote from one of the dozens of articles about infertility treatments I've read over the last several years. "If the sixties was all about sex without babies, then the nineties is all about babies without sex."

Another procedure room, another examination table. Another chance to bare my body to a pair of efficient hands while my husband sits beside me. Only this time it's different. This time I don't have to spread my legs, don't even have to undress. The room is dimly lit, could almost be on the verge of romantic if I don't pay attention to the ultrasound console on my right and the huge pressure below from all the water I drank to fill my bladder.

The technician turns on the monitor, then squeezes some cold jelly on the skin below my navel. She takes something that looks like a man's electric shaver and begins sliding it around on my belly. At first I think I'm going to lose control and pee all over the table. But a moment later I forget about my bladder. There on the screen is a dark pod-shaped object undulating beneath the probe pressing against my belly. Attached along the pod's inner wall is a filmy gray amoebic mass, ghostly and primordial, swirling inward toward the center. At the tip of this mass floats a tiny dot of bright pulsing light. I stare. "There's the heartbeat," says the technician. My husband is up now, leaning over me and staring at the monitor. The technician types out something on the keyboard and the letters B-A-B-Y appear on the monitor screen, with an arrow pointing to the swirling floating mass.

I don't feel pregnant—no morning sickness, no dizziness, no exhaustion—but I think pregnant. I start going to bed earlier, take megadoses of vitamins, and eat regularly from the four major food groups. I foreswear alcohol and drink milk like it's going out of style. I have to pee a lot. Late on a Saturday afternoon at the end of my third month, I'm hefting a new gallon jug of milk onto the top shelf of the refrigerator when I feel the small burst, the trickle soaking my underpants. In the bathroom, I sit and look down between my thighs at the blood leaking into the toilet.

This is what it's come to. All the wanting, all the waiting, and my body is once again asserting itself, rejecting all
my efforts in a steady bright red stream. I scream. I hate my
body. I want to grab it and shake it into submission. I want
to punish it by lashing myself upside down to the wall until
the bleeding stops. But all I can do is try to staunch the flow
with a wad of toilet paper.

I stumble to bed, lie down and call the doctor. No, I'm
not having pain or cramps, I tell him. No, there's really
nothing to be done, he tells me. No, a miscarriage in progress can't be stopped. If it's a miscarriage. Pregnant women
bleed for all kinds of reasons. And no matter what it is,
it's not because of anything I've done, he tries to assure
me.

But I know better. I'm not just any bleeding pregnant
woman. I'm an infertile bleeding pregnant woman. And
now I have a strange and horrifying new thought. It's no
longer just me. At three months, the fetus already has little
hands that can grasp, a mouth that opens and closes and
swallows and even hiccups. Lying there with pillows stuffed
under my hips to stop the flow of blood, I picture my baby
luminous, lit mysteriously from within like the floating
lightbulb, its little hands opening and closing helplessly as it
feels itself dragged downward and out of me until its light
goes out. Once I could occupy myself with idle, inconse-
quential musings about the reasons for my infertility while I
lay plans to overcome it. But no matter what the cause, I
can no longer blame the consequences of my infertility on
either dumb luck or the inexorable movement of some di-
vine plan. I've tricked my body, and my body does not like

it. It's letting me know that whether this baby lives or dies, from now on I'm no longer the betrayed. I'm the betrayer.

March 17 of this year offers not just one but two time-honored excuses for Chicagoans to palsy their brains with alcohol. It's St. Patrick's Day. Coincidentally, it's also the day of the presidential primary. I haven't touched a drop of liquor, but today I'm allowing myself to get high on the blue sky and prematurely springlike air. And the fact that I am four months pregnant. The bleeding has stopped. This time the ultrasound showed us more than we had anticipated—a full frontal view, eye sockets, cheekbones, belly, spinal column. A hand moving, touching the mouth. Heartbeat.

I let the breeze play with my unbuttoned raincoat as I walk to my voting place. Just as I arrive, my neighbors Mike and Nora bustle out the door. Mike is a retired cop. He and Nora are both Irish, decked in green on this day of the Saint. They are all smiles as we greet each other. Mike especially seems happy to see me. Is it my imagination, or is he standing a little close? He's standing too close, invading my space. I nervously pull my coat closed around me as he stares into my face, the whites of his blue eyes webbed with threadlike veins. Finally he asks me whether there's something I want to tell him. "Oh, Mike," Nora protests, tugging at his arm.

I've barely begun to show—I write off my thickening waist as fat (after all, I am eating more) and conceal it beneath big sloppy sweaters. Neither have I told any of my neighbors. But Mike *knows*. How does he know? I'm speechless with not knowing how to answer him. After a pause I manage to say "Could be."

Mike explains that he'd inherited a gift from his mother (God bless her soul in Heaven) who all her life was able to look any woman in the eyes and tell when her baby was due. I imagine fairies and Leprechauns. Magic. I want to believe him, but don't want to trust putting him to the test.

"August," I say.

Over the next few weeks, I have similar encounters with several other men I know casually. "Congratulations," they say to me with a knowing look, apropos of nothing. What is it with these men? I think about the way my husband looks at me, the way he has developed this habit of patting my stomach for good luck. I stand before the mirror and stare at my face, straining to see what they do: a pregnant woman. To myself I look the same as ever. But what I'm beginning to see is this baby floating inside me in all its brightness and its amazing insistence on survival. When I see it, my happiness is almost too much to bear. I'll be cautious, though. I'm not buying any baby clothes. Not yet. Any moment this could all be over. After all, I'm an infertile woman and none of it could be happening anyway.

mirrors

There was a long period of time, almost a year, during which I never looked in a mirror. It wasn't easy; just as you only notice how often people eat on television when you yourself are on a diet, I'd never suspected just how omnipresent were our own images. I began as an amateur, avoiding merely mirrors, but by the end of the year I found myself with a professional knowledge of the reflected image, its numerous tricks and wiles, how it can spring up at any moment: a glass tabletop, a well-polished door handle, a darkened window, a pair of sunglasses, a restaurant's otherwise magnificent brass-plated coffee machine sitting innocently by the cash register.

I hadn't simply woken up one morning deciding not to look at myself as part of some personal experiment, as my friend Sally had attempted once before me: She'd lasted about three days before finally giving in to the need "to make sure I was still there." For Sally, not looking in the mirror meant enacting a conscious decision against a constant desire that, at the end of her three days, she still was at a loss to define as either solely habit or instinct. For me, however, the act of not looking was insidious. It was nihilistic, an insurgence too chaotic even to know if it was directed at the world or at myself.

At the time I was living alone in Scotland, surviving financially because of my eligibility for the dole, the vernacular for Britain's social security benefits. When I first arrived in Aberdeen I didn't know anyone, had no idea just how I was going to live, yet I went anyway because I'd met a plastic surgeon there who said he could help me. I had been living in London, working temp jobs. Before that I'd been in Berlin, and ostensibly had come to London only to earn money for a few weeks before returning to Germany. Exactly why I had this experience in London I don't know, but in my first week there I received more nasty comments about my face than I had in the past three years of living in Iowa, New York, and Germany. These comments, all from men and all odiously sexual, hurt and disoriented me so much I didn't think twice about a friendly suggestion to go see a plastic surgeon. I'd already had more than a dozen operations in the States, yet my insurance ran out and so did my hope that any real difference could be made. Here, however, was a surgeon who had some new techniques, and here was a government willing to foot the bill: I didn't feel I could pass up yet another chance to "fix" my face, which I confusedly thought concurrent with "fixing" my self, my soul, my life.

Sixteen years earlier, when I was nine and living in America, I came home from school one day with a toothache. Several weeks and misdiagnoses later surgeons removed most of the right side of my jaw as part of an attempt to prevent the cancer they found there from spreading. No one properly explained the operation to me and I awoke in a cocoon of pain that prevented me from moving or speaking. Tubes ran in and out of my body and because I couldn't ask, I made up my own explanations for their existence.

Up until this time I'd been having a great time in the hospital. For starters it was in "The City," a place of traffic and noise and dangers and, best of all, elevators. Never having been in an elevator before, I thrilled not just at the ride itself, but also at the game of nonchalance played out in front of the other elevator-savvy children who stepped on and off without thought.

Second, I was free from school. In theory a school existed on the third floor for children well enough to attend, but my friend Derek and I quickly discovered that the volunteer who came each day after lunch to pick us up was a sucker for a few well-timed groans, and once we learned to play straight man for each other there was little trouble getting out of it. We made sure the nurses kept thinking we had gone off to school, leaving us free for a few brief hours to wander the mazelike halls of the ancient hospital. A favorite spot was the emergency waiting room; they had good magazines and sometimes you got to see someone covered in blood come through the door. Derek tried to convince me that a certain intersection in the subbasement was an ideal place to watch for bodies heading toward the morgue, but the one time we did actually see one get wheeled by beneath its clichéd white sheet, we silently allowed each other to save face by suddenly deciding it was so much more fun to steal get-well cards from the gift shop than hang out in a cold basement. Once we stole the cards we sent them out randomly to other kids on the ward, signing them "Love and

Kisses, Michael Jackson." Our theory was to watch them open up what they would think was a card from a famous star, but no one ever actually fell for it; by then we were well pegged as troublemakers.

There was something else going on too, something I didn't know how to articulate. Adults treated me in a mysterious manner. They asked me to do things: lie still for X rays, not cry for needles, things that, although not easy, never seemed equal to the praise I received in return. Reinforced to me again and again was how I was "a brave girl" for not crying, "a good girl" for not complaining, and soon I began defining myself this way, equating strength with silence.

Then the chemotherapy began. In the early seventies chemo was even cruder than it is now, the basic premise of it to poison the patient right up until the very brink of their own death. Up until this point I almost never cried, almost always received some sort of praise and attention in return for this, got what I considered the better part of the deal. But now, now it was like a practical joke that had gotten out of hand. Chemotherapy was a nightmare and I wanted it to stop, I didn't want to be brave any more. Yet I had so grown used to defining myself as "brave," i.e., silent, that even more terrifying was the thought of losing this sense of myself, certain that if I broke down this would be seen as despicable in the eyes of both my parents and doctors.

Mostly the task of taking me into the city for the injections fell upon my mother, though sometimes my father had to take me. Overwhelmed by the sight of the vomiting and weeping, my father developed the routine of "going to get the car," meaning that he left the office before the actual

injection on the premise that then he could have the car
ready and waiting when it was all over. Ashamed of my
suffering, I felt relief when he was finally out of the room.
When my mother was with me she stayed in the room, yet
this only made the distance even more tangible, an almost
palpable distance built on the intensity of our desperate
longing to be anywhere else, anywhere at all. She explained
that it was wrong to cry before the needle went in; afterward
was one thing, but before, that was mere fear, and hadn't I
already demonstrated my bravery earlier? Every week, every
Friday, or "d-day" as we called it, for two and a half years I
climbed up onto that too-big doctor's table and told myself
not to cry, and every week I failed. The injections were
really two large syringes, filled with chemicals so caustic to
the vein that each had to be administered only very slowly.
The whole process took about four minutes; I had to remain
very still throughout it. Dry retching began in the first fifteen seconds, then the throb behind my eyes gave everything a yellow-green aura, and the bone-deep pain of alter-
nating extreme hot and cold flashes made me tremble, yet
still I had to sit motionless and not move my arm. No one
spoke to me, not the doctor who was a paradigm of the cold-
fish physician, not the nurse who told my mother I reacted
much more violently than many of the other children, and
not my mother, who, surely overwhelmed by the sight of her
child's suffering, thought the best thing to do was remind me
to be brave, to try and not cry. All the while I hated myself
for having wept before the needle went in, convinced that
the nurse and my mother were right, that I was "overdoing
it," that the throwing up was psychosomatic, that my

mother was angry with me for not being good or brave enough. So involved with controlling my guilt and shame, the problem of physical pain seemed easy by comparison.

Yet each week, usually two or three days after the injection, there came the first flicker of feeling better, the always forgotten and gratefully rediscovered understanding that simply to be well in my body was the greatest thing I could ask for. I thought other people felt this gratitude, this appreciation and physical joy all the time, and I felt cheated because I only was able to feel it once a week.

When you are only ten, which is when the chemotherapy began, two and a half years seems like your whole life, yet it did finally end. I remember the last day of chemotherapy very clearly for two reasons: one, because it was the only day on which I succeeded in not crying, and because later, in private, I cried harder than I had in years; I thought now I would no longer be "special," that without the arena of chemotherapy in which to prove myself no one would ever love me, that I would fade unnoticed into the background. This idea about not being different didn't last very long. Before I thought people stared because I was bald. I wore a hat constantly, but this fooled no one, least of all myself.

During this time my mother worked in a nursing home in a Hasidic community. Hasidism dictates that married women cover their hair, and most commonly this is done with a wig. My mother's friends were all too willing to donate their discarded wigs, and soon the house filled with wigs. I never wore one of them, they frightened me even when my mother insisted I looked better in one of the few that actually fit, yet we didn't know how to say no to the

women who kept graciously offering their wigs. The cats
enjoyed sleeping on them and the dogs playing with them,
and we grew used to having to pick a wig up off a chair we
wanted to sit in. It never struck us as odd until one day a
visitor commented wryly as he cleared a chair for himself,
and suddenly a great wave of shame overcame me. I had
nightmares about wigs, felt a flush if I even heard the word,
and one night I put myself out of my misery by getting up
after everyone was asleep, gathering all the wigs except for
one the dogs were fond of and might miss, and which they
had chewed anyway into something other than a wig. I hid
all the rest in an old chest where they weren't found for
almost a year.

But my hair eventually grew in, and it didn't take long
before I understood that I looked different for other reasons.
People stared at me in stores, other children made fun of me
to the point where I came to expect it constantly, wherever
I went. School became a battleground, and I came home at
the end of each day exhausted with the effort of keeping my
body so tense and hard that I was sure anything would
bounce off of it.

I was living in an extreme situation, and because I did
not particularly care for the world I was in, I lived in others,
and because the world I did live in was a dangerous one, I
incorporated this danger into my private life. I saw movies
about and envied Indians, imagined myself one. Walking
down the streets I walked down through the forest, my body
ready for any opportunity to fight or flee one of the big cats I
knew stalked the area. Vietnam and Cambodia were other
places I walked through frequently, daily even as I made my

way down the school hall, knowing a landmine or a sniper might give themselves away at any moment with the subtle, soft metal clicks I'd read about in the books I took from the library. When faced with a landmine, a mere insult about my face seemed a frivolous thing.

In the early years, when I was still on the chemo, I lived in worse places than Cambodia. Because I knew it was somehow inappropriate, I read only in secret Primo Levi, Eli Weisel, every book by a survivor I could find by myself without resorting to asking the librarian for. Auschwitz, Birkenau: I felt the senseless blows of the Capos and somehow knew that because at any moment we might be called upon to live for a week on one loaf of bread and some water called soup, the peanut butter sandwich I found on my plate was nothing less than a miracle, an utter and sheer miracle capable of making me literally weep with joy.

I decided I wanted to become a "deep" person. I wasn't exactly sure what this would entail, but I believed that if I could just find the right philosophy, think the right thoughts, my suffering would end. To try to understand the world I was in, I undertook to find out what was "real," and quickly began seeing reality as existing in the lowest common denominator, that suffering was the one and only dependable thing. But rather than spend all of my time despairing, though certainly I did a plenty of that, I developed a form of defensive egomania: I felt I was the only one walking about in the world who understood what was really important. I looked upon people complaining about the most mundane things—nothing on TV, traffic jams, the price of new clothes—and felt both joy because I knew how unimportant those things really were and unenlightened feelings of superiority because other people didn't. Because I lived a fantasy life in which I had to be thankful for each cold, blanketless night I survived on the cramped wooden bunks, chemotherapy—the nausea, pain, and deep despair it brought—was a breeze, a stroll through the country in comparison. I was often miserable, but I knew that to feel warm instead of cold was its own kind of joy, that to eat was a reenactment of the grace of some god whom I could only dimly define, and that simply to be alive was a rare, ephemeral miracle. It was like reliving The Fall a dozen times a day: I was given these moments of grace and insight, only to be invariably followed by a clumsy tumble into narcissism.

As I got older, as I became a teenager, I began to feel very isolated. My nonidentical twin sister started going out with boys, and I started, my most tragic mistake of all, to listen to and believe the taunts thrown at me daily by the very boys she and the other girls were interested in. I was a dog, a monster, the ugliest girl they had ever seen. Of all the remarks the most damaging wasn't even directed at me, but was really an insult to Jerry, a boy I never saw because every day, between fourth and fifth periods when I was cornered by this particular group, I was too ashamed to lift my eyes off the floor. "Hey, look, it's Jerry's girlfriend," they yelled when they saw me, and I felt such shame, knowing that this was the deepest insult they could throw at Jerry.

I became interested in horses and got a job at a run-down local stable. Having those horses to go to each day after school saved my life; I spent all of my time either with them or thinking about them. To keep myself thinking ob-

jectively I became an obsessive reader and an obsessive television watcher, anything to keep me away from the subjec-
tive. I convinced myself I was smarter than everyone else,
that only I knew what mattered, what was important, but by
the time I was sixteen this wasn't true, not by a longshot.
Completely and utterly repressed, I was convinced that I
never wanted a boyfriend, not ever, and wasn't it conve-
nient for me, a blessing I even thought, that none would
ever want me. I told myself I was free to concentrate on the
"true reality" of life, whatever that was. My sister and her
friends put on blue eye shadow, blow-dried their hair, and
went to spend interminable hours in the local mall, and I
looked down on them for this, knew they were misleading
themselves and being overoccupied with the "mere surface"
of living. I had thought like this when I was younger, but
now it was different, now my philosophy was haunted by
desires so frightening I was unable to even admit they existed.

It wasn't until I was in college that I finally allowed that
maybe, just maybe, it might be nice to have a boyfriend. As
a person I had, as they say, blossomed in college. I went to a
small, liberal, predominantly female school and suddenly,
after years of alienation in high school, discovered that
there were other people I could enjoy talking to, people who
thought me intelligent and talented. I was, however, still
operating on the assumption that no one, not ever, would be
physically attracted to me, and in a curious way this shaped
my personality. I became forthright and honest and secure
in the way only the truly self-confident are, those who do
not expect to be rejected, and those like me, who do not

even dare to ask and so also expect no rejection. I had come to know myself as a person, but it would be graduate school before I was literally, physically able to use my name and the word woman in the same sentence.

Throughout all of this I was undergoing reconstructive surgery in an attempt to rebuild my jaw. It started when I was fifteen, several years after the chemo ended. I had known for years I would have operations to fix my face, and sometimes at night I fantasized about how good my life would finally be then. One day I got a clue that maybe it would not be so easy. At fourteen I went first to an older plastic surgeon who explained the process of pedestals to me, and told me it would take ten years to fix my face. Ten years? Why even bother? I thought. I'll be ancient by then. I went to the library and looked up the pedestals he talked about. There were gruesome pictures of people with grotesque tubes of their own skin growing out of their bodies, tubes of skin that were harvested like some kind of crop and then rearranged in ways with results that did not look at all normal or acceptable to my eye. But then I met a younger surgeon, a man who was working on a new way of grafting that did not involve pedestals, and I became more hopeful and once again began awaiting the fixing of my face, of the day when I would be whole, content, loved.

Long-term plastic surgery is not like the movies. There is no one single operation that will change everything, and there is certainly no slow unwrapping of the gauze in order to view the final product. There is always swelling, sometimes grotesque, there are often bruises, and always there are scars. After each operation, too scared to simply go look in the mirror, I developed an oblique method comprised of several stages. First, I tried to catch my reflection in an overhead lamp: The roundness of the metal distorted my image just enough to obscure details and give no true sense of size or proportion. Then I slowly worked my way up to looking at the reflection in someone's eyeglasses, and from there I went to walking as briskly as possible by a mirror, glancing only quickly. I repeated this as many times as it would take me, passing the mirror slightly more slowly each time until finally I was able to stand still and confront myself.

The theory behind most reconstructive surgery is to take large chunks of muscle, skin, and bone and slap them into the roughly appropriate place, then slowly begin to carve this mess into some sort of shape. It involves long, major operations, countless lesser ones, a lot of pain, and many, many years. And also, it does not always work. With my young surgeon in New York, who was becoming not so young with each passing year, I had two or three soft tissue grafts, two skin grafts, a bone graft, and some dozen other operations to "revise" my face, yet when I left graduate school at the age of twenty-five I was still more or less in the same position I had started in: a deep hole in the right side of my face and a rapidly shrinking left side and chin, a result of the radiation I'd had as a child and the stress placed upon it by the other operations. I was caught in a cycle of having a big operation, one that would force me to look monstrous from the swelling for many months, then have the subsequent revision operations that improved my looks tremendously, and then slowly, over the period of a few months or a year, watch the graft reabsorb back into my body, slowly shrink down and leave me with nothing but the scarred donor site the graft had originally come from.

I had little or no conception of how I appeared to other people. As a child, Halloween was my favorite holiday because I could put on a mask and walk among the blessed for a few brief, sweet hours. Such freedom I felt, walking down the street, my face hidden: Through the imperfect oval holes I could peer out at other faces, masked or painted or not, and see on those faces nothing but the normal faces of childhood looking back at me, faces I mistakenly thought were the faces everyone else but me saw all the time, faces that were simply curious and ready for fun, not the faces I usually braced myself for, the cruel, lonely, vicious ones I spent every day other than Halloween waiting to round each corner. As I breathed in the condensed, plastic air I somehow thought that I was breathing in normality, that this joy and weightlessness were what the world was comprised of, and it was only my face that kept me from it, my face that was my own mask, my own tangible barrier that kept me from knowing the true identity of the joy I was sure everyone but me lived with intimately. How could they not know it? not know that to be free of the fear of taunts and the burden of knowing no one would ever love you was all anyone could ever ask for? I was a pauper walking for a short while in the clothes of the prince, and when the day ended, I gave up my disguise with dismay.

I also came to love winter, when I could wrap the lower half of my face up in a scarf: I could speak to people and they would have no idea of who and what they were really speaking to. I developed the bad habits of letting my long hair hang in my face, and of always covering my chin and mouth with my hand, hoping it might be seen as a thoughtful, accidental gesture. My one concession to this came in college, when I cut my hair short, very short, in an attempt to stop hiding behind it. It was also an attempt, though I didn't see it as such at the time, to desex myself. I had long, blond hair, and I also had a thin figure. Sometimes, from a distance, men would see the thin blonde and whistle, something I dreaded more than anything else because I knew as they got closer their tone would inevitably change, they would stare openly or, worse, turn away quickly, and by cutting my hair I felt I might possibly avoid this, clear up any misconception anyone, however briefly, might have about my being attractive.

Once in college my patient friends repeated for me endlessly that most of it was in my mind, that, granted, I did not look like everyone else, but that didn't mean I looked bad. I am sure now that they were right some of the time. But with the constant surgery I was in a perpetual state of transfiguration. I rarely looked the same for more than six months at a time. So ashamed of my face, I was unable to even admit that this constant change affected me at all; I let everyone who wanted to know that it was only what was inside that mattered, that I had "grown used to" the surgery, that none of it bothered me at all. Just as I had done in childhood, I pretended nothing was wrong, and this was constantly mistaken by others for bravery. I spent a great deal of time looking in the mirror in private, positioning my head to show off my eyes and nose, which were not just normal, but

quite pretty, as my still-patient friends told me often. But I
could not bring myself to see them for more than a glimmer:
I looked in the mirror and saw not the normal upper half of
my face, but only the disfigured lower half. People still
teased me. Not daily, not like when I was younger, but in
ways that caused me more pain than ever before. Children
stared at me and I learned to cross the street to avoid them;
this bothered me but not as much as the insults I got from
men. They weren't thrown at me because I was disfigured,
they were thrown at me because I was a disfigured woman.

They came from boys, sometimes men, and almost always a group of them. Only two or three times have I ever
been teased by a single person, and I can think of only one
time when I was ever teased by a woman. Had I been a man,
would I have had to walk down the street while a group of
young women followed and denigrated my sexual worth?

Not surprisingly, I viewed sex as my salvation. I was sure
that if only I could get someone to sleep with me it would
mean I wasn't ugly, that I was an attractive person, a lovable
person. It would not be hard to guess where this line of
reasoning led me, which was into the beds of a few manipu-
lative men who liked themselves even less than they liked
me, and I in turn left each short-term affair hating myself,
obscenely sure that if only I had been prettier it would have
worked, he would have loved me and it would have been
like those other love affairs I was certain "normal" women
had all the time. Gradually I became unable to say "I'm
depressed," but could only say "I'm ugly," because the two
had become inextricably linked in my mind. Into that uni-
versal lie, that sad equation of "if only" which we are all

prey to, I was sure that if only I had a normal face, then I would be happy.

What our brains know is one thing, yet what our hearts know is another matter entirely, and when I met this new surgeon in Scotland, I offhandedly explained to my friends back home "why not, it's free, isn't it?" unable to admit that I believed in the fixability of life all over again.

Originally, it was planned I would have something called a tissue expander, followed by a bone graft. A tissue expander is a small balloon placed under the skin and then slowly blown up over the course of several months, the object being to stretch out the skin and create room and cover for the new bone. It is a bizarre, nightmarish thing to do to your face, yet I was hopeful about the end results and I was also able to spend the three months the expansion took in the hospital. I've always felt safe in hospitals: It's the one place I feel justified, sure of myself, free from the need to explain the way I look. For this reason the first tissue expander was bearable, just, and the bone graft that followed it was a success, it did not melt away like the previous ones.

However, the stress put upon my original remaining jaw from the surgery instigated a period of deterioration of that bone, and it became apparent that I was going to need the same operation I'd just had on the right side done to the left. I remember my surgeon telling me this at an outpatient clinic. I planned to be traveling down to London that same night on an overnight train, and I barely made it to the station on time, I was in such a fumbling state of despair. I could not imagine doing it all over again, and just as I had done all my life, I was searching and searching through my

intellect for a way to make it okay, make it bearable, for a
way to do it. I lay awake all night on that train, feeling the
tracks slip quickly and oddly erotic below me, when I remembered an afternoon from my three months in the hospital. Boredom was a big problem those long afternoons, the
days punctuated and landmarked by meals and television
programs. Waiting for the afternoon tea to come, wondering
desperately how I could make time pass, it suddenly occurred
to me I didn't have to make time pass, that it would do it of
its own accord, that I simply had to relax and take no action. Lying on the train, remembering that, I realized I had
no obligation to make my situation okay, that I didn't have
to explain it, understand it, that I could invoke the idea of
negative capability and just simply let it happen. By the
time the train pulled into King's Cross Station, I felt able to
bare it yet again, not entirely sure what other choice I had.

But there was an element I didn't yet know about. I
returned to Scotland to set up a date to go in and have the
tissue expander put in, and was told quite casually that I'd
only be in the hospital three or four days. Wasn't I going to
spend the whole expansion time in the hospital? I asked
almost in a whisper. What's the point of that? You can just
come in every day to the outpatient to have it expanded.
Horrified by this, I was speechless. I would have to live and
move about in the outside world with a giant balloon in my
face? I can't remember what I did for the next few days
before I went into the hospital, but I vaguely remember that
these days involved a great deal of drinking alone in bars
and at home.

I went in and had the operation and, just as they said,

went home at the end of the week. The only thing I can truly say gave me any comfort during the months I lived with my tissue expander was my writing and Kafka. I started a novel and completely absorbed myself in it, writing for hours and hours every day. It was the only way I could walk down the street, to stand the stares I received, to think to myself "I'll bet none of them are writing a novel." It was that strange, old familiar form of egomania, directly related to my dismissive, conceited thoughts of adolescence. As for Kafka, who had always been one of my favorite writers even before the new fashion for him, he helped me in that I felt permission to feel alienated, and to have that alienation be okay, to make it bearable, noble even. In the way living in Cambodia helped me as a child, I walked the streets of my dark little Scottish city by the sea and knew without doubt that I was living in a story Kafka would have been proud to write.

This time period, however, was also the time I stopped looking in the mirror. I simply didn't want to know. Many times before in my life I have been repelled by the mirror, but the repulsion always took the form of a strange, obsessive attraction. Previously I spent many hours looking in the mirror, trying to see what it was that other people were seeing, a purpose I understand now was laughable, as I went to the mirror with an already clearly fixed, negative idea of what people saw. Once I even remember thinking how awful I looked in a mirror I was quickly passing in a shopping center, seeing perfectly all the flaws I knew were there, when I realized with a shock that I wasn't looking in a mirror, that I was looking through into a store at someone who had the same coat and haircut as me, someone who, when I looked closer, looked perfectly fine.

The one good thing about a tissue expander is that you look so bad with it in that no matter what you look like once it's finally removed, it has to be better. I had my bone graft and my fifth soft tissue graft and yes, even I had to admit I looked better. But I didn't look like me. Something was wrong: Was this the face I had waited through twenty years and almost thirty operations for? I somehow just couldn't make what I saw in the mirror correspond to the person I thought I was. It wasn't just that I felt ugly, I simply could not associate the image as belonging to me. My own image was the image of a stranger, and rather than try to understand this, I simply ignored it. I reverted quickly back to my tissue expander mode of not looking in the mirror, and quickly improved it to include not looking at any image of myself. I perfected the technique of brushing my teeth without a mirror, grew my hair in such a way that it would require only a quick simple brush, and wore clothes that were simply and easily put on, no complex layers or lines that might require even the most minor of visual adjustments.

On one level I understood that the image of my face was merely that, an image, a surface that was not directly related to any true, deep definition of the self. But I also knew that it is only through image that we experience and make decisions about the everyday world, and I was not always able to gather the strength to prefer the deeper world over the shallower one. I looked for ways to relate the two, to find a bridge that would allow me access to both, anything no matter how tenuous, rather than ride out the constant swings between peace and anguish. The only direction I had to go in to achieve this was simply to strive for a state of awareness and self-honesty that sometimes, to this day, rewards me and sometimes exhausts me.

Our whole lives are dominated, though it is not always so clearly translatable, with the question "How do I look?" Take all the many nouns in our lives: car; house; job; family; love; friends; and substitute the personal pronoun—it is not that we are all so self-obsessed, it is that all things eventually relate back to ourselves, and it is our own sense of how we appear to the world by which we chart our lives, how we navigate our personalities that would otherwise be adrift in the ocean of other peoples' obsessions.

One particular afternoon I remember very lucidly, an afternoon, toward the end of my yearlong separation from the mirror. I was talking to someone, an attractive man as it happened, and we were having a wonderful, engaging conversation. For some reason it flickered across my mind to wonder what I looked like to him. What was he seeing when he saw me? So many times I've asked this of myself, and always the answer was a bad one, an ugly one. A warm, smart woman, yes, but still, an unattractive one. I sat there in the café and asked myself this old question and, startlingly, for the first time in my life I had no answer readily prepared. I had literally not looked in a mirror for so long that I quite simply had no clue as to what I looked like. I looked at the man as he spoke; my entire life I had been giving my negative image to people, handing it to them and watching the negative way it was reflected back to me. But now, because I had no idea what I was giving him, the only thing I had to judge by was what he was giving me, which, as reluctant as I was to admit it, was positive.

That afternoon in that café I had a moment of the freedom I had been practicing for behind my Halloween mask as a child. But where as a child I expected it to come as a result of gaining something, a new face, it came to me then as the result of shedding something, of shedding my image. I once thought that truth was an eternal, that once you understood something it was with you forever. I know now that this isn't so, that most truths are inherently unretainable, that we have to work hard all our lives to remember the most basic things. Society is no help; the images it gives us again and again want us only to believe that we can most be ourselves by looking like someone else, leaving our own faces behind to turn into ghosts that will inevitably resent us and haunt us. It is no mistake that in movies and literature the dead sometimes know they are dead only after they can no longer see themselves in the mirror. As I sat there feeling the warmth of the cup against my palm this small observation seemed like a great revelation to me, and I wanted to tell the man I was with about it, but he was involved in his own topic and I did not want to interrupt him, so instead I looked with curiosity over to the window behind him, its night-darkened glass reflecting the whole café, to see if I could recognize myself.

d o r i s   g r u m b a c h

coming into
the end zone

It is eccentric and inaccurate to claim that the July of my seventieth birthday is a landmark in my life. Surely there were other important Julys scattered throughout those many years. For instance, that month of my fifth year when I realized I had to go to school in September. It was a prospect I dreaded, believing in my heart that I was already sufficiently educated by Central Park, by the books I had read since I was three and a half, and by the disruptive arrival that year of a baby sister who taught me terrible lessons in displacement, resentment, hatred.

In the July of my twentieth year after I had graduated from college, I ignored the event because I was in a state of shock. During the May that preceded it, my friend and classmate John Ricksecker had jumped from the roof of the School of Commerce at New York University, ending his troubled life and my innocence about how good life was and how hopeful our future. It was May 1939, a few months before Hitler marched into Poland. Was he determined not to be made to go to war? I never knew why he chose to jump, or whether he did. For he said as he was dying that he "climbed up and fell." I have always mourned him and felt responsible for his death. As a woman not liable to be "called up," I was overwhelmed by the unfairness of the draft, making me realize the destructive power of sexual inequities and the injustice of death.

There was the July two years later after I married in May. I began to see that legal unions did not solve problems of inner turmoil and loneliness. . . . The Julys in my middle years after two of my children were born and I began to have serious doubts about my capacity for motherhood. The July I lay in bed in a tiny room in a country house, afflicted with viral pneumonia, listening to the sounds of husband and children downstairs, and wondering how to escape from everything and everyone I knew.

My sixtieth July was terrible. I remembered, as though I had been struck a blow, that my mother had died at fifty-nine. Somehow, to have exceeded her life span by a year seemed to me a terrible betrayal. It was worse than the guilt that choked me later at the thought of having lived eighteen years longer than the little sister I had once hoped would disappear from her crib during the night, stolen by an evil fairy, or dead at the hand of a careless Fräulein.

At sixty-five I must have been resigned to aging and death: I can remember no raging against the night, no anger about what Yeats described as "decrepit age that has been tied to me / As to a dog's tail."

But seventy. This is different. The month at seventy seems disastrous, so without redeeming moments that, in despair, I am taking notes, hoping to find in the recording process a positive value to living so long, some glory to survival, even vainglory if true glory is impossible.

• • •

The terrible Twelfth goes on. I invite Peggy, our host, to share May Sarton's gift of champagne with us. Friends from up the road, Ted Nowick and Bob Taylor, will come too. I suddenly think: A more suitable way to celebrate this dread event would be alone, not in society. I ought to let go of the cheerful illusions of company and surrender to the true state of old age, remembering Virginia Woolf's conviction that at bottom we are all alone and lonely.

The sun moves to the other side of the house. I go in to change to slacks and a shirt with sleeves. In the process I do an unusual thing. I look skeptically, exploringly, at my body in the floor-length mirror. In my young years I remember that I enjoyed feeling the firmness of my arms and legs, neck and fingers, chin and breasts. Once the result of such examinations was less reassuring I stopped doing it. Thereafter, I never resorted to a mirror, believing it would be better not to know the truth about change and decline. In my memory of my body nothing had changed.

Now I look, hard. I see the pull of gravity on the soft tissues of my breasts and buttocks. I see the heavy rings that encircle my neck like Ubangi jewelry. I notice bones that seem to have thinned and shrunk. Muscles appear to be watered down. The walls of my abdomen, like Jericho, have softened and now press outward. There is nothing lovely about the sight of me. I have been taught that firm and unlined is beautiful. Shall I try to learn to love what I am left with? I wonder. It would be easier to resolve never again to look into a full-length mirror.

. . .

October 10. I put down this date, although my habit in journals is not to do so. If something is worth recording, I have always thought, it ought to be general enough to be free of dull, diurnal notation. But this day:

I take the very early Metroliner (six-fifty, an unusual hour for me to take a train) to New York for a meeting of the board of the National Book Critics Circle, a group I have belonged to for many years. A law has been passed that, I believe, makes this the last year of my term, so I am determined to attend every meeting, despite the cost of travel. We are reimbursed only for the two last meetings in the year if we do not serve an institution that pays our way. National Public Radio does not do this for me.

We talk about NBCC business and possible recommendations of books deserving of nomination for an award. It is always fun to meet with other critics and editors. We hole up on the third floor of the Algonquin Hotel, and argue, insult each other pleasantly by challenging the validity of views different from our own, eat a buffet lunch together as we work, and take notes on books of interest we have missed and ought now to read.

At four o'clock the meeting is over. I planned to meet my daughter Jane at the public library for a cocktail party a publisher is giving to celebrate the appearance of the first volume of T. S. Eliot's letters. I need coffee, as I always do between events. Caffeine acts as oil with which to shift gears, sustenance for my flagging spirits. Flagging: Why is that adjective always used for spirits? The *Oxford English*

Dictionary informs me that the usage is three hundred years old and first referred to falling down through feebleness. It then was used for the heart, then the circulation. Matthew Arnold was the first to speak of "a spiritual flagging." I buy coffee in a plastic cup and carry it to the benches on Forty-fourth Street and Sixth Avenue (now called, grandly, the Avenue of the Americas, but in my youth known simply by its common number).

While I drink I watch a street lady eating a hot dog on a roll. Behind her and across Sixth Avenue is the store from which her food must have come. There is a huge sign over the door that reads: AMERICA'S 24 HOUR HOST. STEAK'N'EGGS. She converses with herself between bites in a loud, harsh voice and shakes her head at what I assume are the answers she hears in the air.

Her hair is composed of switches pinned, it seems, to a wig base, and at the top there is a great heavy bun. Her eyebrows are crusted and red, the same flush that covers her light-brown skin and culminates in an angry red ball at the end of her nose. Her body is very thin under a coat composed, like her hair, of parts that are pinned together, but her thinness disappears at her neck, which is full of thick folds of skin, like the necklaces African women wear to elongate their necks for beauty.

She finishes her hot dog, rises slowly, and walks to the trash container near the door to the office building. She moves as if her steps were painful. Her face suggests misery and resentment, as though the weight of all the bunches of cloth tacked on to her were depressing her spirits. She returns to her bench. Her profile is Flemish: the long, thin nose, the chin that falls away, a large black mole on her cheek. She wipes her mouth and her nose on her fingers and then puts them in her mouth. I shudder.

I finish my coffee, stand up to walk to the trash container, and, inexplicably, fall on my face. There is pain in my right ankle that turned and caused me to fall, and greater pain in my left shoulder, so intense that I cannot get up. I lie there, seeing two sets of feet in well-shined shoes pass me by without breaking stride. I try to think of a strategy that will get me on my feet, but without the use of my left arm and hand nothing works.

Then I see a brown hand near my face and hear the street lady's rough voice say: "Here. Hold on here."

I do as she says, doubling my arm against hers and gripping her loose flesh as she holds mine. She pulls hard. I hold tight, I am up, dizzy. She puts her arm around my shoulders and puts me down on the bench. She sits beside me.

The next hour I remember with disbelief. The street lady, Nancy, and I talked about her life while she inquired about my pain and dizziness and advised me about therapy. "Don't get up yet," she said, "or you'll conk out." I think about finding a telephone to tell my daughter, who might still be at work at the Ballet Society, to meet me here instead of in front of the library. Is there a telephone in this office building? I ask her. "Yes," she says, "but whatever you do don't use it. The AT and T puts devils on the wires and they get into your ears." I give up my idea of calling Jane for fear of offending Nancy.

She tells me that she has money to buy a winter coat but storekeepers won't let her try their coats on. Silently I determine to come back and find her, take her to a store for a coat, try it on, and then let her buy it. She tells me she went through high school, took an "industrial" course, got a good job, married, had a daughter who lives now in another part of the city. "She never comes by to see me. I don't know her address."

In the same year she lost both her husband and her job "and never could get ahead again." She shares a room in a welfare hotel on Forty-sixth Street with three other women; they sleep in one bed in shifts. In warm weather she prefers to bed down in the doorways of her street, where the mattress devils can't get at her. And the evil spirits in the pillows. "But I like to have an address. Welfare checks come to me there. So I have some little to get by on," she tells me.

"Winter is worst," she says. "Even now, in October, it's too cold." Her parents came from Haiti, she says with some pride. Her mother told her she never was warm once she got here. "But she saw I went to high, and then she died from her lungs and I married a bum, a devil."

Five-thirty. I get up with difficulty. "I'll walk with you," she says, but I say no. I can make it now. I thank her and give her a hug and tell her I hope to get back to New York soon and then I will look her up at her hotel. She says, "Oh yeah. Watch out for that devil at the front door. She's into voodoo and hexing." I say I will, and limp down Forty-second Street to find an Ace bandage for my swollen ankle.

My daughter takes me to her apartment and then, this morning, to the ballet's orthopedic fellow. He says my shoulder is broken, gives me pills and a sling and a warning to do therapeutic exercises after a week or else suffer permanent stiffness. I resolve to do as he says. But already, in all the night's pain and the next day's scurry to be relieved by a doctor and medicine, the memory of Nancy seems less distinct. Will I look her up if I come to New York at the end of the month for the ballet's trip to Paris? Probably not, knowing how such resolves usually end for me.

Yesterday I sat in the waiting room of the physician who is taking care of my slowly healing shoulder. Around me are elderly patients with casts on ankles, arms, necks, a few in wheelchairs accompanied by exasperated-looking middle-aged children. There is a look I have grown to recognize on the faces of captive offspring caring for parents they have long since ceased to love.

A white-gowned young blond woman with the high, structured hairdo called a beehive appears at the door of the waiting room and says:

"We're ready for you now, Lucy."

One of the annoyed-looking men stands up and wheels "Lucy," who is clearly over eighty, through the door. He is carrying the pink slips that indicate "Lucy" is a first-time patient.

I am in my customary state of fury. How dare that receptionist, surely not more than twenty years old, address the elderly woman by her first name. She has never met her before, knows nothing about her except that she is old, and sick. *Lucy!*

I sit there fuming, remembering a visit I made a few years ago to a nursing home on Wisconsin Avenue in Washington. My acquaintance, a professor emeritus of English literature, had broken her hip, and was here to recuperate. We talked for a while, about the study of Whitman by Paul Zweig she had been reading, about the new Marguerite Yourcenar I was reviewing. Then a young woman in white carrying a pail and mop came into the room, smiled brightly to the professor (whose doctoral work had been done, as I recall, at Oxford), and said:

"Hiya, Eda Lou. Don't mind me. I'll be out in a minute."

Professor Morton shut her eyes.

"That's a good girl. Don't need to watch while I clean."

I said: "She is Dr. Morton, not Eda Lou."

But the young woman, engrossed in her task, which took her through the middle of the professor's room but under nothing, seemed not to hear me. She finished quickly while I sat stonily and the professor lay with her eyes closed as if waiting for the final assault. It came as the young woman went out the door, calling behind her:

"Be good, Eda Lou. See ya tomorra."

Let neither the peculiar quality of anything nor its value escape you. The peculiar quality of this encounter has stayed with me, sensitizing me to the indignity, in hospitals and nursing homes and waiting rooms, of reducing the elderly sick to children, ignoring the respect due their years and accomplishments, and the dignity of their adult titles or married names.

My turn comes for the orthopedic surgeon's attention.

"Ready for you now, Doris," the woman with the bee-hive head says, the same bright smile on her face as the cleaning woman had in the nursing home, displaying her affected charm and familiarity with the patient.

This time I am ready. I do not move.

"Doris?" the young woman says, somewhat louder, suggesting by her tone that I, the only woman left in the room, must be deaf.

Aha, I think, I have her. She comes toward me, by now convinced I must be both deaf and, as we used to say, dumb.

"DORIS?" she shouts almost in my ear.

I stand up, forcing her to step back.

"Miss," I say, "I am Mrs. Grumbach. A stranger to you. About fifty years older than you, I would guess. Don't call me by my first name. What is *your* name, by the way?"

"Susan, er, I mean, Miss Lewis."

To her credit, she blushes furiously, apologizes, and follows me into the doctor's office. "Please be seated, Mrs. Grumbach," she says. "Dr. Moore will be with you in a moment."

"Thank you, Miss Lewis," I say. The war, of course, is still to be waged, but I have won this small skirmish. As it turns out, my shoulder appears to be better. Probably because the weight of my indignation has been lifted from it.

I need new batteries for my hearing aids. They are tiny things, little curls the size of infant snails. Last year I was made to face my loss of hearing, which had clearly begun to annoy Sybil, my dear friend and housemate of many years, and others to whom I turned an almost deaf ear—indeed, ears. But the compelling force to acquire two disturbing, overmagnifying instruments was my realization that the music I heard so clearly in my head (and could remember well although I could not sing it) was not what I was actually hearing, hard as I tried to listen more intently to records and tapes, the radio and television.

When I was young I made sure I heard everything, listened in on every conversation, as though widening my sphere of sound would permit me entry into the larger world. "I have heard that . . ." was a customary start to my sentences, and "Have you heard that . . . ?" another. I relied heavily on what I heard in order to fill my conversation and the page.

Losing a good part of my hearing reduced my avidity. Now I am grateful for hearing less, being left alone with my own silences, away from the raucous world of unnecessary talk, loud machines, the shrill chatter of cicadas in our American elm tree, the unending peeps of baby sparrows that nest under the air conditioner outside the bedroom window, the terrified nightmare screams of the neighbor's child through our wall at three o'clock in the morning.

I acquired hearing aids for use in public places— speeches in large auditoriums, classes, workshops, restaurants, theaters, concerts, and other such places. But I find I wear them less and less, preferring not to listen to the conclusions of most speeches, the sounds of dishes at a distant waiter's station, and the confidences exchanged at a nearby table. At some plays it is a comfortable kind of literary criticism to turn the little buttons off so I hear less of the inane dialogue being exchanged by unbelievable characters in a dull and unconvincing situation.

. . .

July 12, 1989: No longer am I burdened by the weight of my years. My new age today, a year later, does not worry me. Alone for most of the day, until the promise of dinner with friends tonight, I went for a swim in the cove (outside our house in Sargentville, Maine), conquering its temperature (sixty degrees) by thinking it was not as cold as I expected it to be.

Nor is this day as painful as I thought it might be. I seem not to have grown older in the year, but more content with whatever age it is I am. I accept the addition, hardly noticing it. There may well be the enduring challenge of the 365 steps up the face of the Temple of the Dwarf at Chichén Itzá, but the certainty that I shall never again climb them no longer disturbs me.

O'Henry's last words are said to have been: "Turn up the lights—I don't want to go home in the dark." I've begun to try to turn up the lights on what remains of my life.

Waiting on the deck for Ted, Bob, and Peggy to take me to a birthday dinner, I watch my unknown neighbor bring his sailboat to anchor in the cove, furl and wrap his sails, and stand for a moment in the prow looking out to the reach. The light is dimming, the water flattens out from gray to dark-blue calm, the sun sets, coloring the sky like an obscured klieg light, out of my sight.

Now I shall sail by the ash breeze, standing still on the deck.

Living in this beautiful place, I look forward to the soli-

tude it affords me, and to friends to break it with. At the end
of the day I shall welcome them to share my board and my
luck. Who knows, I may be entertaining angels.

Unlike Anna Pavlova, I have no immediate use for a
swan costume. I am ready to begin the end.

margaret atwood

the female body

. . . *entirely devoted to the subject of "The Female
Body." Knowing how well you have written on this
topic . . . this capacious topic . . .*
          —Letter from *Michigan Quarterly Review*

1.

I agree, it's a hot topic. But only one? Look around,
there's a wide range. Take my own, for instance.

I get up in the morning. My topic feels like hell. I sprin-
kle it with water, brush parts of it, rub it with towels, powder
it, add lubricant. I dump in the fuel and away goes my topic,
my topical topic, my controversial topic, my capacious topic,
my limping topic, my nearsighted topic, my topic with back
problems, my badly behaved topic, my vulgar topic, my out-
rageous topic, my aging topic, my topic that is out of the
question and anyway still can't spell, in its oversized coat
and worn winter boots, scuttling along the sidewalk as if it
were flesh and blood, hunting for what's out there, an avo-
cado, an alderman, an adjective, hungry as ever.

2.

The basic Female Body comes with the following accessories: garter belt, panty girdle, crinoline, camisole, bustle, brassiere, stomacher, chemise, virgin zone, spike heels, nose ring, veil, kid gloves, fishnet stockings, fichu, bandeau, Merry Widow, weepers, chokers, barrettes, bangles, beads, lorgnette, feather boa, basic black, compact, Lycra stretch one-piece with modesty panel, designer peignoir, flannel nightie, lace teddy, bed, head.

3.

The Female Body is made of transparent plastic and lights up when you plug it in. You press a button to illuminate the different systems. The circulatory system is red, for the heart and arteries, purple for the veins; the respiratory system is blue; the lymphatic system is yellow; the digestive system is green, with liver and kidneys in aqua. The nerves are done in orange and the brain is pink. The skeleton, as you might expect, is white.

The reproductive system is optional, and can be removed. It comes with or without a miniature embryo. Parental judgment can thereby be exercised. We do not wish to frighten or offend.

4.

He said, I won't have one of those things in the house. It gives a young girl a false notion of beauty, not to mention anatomy. If a real woman was built like that she'd fall on her face.

She said, If we don't let her have one like all the other

girls she'll feel singled out. It'll become an issue. She'll long for one and she'll long to turn into one. Repression breeds sublimation. You know that.

He said, It's not just the pointy plastic tits, it's the wardrobes. The wardrobes and that stupid male doll, what's his name, the one with the underwear glued on.

She said, Better to get it over with when she's young. He said, All right, but don't let me see it.

She came whizzing down the stairs, thrown like a dart. She was stark naked. Her hair had been chopped off, her head was turned back to front, she was missing some toes and she'd been tattooed all over her body with purple ink in a scrollwork design. She hit the potted azalea, trembled there for a moment like a botched angel, and fell.

He said, I guess we're safe.

5.

The Female Body has many uses. It's been used as a door knocker, a bottle opener, as a clock with a ticking belly, as something to hold up lampshades, as a nutcracker, just squeeze the brass legs together and out comes your nut. It bears torches, lifts victorious wreaths, grows copper wings, and raises aloft a ring of neon stars; whole buildings rest on its marble heads.

It sells cars, beer, shaving lotion, cigarettes, hard liquor; it sells diet plans and diamonds, and desire in tiny crystal bottles. Is this the face that launched a thousand products? You bet it is, but don't get any funny big ideas, honey, that smile is a dime a dozen.

It does not merely sell, it is sold. Money flows into this

country or that country, flies in, practically crawls in, suitful after suitful, lured by those hairless preteen legs. Listen, you want to reduce the national debt, don't you? Aren't you patriotic? That's the spirit. That's my girl.

She's a natural resource, a renewable one luckily, because those things wear out so quickly. They don't make 'em like they used to. Shoddy goods.

6.

One and one equals another one. Pleasure in the female is not a requirement. Pair bonding is stronger in geese. We're not talking about love, we're talking about biology. That's how we all got here, daughter.

Snails do it differently. They're hermaphrodites, and work in threes.

7.

Each Female Body contains a female brain. Handy. Makes things work. Stick pins in it and you get amazing results. Old popular songs. Short circuits. Bad dreams.

Anyway: Each of these brains has two halves. They're joined together by a thick cord; neural pathways flow from one to the other, sparkles of electric information washing to and fro. Like light on waves. Like a conversation. How does a woman know? She listens. She listens in.

The male brain, now, that's a different matter. Only a thin connection. Space over here, time over there, music and arithmetic in their own sealed compartments. The right brain doesn't know what the left brain is doing. Good for aiming though, for hitting the target when you pull the trigger. What's the target? Who's the target? Who cares? What matters is hitting it. That's the male brain for you. Objective.

This is why men are so sad, why they feel so cut off, why they think of themselves as orphans cast adrift, footloose and stringless in the deep void. What void? she asks. What are you talking about? The void of the universe, he says, and she says, Oh, and looks out the window and tries to get a handle on it, but it's no use, there's too much going on, too many rustlings in the leaves, too many voices, so she says, Would you like a cheese sandwich, a piece of cake, a cup of tea? And he grinds his teeth because she doesn't understand, and wanders off, not just alone but Alone, lost in the dark, lost in the skull, searching for the other half, the twin who could complete him.

Then it comes to him: He's lost the Female Body! Look, it shines in the gloom, far ahead, a vision of wholeness, ripeness, like a giant melon, like an apple, like a metaphor for "breast" in a bad sex novel; it shines like a balloon, like a foggy noon, a watery moon, shimmering in its egg of light.

Catch it. Put it in a pumpkin, in a high tower, in a compound, in a chamber, in a house, in a room. Quick, stick a leash on it, a lock, a chain, some pain, settle it down, so it can never get away from you again.

thicker than water

When I was lost to girlhood and became a woman, that is, when I moved in with a man and Mom-mom was forced to perceive me as a woman, my grandmother gave up her parental pretenses and grew much more candid about matters she considered private and vulgar—which is to say, female. She told me all the stories I had heard previously from my mother who loved to reveal the indiscretions of those near to her. Anything that I had suspected my mother might have embellished (or *embroidered*—the family word for lying) and made juicier, I have now heard from the heroine herself of these romantic and, yes, often indiscreet adventures. I know that Mom-mom did have an affair with a White Russian. And that, as with all the other men my grandmother loved, her father found him dangerous and boorish, and obviously after her money. It is hard to protect a daughter with a fortune.

"God in heaven," he yelled, a tall man with a deep voice, "the man is a Mohammedan! He could have another wife!"

I have now heard from both my mother and my grandmother about how the chauffeur tried to blackmail my young bold grandmother, and how she tricked him. She had affairs when it was not fashionable to do so; she could not force herself to marry any of the men who were chosen for her—one she jilted on the wedding day and spent months returning outlandishly extravagant gifts. Her wedding gown and trousseau, made to order by Lanvin, were of course not returnable. Donated to charity, together they fetched the highest bid for the Shanghai Smallpox Hospital. After her father died and she realized that she hadn't the courage, quite, to bear children out of wedlock, Mom-mom married my grandfather.

"He was no wiz," she told me once, and from that I was supposed to understand that he was not very skilled as a lover. Briefly, sharply, I was humiliated for Opa, my only gentle parent, and at the red light on the corner of Wilshire and Santa Monica boulevards, I blushed deeply.

My grandmother was far more likely to make such revelations in the car; like me, she was lulled by the movement and the fact that she was in transit: not anywhere for the moment and freed from responsibilities implied by place. Urged toward contemplation, perhaps by the illusion of forward progress, the neat equation of getting from there to here, she thought and spoke her thoughts aloud.

Well, in truth I can't imagine Opa was a "wiz." About matters of sex he remained a true Victorian well into the 1970s, his nineties. While Mom-mom feigned the delicacy she had been taught to display, my grandfather really was a prude, incapable, for instance, of fathoming Mom-mom's pleasure in ribald jokes. Any report that Opa had been a great lover would not have rung true, but still I felt acutely the shame he would have suffered if he knew that his most private and, as he would have considered them, low or animal urges had ever been the topic of discussion with anyone, let alone with me.

My grandmother had not always been so forthcoming about sex. For many years, she assumed a false mantle of modesty and seemliness. As for my mother, when I was a teenager she undressed and bathed in the dark so that not even she could witness her nudity. As I grew older, the woman with whom I showered as a child of four or five became pathologically modest.

She had been lovely nude, when I was little more than an infant. Having concluded, in her fastidiousness, that it was a tidier operation simply to bathe with me than to lean over a churning tub of child and water and soap and toys, my mother would strip with me and wash us together in my grandparents' big stall shower. Today I can tip my head back, eyes closed, and still see her as I did then, a great tall expanse of fair flesh, the dark surprises of pubic hair and nipples—hers always so much redder than mine, livid even —the shower boiling like a cauldron. My mother taught me to like showers so hot that I have never been able to bathe with anyone else without ultimately feeling damp and chilled; no one can bear the bath to be as hot as I want it to be.

My mother would stand like a Madonna, lather and shampoo rolling down her shoulders. I could hardly see her face for the steam, her strong fingers moving over my scalp, our skins turning pink then red in the spray. I hated to get out. A few years later, when I was bathing by myself, and after she had moved out of my grandparents' home for the last time, I remember bath time differently. When I showered, I did so alone, and the water was simply wet, not pleasurable or seductive. Our household frowned upon my tears, and as the tiled shower stall was one place where I could cry undetected, a red wet face being natural after a good washing, I fell into the practice of crying in the shower. Since I hardly ever cried at any other time, I saved all my sorrow for the shower and would begin weeping as I took my clothes off, not for any particular reason I could identify, but out of habit. Even today, when I bend to fill the tub or to adjust the water temperature before turning on the shower, I feel the ache in my throat. I am probably one of very few people who shed Pavlovian tears when the water pours forth from the tap over my hands and feet.

After Mother had left home, and before I was trusted to wash competently by myself, Mom-mom took charge of my baths. They occurred at six o'clock, just before dinner, and they were not particularly recreational. Occasionally, in a rare mood, my grandmother would sit on the side of the tub and tell me a story while I slowly soaked clean. But usually she would instruct me as I learned how to wield a washcloth properly.

The dirtiest place, the spot that had to be washed not once but twice at least, was *down there*, which I immediately understood to mean my genitals. I scrubbed myself; frightened, I washed there four or five times, my fingers never touching the soft folds of flesh, a washcloth doing the job; I scrubbed myself raw. And I never looked to see what I was washing. I didn't want to know what was so mysteriously dirty, what clearly got dirty by itself, of itself. My knees, gray with grime from play, required only one cursory soaping.

Only when I was almost eighteen and considering the curious fact that I had allowed a man to see what I never had did I stand naked in a dorm bathroom one night, behind a locked stall door, and put a mirror between my thighs to look, to find with my eyes the place that I had learned, like the blind, by touch. It was in college that I spent several tearful consultations with a patient doctor who asked me, please, to take only one shower a day, to give up scrubbing *down there*, to stop using feminine hygiene spray. I was so clean, so squeaky clean, that it hurt to walk; intercourse was impossible, nearly, and I had concluded that I had some horrible social disease. Between that fear and my chronic requests for pregnancy tests if my period was even a day late, I visited Student Health often enough that one concerned nurse redirected me to Student Mental Health.

Both things are true. I have never wanted not to be a woman; I have always believed that being a woman was dirty, inherently and unavoidably dirty. Once, many years after the happy hours we spent showering together, my mother told me that there were only two things that smelled like fish, and one of them was fish. I hear those words over and over, the refrain to my period, but not only then; I check during the rest of the month too. At the end of the day I pull down my underpants and cannot drop them into the hamper without smelling the crotch, trying to decide if I should take the extra, second shower. It has been years since I have purchased or used a feminine hygiene spray, but I remember once going home from high school after my third class, because I had forgotten to use that pink aerosol can, the sweet, flowery blast of powder, cold and frosting my pubic hair like a winter beard, dusting the cotton crotch of my underwear. I went through a can every two weeks, wouldn't buy it myself, afraid that a checker might think I was a peculiarly smelly sort of girl.

My grandmother and I had some bitter, if absurd, quarrels in the supermarket. When I was fourteen or so and at the insane height of my self-consciousness, I would not buy certain products. I had the money, could get to a drugstore, but couldn't make myself gather and pay for what I needed: Kotex, Midol, feminine hygiene spray. Anything that indicated that I menstruated or smelled was too humiliating to handle in public. And the size of the Kotex box—too horrible to imagine. I wished I could use tampons, but I was too frightened, and Mom-mom was of the opinion that only fast girls, those who had been penetrated by something other than a sterile plug of cotton, used tampons.

When I finally developed the courage to push that little white applicator inside, to feel my way between my thighs, my grandmother didn't speak to me for days, assuming I had also had the nerve to leap out of virginity, and not only out of the humiliation of wearing a heavy, bloodied napkin strung between my legs by an absurd elastic belt whose clasps pinched my bottom in the back and plucked out hairs from the front. So, at the market, in the aisle marked

"Health Care Products," my grandmother and I waged a desperate war. It was my habit to drop what I wanted into the cart surreptitiously—if one can sneak a two-foot box of Kotex past a spry old woman of substantial stature—and then disappear when it was time to go through the checkout, leaving my grandmother to face the indignity alone.

"Don't you see that it is much more embarrassing for a woman of my age to buy these?" she would say in a loud angry whisper. "I want you in line with me." In response I could only shake my head, tears of embarrassment smarting already in my eyes.

Ironically, the only place in the market where Mom-mom wouldn't pursue me was to the magazine stand where I would publicly page through a copy of *Playgirl*, rendering my grandmother mute with rage—she would not speak to me with that magazine before my face. I was unabashed about looking at pictures of men's penises in public—I had followed Opa to the garden toilet once when I was five, to the pool house where the floors were covered in hemp mats that smelled of chlorine. Frustrated by the gray light through the keyhole, seeing nothing more than a dark mass, ancient and larger than anticipated, I had been looking ever since at men's genitals wherever I could, trying to penetrate some mystery. I could look at *Playgirl*—relishing my grandmother's fury—but could not stand in line and pay for any product that told other people that I was a girl: that I bled and smelled. Later we would meet, Mom-mom and I, at the car as the bagger was lifting our purchases into the trunk, she too livid to speak, and I silent in my triumph.

. . .

I was apprehended late one summer night by the store detective at Barrington's supermarket. It was very hot, still in the nineties at ten o'clock; I was wearing a short tennis dress and sneakers, a cotton cardigan—not an outfit that afforded much place to secrete stolen goods. The detective who took me by the elbow in the parking lot, the Santa Ana wind scattering trash between the cars, was a sober balding sweaty man with yellow teeth. He smiled as he asked me to follow him, and I started to cry, both with fear at the prospect of what I imagined would be a police record, and with humiliation because I had been caught with a box of ten tampons stuffed up my sleeve. When the time had come to pay for them, all the checkers had been men. I had developed the ability to purchase tampons from women—after all, they too secretly bled and smelled—but I could not let a man ring up my Tampax. And so I stole them: It seemed reasonable, I wasn't frightened walking out. After all, I'd been shoplifting for years, nothing expensive and not from good stores, but I was practiced at the art.

Upstairs in a room over the supermarket, the noise of shoppers and cash registers rising distant and dull through the floor, the kindly exasperated manager explained that the store's policy was to involve the police only after a second violation. But, since I was not yet eighteen, whoever was responsible for me would have to come pick me up from the market, they would have to be informed of my transgression. I settled into a sullen miserable heap in a yellow vinyl chair as the manager called my home. I could imagine my grandparents sitting in the living room, watching television, the phone call startling them. I had always been such a very good girl.

No amount of pleading could induce the manager to let me go home alone. I promised that I would never return. I promised that he could arrest me if I so much as stepped through the automatic doors and into the chill wind of air-conditioning. But he was unmoved, and my grandparents soon arrived, in their overcoats, with sleepwear showing underneath. I was sure that I had finished crying until I saw the limp striped flannel legs flopping over my grandfather's gardening shoes, and noticed the frayed lace nightgown collar under Mom-mom's coat. I had sunk into an insulted silence and was glaring blackly at the door, waiting for their arrival; but that pathetic glimpse of their pajamas, the implication of crisis, of their struggling hurriedly into winter coats on a hot summer night, stepping out of slippers and into garden shoes, driving too fast to the store, only blocks from the house: This was too much. And my grandfather's shocked insistence that the store had made a mistake, that I was *incapable of stealing*, foolishly clothed in striped flannel, his red-faced choleric indignation that was sufficient to rupture my hard-won self-containment and unstick my insulted glare from the window.

Fifteen minutes later we were driving home. Mom-mom had not said one word after "What has she done?"; she was always ready to believe the worst of those she loved. So very unlike my grandfather, whose love did not allow for another's frailties. It was for him that I tried never to cry in public, always to uphold the code of stoic dignity. He was shaking his head as Mom-mom drove, apparently unable to fathom such bull-headedness on the part of the store detective who had not ultimately backed down, admitted he had been wrong, had made a mistake, had seen some other girl walk out with a box of tampons.

The lasting fear of that night was not from the sting of humiliation. As I had promised the manager, I never returned to the market, and a blush of shame rose every time I passed the store or even saw a billboard advertising one of their specials. But that was incidental, not so very troubling. What mattered most was that my grandfather refused to know me, refused to know the part of me that was wrong, that would be weak, criminal even. And because I had been caught stealing tampons, a product that was intimately connected to the Undiscussable, I could never go to him and explain my transgression. I was never allowed to have his honest love of my weakness, but only that which disallowed imperfection in his love-object. For I understood that night that my grandfather fully subscribed to the chivalric code; he could have only a reproachless princess.

When we returned to the house—the television still speaking softly into the empty living room, Mom-mom having turned down the sound as she always did when answering the phone—my mother was standing in the hall looking perplexed. She was dressed formally, in a black dress and impossibly high heels, her makeup flawless even after a long evening. She watched as Mom-mom and Opa hung up their overcoats and walked back to the living room in their pajamas. "What happened, where were you? I was frightened," she kept saying. But no one answered her.

beauty tips for the dead

"Can't you cut it out, Doc?"

"I'd have to gut you like a fish."

In *The Shootist*, John Wayne, playing an aging gunfighter with cancer, has this tête-à-tête with his crusty doctor, played by Jimmy Stewart. I happened to catch a few minutes of the film on television shortly after being diagnosed with breast cancer. It occurred to me that I was fortunate to be living in an era when doctors avoid using language such as "gut you like a fish," and instead toss around terms like "five-year survival rates" and "positive axillary nodes," which are not quite so chilling if you don't look closely. I was also grateful that my surgery consisted of a simple lumpectomy and removal of the lymph glands in my armpit, which certainly fell far short of being gutted like a fish, although it robbed me of any possible career I might have had as a centerfold.

I was forty-one years old and way too old for centerfolds, of course, but as a late bloomer and the mother of a three-and-a-half-year-old I still harbored the illusion that I was in the stage of life known as "young motherhood." My idea of a big problem was that my son refused to eat anything but pizza and that I wasn't yet "living off my royalties," which was one of my original purposes for becoming a writer. With the suddenness of a sniper's attack, I woke up to the end of all that. From that moment on, my former life would take on the coloring of a remote and inaccessible state, Eden before the fall, a dimly remembered lost paradise. An anonymous pathologist—for some reason I envision him skimming a travel article in *Medical Economics* before typing up the biopsy report—scrutinized the bits of tissue under the microscope and reported that ten axillary nodes were positive. Translation: ten armpit glands contained cancer. This is what is known in the trade as "poor prognosis breast cancer."

There is a line in a Samuel Beckett novel that equates life to having a tooth filled when you are dying of cancer, and, as it happened, on the day I got my diagnosis I had a dental appointment. Back in college I had underlined the Beckett passage in yellow highlighter, perhaps writing "existential" in the margin next to it. I did not know then that what seemed existential, even surreal, could be utterly real. I considered canceling the dentist, but then thought, Why *not?* Perhaps sitting around in a bland, Muzak-filled space in which the coffee tables are strewn with Whittle publications would be just the antidote for the existential dread that was congealing in my veins. So I went to the dentist and was uncharacteristically nonchalant when the hygienist lectured me about plaque. (I would learn that when you're on chemotherapy you need to take plaque very seriously, but that's another story.)

• • •

The moment you get cancer you are plunged into the medical gulag, a universe as complex and multilayered as Dante's purgatorio, each level with its own special torments. (To your right, ladies and gentlemen, the Realm of the Incurables; through that door wander the Maimed and Mutilated, with their prostheses. . . .) No longer are you a simple civilian. With your first intake form (When was your last menstrual period? Do you drink alcohol? Relatives with cancer?) you are data in a computer, cross-linked to millions of other unfortunate people, destined ineluctably to be a minuscule point on a hundred graphs and shaded tables. You pray you end up in the right part of the graph.

While there is no cure for cancer, as of this writing, there is a surfeit of information. By calling an 800 number one can obtain the entire spectrum of cancer-related pamphlets published by the National Cancer Institute and the American Cancer Society. These range from the mildly disturbing ("Breast Exams: What You Should Know" and "Questions and Answers about Breast Lumps") to the undeniably grave: "Advanced Cancer: Living Each Day." They are illustrated, in the style of elementary-school health textbooks, with drawings of kindly-looking doctors examining X rays, diagrams of axillary lymph nodes that look like pinto beans, women serenely doing breast self-exams.

I used to think that the American Cancer Society was the organization in charge of finding a cure for cancer. Actually, it is the National Cancer Institute, part of the giant, sprawling National Institutes of Health complex in Bethesda, Maryland, that oversees cancer research. The American Cancer Society is the public relations side of the business, a sort of kindly aunt who reminds you to go get a baseline mammogram if you're over thirty-five and nags you for not doing those breast self-exams. Its gentle counseling about the seven warning signs and changes in moles and bowel habits are now part of the collective unconscious, and most of us have probably sent donations to the Society in the names of departed friends.

Lately I've been wondering if my departed friends would appreciate the American Cancer Society's current "LOOK GOOD—FEEL BETTER" campaign. This was developed in March 1989 in partnership with the Cosmetic, Toiletry and Fragrance Association and the National Cosmetology Association as "an opportunity for people undergoing cancer treatment to develop skills to improve their appearance," in the Society's words. Skills covered include using eyebrow pencil when therapy has robbed you of your eyelashes and eyebrows; shopping for and caring for a wig when you're bald; disguising sunken cheeks and bad color with blusher; shopping for a special bathing suit when you're missing a breast. From the hospital walls "LOOK GOOD—FEEL BETTER" signs hover above the emaciated, wheelchair-bound patients with breathing tubes, the woman on a gurney with a black Magic Marker on her forehead, the man without a voice box reading a six-month-old copy of *Newsweek*.

While this information is useful (I myself have found that long, dangly earrings can do a lot to compensate for the lack of a hairdo), it doesn't help much with the real problem —a problem the pamphlets don't really address until we get to "Advanced Cancer: Living Each Day." Does the American Cancer Society imagine that a woman with a deadly disease will really feel a whole lot better once she gets some expert cosmetological advice? It is as if the characters in *The Plague* were handed pamphlets full of tips like "The hot sun in Algeria can be a problem when you're dehydrated." Okay, okay, I know I am being unfair.

The booklets that corresponded to my situation fell somewhere in the middle range of horrors. Among other things, my diagnosis meant I needed chemotherapy, a word that sounds scarcely more pleasant than "gut you like a fish." It is not a word you will ever find on a Hallmark Card or a cruise brochure. It just *sounds* bad. "Chemotherapy and You" contained a list of possible side effects of the most common cancer drugs. Among the symptoms I might experience, I learned, included diarrhea, fever, chills, black, tarry stools, unusual bleeding or bruising, sores in the mouth, darkening of skin and fingernails, hair loss, missed menstrual periods, swelling of the feet or lower legs, etc. And, of course, the two biggies: nausea and fatigue.

> *Cancer cells grow in an uncontrolled manner, and they may break away from their original site and spread to other parts of the body. Anticancer drugs disrupt the cancer cells' ability to grow and multiply.*
> —"CHEMOTHERAPY AND YOU"

Adriamycin (generic name: doxorubicin) is a vivid reddish-orange liquid, which, streaming through the IV tubing, looks something like cherry Kool-Aid. It is the first term in the three-drug cocktail known as "CAF," for Cytoxan, Adriamycin, fluorouracil, which is a standard adjuvant chemotherapy for Stage II breast cancer. (Stage II means that some lymph nodes are involved and/or that the original tumor is between two and five centimeters in diameter.) In a positive-thinking frame of mind one can relate Adriamycin's color to the saffron robes worn by Tibetan Buddhist monks and imagine it transformed into thousands of tiny saffron-robed monks gliding through the bloodstream, chanting "Om mane padme hum" and zapping cancer cells with their *vajras* of incomparable diamond wisdom. Fluorouracil, or 5-FU, as it is known, is colorless. The third member of the cocktail, Cytoxan (generic name: cyclophosphamide), is a member of the charming nitrogen mustard family—as in the poisonous mustard gas used in the trenches during World War I. It is taken in pill form. I took three each night before bed, washed down with a tall glass of water to save my kidneys. These tablets, with their sinister greenish flecks, began to provoke a Pavlovian response in me: I felt queasy as soon as I looked at them.

The intravenous part of my chemotherapy took place two days a month for six months in a comfortable lounge at the doctor's office; with an IV in my vein I sat and read in an armchair within arm's reach of a jar of candy with a drug company's name on it. Here the unthinkable became commonplace, even mundane. The chemo room chitchat ("My blood counts were under a thousand, so I didn't get chemo last week"); the signs reminding you that if you're on 5-FU you need to stay out of the sun; if you're on Cytoxan you need to drink plenty of fluids. And, yes, even the nail-care tips from the Look Good—Feel Better campaign had a reassuring quality, as if having body parts destroyed by poison were no more remarkable than split ends.

At the doctor's office, I noticed, there are two castes of people, those with cancer—the patients—and those without —the doctors, nurses, secretaries, and receptionists. The latter gossip among themselves and treat the patients with the mild contempt reserved for those on the other side of the glass, the diseased ones. What they don't realize is that the glass partition separating us is an illusion. They don't know they are not safe either; that human life is a space shuttle full of Krista McAuliffes. This is what cancer patients know. It is our little secret.

> *The hair follicles of the head and body are made up of cells that grow and divide rapidly, so they can react to some of the anticancer drugs. . . . Severe hair loss can begin within a few days or weeks of treatment. You may notice a greater than normal amount of hair loss when brushing, combing or washing your hair. Loss of hair may stop at severe thinning or may continue to total baldness.*
>
> —"CHEMOTHERAPY AND YOU"

About two or three weeks into chemotherapy, I began to wake up to a tangled wad of hair on my pillow. Hair fell into my plate as I ate. It fell on my clothes, on the floor, on my son's bed when I read him a bedtime story (prompting him to call "Mommy, you forgot your hair!"). It clogged the vacuum cleaner, filled the plastic, handle-tie garbage bags. When the part in my hair became an inch wide, I knew it was time to visit Audrey's Wigs.

Audrey was in her late fifties, I estimated, and sported a

lemon-yellow cascade of hair resembling the hair on a doll I had as a little girl. I don't think it was a wig, but it looked like one. She confided that the bulk of her clients were chemotherapy patients or country-and-western singers. I could tell that she disapproved of me, perhaps because I was not wearing makeup or perhaps because my head was too small for most of her wigs. She produced a longish light-brown wig with a shag cut. When I put it on, I looked like a failed cocktail-lounge act. "Do you have anything else?" I asked. She trotted out some more wigs, *all* of which made me look like a cocktail-lounge singer. Finally we settled on a short curly wig that didn't look anything like me, but did look vaguely human. I bought a couple of terry-cloth tur-bans too. I never wore the wig. I did wear the turbans day in and day out, often coordinating them with my outfits.

> *Some anticancer drugs cause nausea and vomiting because they affect the stomach lining and the part of the brain that controls vomiting.*
> —"CHEMOTHERAPY AND YOU"

Everything I know about nausea comes from the second week of my treatment, hereafter to be known as Nausea Week, or, if I am in an existential, Satrean mood, *La Semaine de la Nausée*. On this particular late August week it was 92 degrees and humid, and somehow the humidity and nausea mingled to form a sort of hideous inner weather front. The physical world, which seems so enthralling to people who make their own fresh pasta and mull over lever-aged buyouts in their Jacuzzis, loses its appeal totally when you are nauseated. My inner being, my soul, screamed, "Beam me up, Scotty!" I considered reading books on astral projection and soul travel—anything—in the hopes of escaping, happily incorporeal, to one of those misty, pastel astral planes you see depicted in Theosophical literature. Then, inexplicably, the nausea passed into mere queasiness.

> *Many people use distraction without realizing it, when they watch television or listen to the radio to take their minds off their worries or discomfort. Any activity that holds your attention can be used for distraction.*
> —"CHEMOTHERAPY AND YOU"

One thing that can distract you from a bad diagnosis, I have found, is a very stupid TV sitcom, preferably with a laugh track. This is not because it truly amuses you—à la Norman Cousins—but because it is so banal it disconnects your anxiety circuits briefly. This is especially useful medicine during the first few days or weeks when you feel like an earthquake victim clawing your way out of the rubble, a Hiroshima survivor wandering dazed and confused in the ruins of what used to be your city. I do not truly mean to compare my situation to that of a Hiroshima victim, of course; this is only a very crude approximation. But one side effect of cancer is an instant, indelible, searing empathy for victims of misfortune everywhere in the world. Flood victims in Bangladesh are truly your brothers and sisters; their pain reaches out to you across the continents. This sometimes makes the eleven o'clock news an impossibility; what is called for (when one is not perusing the Book of Job, always instructive reading for the cancer patient) is something on the order of *Three's Company*.

At times I could not shake the feeling that I was in a made-for-TV movie. I suppose this is a modern form of depersonalization. Not even a real movie, but one of those NBC specials in which some youngish person deals gallantly and, of course, attractively, with a loathsome disease. I found myself inventing witty dialogue and spunky gallows humor for my interludes with doctors and other medical personnel, who are invariably serious. Who did I think I was—Nancy on *Thirtysomething*? I've only watched *Thirtysomething* twice in my life, but I did happen to catch the episode where the Nancy character, stricken with ovarian cancer and a propensity for morbid jokes, is undergoing chemosomething. She does not lose her waist-length blond hair and explains to a friend that she is taking a new hair-loss–prevention drug. She—and her entire cancer-patient support group, for that matter—looked as if they had just come from an aerobics class. I couldn't help comparing their good color, stylish clothes, and yuppie worldview to the gray-green skin tones and real-life problems of my support group. I am especially haunted by the vision of one lovely man in my group who, while receiving killer doses of chemotherapy for a poor-prognosis brain tumor, had to stagger out of the hospital, half dead, to oversee the apple harvest at his small, family-owned orchard.

Most anticancer drugs affect the bone marrow, decreasing its ability to produce blood cells. The white blood cells produced by the bone marrow help to protect your body by fighting bacteria that cause infection. If the

number of white cells in your blood is reduced, there is a
higher risk of getting an infection.
—"CHEMOTHERAPY AND YOU"

There is one week when I was so sick I couldn't get out
of bed. It wasn't that I was sick from chemo exactly; it was
more indirect. My white blood count was low—hovering
around 1,200 at the nadir (6,000 is normal)—and I caught a
cold from my son. Because I had almost no resistance to
infection, it turned into a killer cold, an Ur-cold, a cold
from hell, and it would not leave. My throat was so sore I
could only sleep for an hour or two before the pain woke me
up. I couldn't eat at all, partly because of the sore throat and
partly because of the most horrible of all chemotherapy side
effects: mouth sores. Mouth sores arise because the epithelial
cells lining the mouth (and the entire digestive tract, for
that matter) are rapidly dividing and thus vulnerable to cell-
killing agents. When you have mouth sores you think very
carefully before even trying to take a bite of food; even
something as innocuous as a yogurt smoothie is like swallowing a handful of nettles. This also happened to be the time
that my hair truly fell out. Because I couldn't eat my weight
had dropped alarmingly. I happen to be one of those people
who look a wreck when I have a mere head cold; I look
horrible out of all proportion to my symptoms. This time
when I looked in the mirror I was truly alarmed. This was
not a case that the Look Good—Feel Better people could
solve. In the wink of an eye I had been transformed into an
eighty-year-old woman; or more precisely, I looked near
death. To have such a thing happen to your body, even
briefly, is to see your own mortality rising up to greet you,

like one of those gaudily dressed skeletons in a medieval dance of death.

Although I knew that it would be absurd and even undignified to die from a cold, at the time I felt that I might. It did not seem possible that I would ever get better, and indeed for ten days I did not. Desperate for an antidote, I sent my husband to the video store to rent Richard Attenborough's documentary about Mother Theresa of Calcutta. This particular video became famous in the annals of psychoneuroimmunology a few years ago when it was found to actually enhance the immune response of students who watched it. I forget what was measured—T-lymphocytes or something—but I was willing to try anything. So I watched the film, and to this day I am convinced it turned me around. The documentary records a meeting between Mother Theresa and the American ambassador (or consul or some other official) in which the nun insists against all reason that there will be a cease-fire next week that will allow her nuns to cross into West Beirut (or was it East Beirut?) to rescue sick children. And, against all reason, there is. It is hard not to be convinced of a force of love in the universe that can illumine the darkest pits of hell. Despite differences in philosophy about abortion and other issues, I feel that on that day I was healed by Mother Theresa. I knew that white-cell counts and statistics were not going to undo me. I knew that all things were possible.

When you start chemotherapy, your lifestyle may change; you may have to adjust your routine. . . . These kinds of changes are not pleasant, but you can handle most of them by adjusting your own attitudes and

*behavior. It is important to remember that you are not
alone and that many other cancer patients have success-
fully dealt with similar feelings and problems.*
                                   —"CHEMOTHERAPY AND YOU"

After a few months on chemo, I had no eyebrows, eyelashes, or pubic hair, and my deathly pale, almost translucent skin looked like some fairy-tale princess bewitched into
a premature sleep/death. I began to know what it is like to
walk through life looking different. At a children's Halloween party in our town, my son was dressed as a bat and I was,
as usual, wearing a turban. When I complimented one of the
other mothers on her spider costume, she said, "I like yours
too. Are you a fortune teller?" I said I was.

I began in a small way to understand the pain of the
handicapped and disfigured, the stares and averted glances,
and at times I experienced paroxysms of envy of other people's youth, good looks, and physical robustness. The Look
Good issue became more problematic when I was undergoing radiation and my chest and shoulders were decorated
with garish Magic Marker lines, extending up to the middle
of my neck. I once pointed out to the technician that it was
a bit embarrassing when wearing a bathing suit to look like a
butcher's diagram of the cuts of beef. She said, "Well, more
and more people have it these days," pointing out that many
patients had the stigmatic marks on their faces and heads.
She added, "When I see it I don't think anything about it."
You don't of course, I think to myself. You work in radiation
therapy. But I can assure you that I am the only person at
my health club who is covered with black and purple stig-
mata.

It is at my health club that the gulf between a cancer patient and a "normal" person seemed most striking. The conversations in the dressing room—the pleasant, everyday conversations of normal, healthy, well-adjusted people— sounded as alien to my ears as if I were the Man Who Fell to Earth. "I would be happy if I could just lose five pounds," one woman remarked to her friend. "Yeah, five pounds—I used to think ten, but now I would settle for five." Another woman in workout gear confided that she had planned to have two sons five years apart, both conceived in October and born in June, and that she had managed to accomplish just that. To make things even more complete, it appeared, both sons were extremely gifted. I was stunned by the con- trol she exerted over her life; I wondered how she and others like her managed this. Had I missed something vital some- where along the line? Not only did I lack the ability to time a child's conception, predestine its sex or degree of gifted- ness; I couldn't alter the fact that it was no longer possible for me to conceive a child at all. There were other things I couldn't control either—like the fact that my son was not acting at all gifted at the moment and still refused to eat vegetables. And I certainly wouldn't be able to ensure that he gets the best teacher in fifth grade if I succumbed to the NCI's statistics. And as for building a perfect body for myself —that seemed about as attainable as the philosopher's stone.

> *Women having some types of chemotherapy may notice changes in their menstrual cycles.*
> —"CHEMOTHERAPY AND YOU"

Another little side effect of chemotherapy—glossed over in the pamphlets, I notice—is instant menopause. The result of having one's ovaries fried by chemotherapy, "cessation of ovarian function" is usually temporary in twenty-five-year-olds, permanent in forty-year-olds. My doctor scarcely mentioned the phenomenon either, so for several months I was not sure why I suddenly felt an urge to rip off all my clothes when the inside temperature was a Spartan 62 degrees. Driving down the interstate I was a strange hot-house flower, a tropical orchid in a northeast climate. Over the dishes I was engulfed in inner flames. At night I'd have night sweats and wake up clammy. One evening I got a phone call from a statistician who was interviewing the women in the study I was in. "I have a strange question," she announced. "Have you been having hot flashes?" Suddenly it clicked. "Yes!" I shouted. "Yes, I have! I was wondering what those were."

Instant menopause brings a new meaning to the word midlife crisis. Abruptly, in a few weeks' time, you are plunged, medically speaking, into deep middle age; you are postmenopausal. Gone are the biological cycles linked to the moon and the tides, the inevitable ebb and flow of estrogen and progesterone, the rich female humours. You're now living in a hormonal milieu that is shockingly alien, made all the more so by the estrogen-blocking drugs like tamoxifen. Now you get to worry about your bones becoming so brittle from osteoporosis that you'll break your hip falling on the ice in the driveway one day and become an invalided old woman with a child still in Cub Scouts. You can never take estrogen replacement therapy, of course, as estrogen promotes breast cancer. But you get used to it; you get used to anything.

> *Many people do not understand cancer and they may avoid you because they're afraid of your illness. Others may worry that they will upset you by saying the wrong thing.*
>
> —"CHEMOTHERAPY AND YOU"

What the booklets fail to tell you is that some of the people "who do not understand cancer" are doctors. (The booklets are always urging you to "discuss your feelings" with your doctor, as if doctors were adept at handling complex emotions.) Just last week a friend of mine who is a six-year breast cancer veteran consulted an endocrinologist about an adrenal hormone abnormality. In the course of the exam the doctor remarked casually, "When I've done autopsies on breast cancer patients I've often found endocrine cancer." Now, "autopsy" is not a word one wants to hear when one is lying on the examining table; it suggests that the doctor who is palpating your flesh sees you more as a potential cadaver than as a person. Fortunately, tests later proved that my friend did not have endocrine cancer, but that doctor's thoughtless words had plunged her into a week of despair. There are worse stories—like the doctor who told a tearful woman, newly diagnosed with lung cancer, "Well, we all die. You'll just die sooner."

I myself have had my peace of mind shattered by doctors who lacked the most rudimentary interpersonal skills. Once when I was trying to make a decision about endocrine (estrogen-blocking) treatment, I called up a high honcho in the field, a colleague of an NIH scientist friend of mine. After I briefly described my health status, the expert opined that endocrine therapies would probably be of little value and then added, somewhat gratuitously, "You'd just better hope the chemotherapy worked!" This was delivered in such a hostile, aggressive tone that for a moment I felt I should apologize for being such an unpromising case. His delivery suggested that what he really meant was "Lady, you don't have a snowball's chance in hell." Alternative doctors can be just as ungracious. One doctor I consulted announced as soon as I entered his office, "Well, you know, if you've had chemotherapy none of this other stuff will work." But I have my own revenge. When a doctor casually hands me a death sentence, I silently vow to outlive him.

Breast cancer is largely a communication problem.
—DOCTOR INTERVIEWED IN A CNN NEWS SHOW

Having cancer makes you acutely attuned to the peculiar semiotics of medical public relations. You know that those "Cancer Cure in Sight" newspaper headlines are no accident; they have been planted in a writer's brain by selected voices of the cancer establishment. Even more subtle are the subtexts, the images, the spaces between the words. A case in point is a short news segment I caught recently on CNN about an American Cancer Society program to educate Spanish-speaking women about breast cancer. While this is a commendable project, I got the feeling that there was a hidden agenda in this footage of benevolent white

doctors bringing supposedly life-saving information (get regular mammograms) to the poor and benighted. "Look how
much we're doing; look what great strides we're making,"
the cancer establishment is telling us subliminally, while the
camera lingers on a breast cancer patient who is Hispanic
(subtext: doesn't speak English), poor (no access to medical
care), uneducated (doesn't get mammograms), and obese
(doesn't take care of herself). In case we missed the point,
an expert observes, "Breast cancer is largely a communications problem," i.e., in this age of dazzling medical break-
throughs the only people who don't "catch it early" don't
have the wherewithal to take care of themselves. If we *don't*
catch it at an early, curable stage, the establishment suggests, it is *we* who are somehow to blame—not the medical
industry that after three decades of intense funding still
doesn't have a clue about how to save our lives.

Obviously, being poor and having breast cancer is an
almost unendurable double whammy, and the dismal survival statistics of nonwhite women are a national disgrace.
The fact remains, however, that the highest incidence of
breast cancer is among women of European ancestry. And
higher education, for some mysterious reason, seems to be a
risk factor. Many women do not "catch it early," not because of a "communication problem" but because of the
unpredictable, elusive nature of the disease and the fact that
mammograms are not entirely reliable. (Fifteen percent of
malignancies do not show up on a mammogram at all, and,
to complicate matters further, mammograms themselves may
be carcinogenic.) Another way the American Cancer Society distracts us from absence of real progress in *treating* breast

cancer is by continually harping on the good news—mammograms (catch more early cancers), lumpectomies (now standard treatment), and breast reconstruction.

The only sure thing in this whole business is that your hair will grow back.

—MY ONCOLOGIST

My chemotherapy ended in mid-January. As soon as I finished the last creepy, green-flecked Cytoxan I immediately felt better. In an all-out effort to flush the poison residues out of me, I went on a heavy-duty detoxifying diet consisting of vegetables, fruits, and nauseating quantities of carrot and green vegetable juice. I felt purified, radiant. By mid-February I had eyebrows and eyelashes and my skin had returned to normal Earthling color. I was even pleased to see tiny hairs appear on my arms and legs. During the late turban and early hair-stubble phase, which happened to coincide with late winter/early spring in this latitude, I felt that I was a creature undergoing a profound metamorphosis. I was cocooning, molting, transforming. The new being that would emerge from this process, I visualized, would be beautiful, transcendent, rising phoenixlike from the ashes of medical mortification. I am not really talking about physical beauty; I was realistic enough to know that I was not about to begin a modeling career as a forty-two-year-old chemotherapy-radiation-surgery veteran. But even while ignorant observers saw an unresplendent woman with sallow skin and an unbecoming hairstyle, I knew I was incubating my reborn self. About the time blossoms and new pale-green leaves appeared on the trees I was growing my new foliage.

Meanwhile, bizarre things were happening to my fingernails. It is fortunate I have never been a fingernail freak because a woman who cared at all about her fingernails would be driven mad by chemotherapy. What occurs is that each infusion of chemotherapy murders a population of fingernail cells, leaving a striated pattern of horizontal white bands. When each band reaches the end of the nail bed it breaks off in jagged edge. Like the concentric rings that date the growth of a redwood tree, each of my nail striations recorded an event in time, an act of poisoning. They persisted, souvenirlike, for months after chemotherapy, edging slowly toward the end of the fingernail before disappearing like a bad dream.

I threw out my turbans once and for all in April, on a vacation in the Yucatan where the temperature was 96 degrees. (The turbans are now in my son's dress-up collection along with pirate hats and cowboy gear.) I still looked like a cross between Gertrude Stein and Sinead O'Connor, and, unlike them, I had no extreme personal philosophy to go with my hairstyle, but it was exhilarating to feel the wind in my hair, or my stubble, shall we say, as I walked up the steps of Mayan temples. By June I was on the cusp of normal-looking, close-cropped, to be sure, but the disinterested observer might deem it possible that I had actually chosen this look. Around this time it was apparent that my new hair would be curly. I had gotten a $15,000 perm! I was relieved that my new hair was my normal color rather than, say, snow white.

There will be days that your spirits will be low—not only because you are dealing with an uncertain future but also because you have been through a hard time. Pretending you're always happy, without admitting that sometimes you feel upset, can cut off channels for communications and will not make your recovery period any easier.

—"AFTER BREAST CANCER"

"When will you know if the chemotherapy is working?" a friend asks.

The correct answer is "Never." The cancer cells that may or may not be circulating through my bloodstream are too small to detect—they are known in the trade as micrometastases—and there is no telling whether in three months or five years or seven years they will stick to my bones, liver, lungs, or brain. Or perhaps, in spite of everything, I will live to be ninety-five, like most of my ancestors. Or perhaps I will be killed in an avalanche. Because of the precarious lack of certainty in my life I have become as superstitious as an Italian grandmother. I see signs and omens everywhere—but especially in published statistics.

I have a theory about cancer cells. I do not think they are evil in the sense that Hitler was evil. They are simply buffoons, so dumb they can't even transcribe the DNA message right. Duh! Back there in my genes, is the master program of my organism, perfect, created by God himself. When I was born I was born perfect, then something happened. Maybe one of the cells got bored and came up with the notion of a mutiny. Screw the system! *Viva la revolución!*

Then, like a microscopic Che Guevara, it talked other cells into going along with this. "We want to build a different kind of cell. We have a better idea for a cell."

Maybe what the cells really have in mind is to make a new person. What they don't know is that they will end up killing me (us) in the process. I try to talk to them. "Hey, cells," I say. "Enough already. If there is something you want, let me know; maybe we can come to some sort of compromise." They seem to be telling me that they want to grow. So I tell them, "Look, cells, let's examine this growth issue together. I think maybe you've taken this a bit too literally. Maybe what we really want here is spiritual or psychological growth. Okay? Is that it?"

As ancient Greeks consulted entrails for clues to the future, we cancer patients scrutinize the statistics churned out of places like NCI, Sloan-Kettering, Dana Farber, the University of Pittsburgh. "Cancer Facts and Figures 1991," based on rates from NCI's Surveillance, Epidemiology, and End Results (SEER) program, tells us that 175,000 women will be diagnosed with breast cancer in the United States this year; an estimated 44,800 will die. I read in "Cancer Facts and Figures" that breast cancer rates were soaring—by about 3 percent a year since 1980—and no one knew why. Hunting for survival rates, I turned to the "Breast Cancer" page in the SEER pamphlet and learned that 91 percent of women with localized breast cancer survive today; referring to another table, I found that this apparently represented an improvement from the 78 percent rate of the 1940s. If the cancer has spread regionally (that is, to the neighboring lymph nodes in the armpit), the five-year survival rate is 69 percent, I learned. For distant metastases (e.g., bones, lungs, chest wall, brain, liver, et cetera), the rate drops to 18 percent.

With a cure rate approaching 100 percent, you may wonder, what's all the fuss about? I spread out the mountain of papers and pamphlets the NCI had mailed me and concentrated on it as if it were a sort of bureaucratic mandala. I began to notice some things, the very things, I believe, the NCI hopes we *won't* notice: (1) When they are happily touting a 91 percent survival rate, they are not talking about *all* breast cancer patients, only about the fortunate subset known as Stage I, with no lymph node involvement. (2) Since Stage I patients traditionally receive no chemotherapy, their lives are saved by Mother Nature, not by any great medical advances. Yet, to confuse you, "greatly improved chemotherapy" is frequently mentioned in the same breath as "91 percent curable." (3) They are giving us the *five*-year survival figure, as if this represented a cure. Later, squinting into the fine print, we might stumble on the fact that a sizable number of patients even in this good-outcome, highly treatable group actually die—but after five years, when nobody's looking. (In the morass of material I was sent by NCI I was hard-pressed to find any ten-year survival data at all. But an NIH monograph, *1987 Annual Cancer Statistics Review*, does concede that "of the five-year survivors [of breast cancer] about 17 percent will die in the next five years." A recent issue of the American Cancer Society journal *Ca: A Journal for Clinicians* mentions in passing a large study in which the ten-year survival was 71 percent for women with negative nodes, 48 percent for women with positive nodes. (Certain subgroups fare much worse.) Obviously, then, if you have hopes of one day cashing in your

IRA and taking AARP field trips to Arizona, you can't necessarily pin your hopes on that oft-quoted 91 percent. (4) NCI maintains separate survival tables for whites and nonwhites, and wherever you find wonderful, soaring cure rates you'll probably find nonwhites excluded. In some cases, current survival statistics for whites are compared with overall survival statistics in, say, 1969, so, *of course*, 1990 looks better. Another reason 1990 looks better is that in the early 1970s the NCI switched statistical methods, so that about 7 percent of the improvement in survival is merely a statistical artifact. And yet:

CANCER-CURE REPORT: SAVING YOUR BREASTS; NEW TREATMENTS, NEW HOPE proclaimed a recent coverline in *Self* magazine, which I bought from the newsstand one day in mid-chemotherapy, hoping for new treatments and/or new hope. Inside the magazine, awash in a floral cheap-cologne scent, I came upon even giddier optimism. "Many of us believe that we're now on the edge of totally curing breast cancer," noted Larry Norton, M.D. The rest of the article was unfailingly upbeat, barely distinguishable from "Looking Great at the Gym" and other features in the issue. I learned that chemotherapy had improved dramatically in recent years, becoming little more bothersome than a pedicure and considerably more effective. "An array of drugs, for example a combination of cyclophosphamide, methotrexate, and fluorouracil, better known as CMF, has dramatically improved results." Oh yeah? I thought. Even I knew that CMF was old news, that state-of-the-art treatments included Adriamycin, which is more potent as well as more toxic than methotrexate. Furthermore, the most optimistic studies reveal that in premenopausal women chemotherapy saves 10 to 12 percent of those who would otherwise die, which is nice but small comfort to the other 90 percent. A few months later I would read that, in the latest, much-ballyhooed *Lancet* "meta-analysis" of the statistics, chemotherapy was found to be exactly as effective as ovarian ablation, the destruction of the ovaries by surgery or radiation, a treatment that fell out of favor in the 1950s. Indeed, it has been suggested that chemotherapy works by effectively destroying the ovaries of premenopausal women, thereby suppressing estrogen production. In postmenopausal women there is scant evidence that chemotherapy improves life expectancy at all.

Later in the *Self* article, next to the photo of a naked baby girl, came a blurb from Dr. Norton: "It's realistic to expect that no one of her generation will die of breast cancer." That's a nice thought, I muttered to myself, but given the current epidemic—one out of every nine women— wouldn't it be more realistic to expect that one out of every two or three women will get breast cancer by the time Baby X turns forty?

As a result of such articles, a lot of people have the impression that breast cancer is little more than a fashion and lifestyle bummer: You might lose a breast or your hair and become a little less productive in your job, but then, after your hair grows back and you look healthy again, you're fine. It is hard to explain that, at the tail end of the twentieth century, you have an essentially incurable disease.

Q: *Why are such people [practitioners who offer "unproven methods of cancer management"] dangerous?*

A: *They cause the patient to lose valuable time before
   getting proper treatment. The loss of time could
   prove fatal. These purveyors of unproven methods
   often convert a hopeful clinical situation into one of
   hopelessness and despair by delaying adequate therapy or avoiding qualified consultations that could be
   of benefit.*
            —"ANSWERING YOUR QUESTIONS ABOUT CANCER"
            (THE AMERICAN CANCER SOCIETY)

A brief note to the American Cancer Society: I have
already completed your program of "slash, poison, and
burn," in the words of Harvard breast surgeon Dr. Susan
Love. At this point you have nothing more to offer me
except an autologous bone marrow transplant, which I have
already rejected as too scary (the death rate *from the procedure* is 10 percent). Following your frequent urgings, I go in
for regular checkups and tests, but if any of those tests were
to reveal cancer, you would write me off. I think of an acquaintance with liver metastases who was told by her
oncologist: "There's nothing really to do. It's just a matter of
time." Later, when this woman mentioned that she had seen
an alternative physician, the oncologist said, "I'm really dis-
appointed in you." You assume I am naive, desperate, an
easy prey for alternative snake oil salesmen. Although all
you can promise me is that I might be among the 10 percent
of breast cancer patients who are saved by chemotherapy,
you warn me that, no matter what, I should never, ever
contemplate an "unproven" remedy—even vitamin C.
Speaking of unproven: How about the fact that for years you

have been prescribing harmful chemotherapy for many types of cancer (pancreas, colon, et cetera) when your own statistics show it does not prolong life one iota?

Because cancer patients are so vulnerable, you maintain a list, compiled in a freely available document called "Unproven Therapies"—by which you really mean "quacks"—to warn us about questionable cancer remedies that originate outside the NCI–Sloan Kettering–Dana Farber axis. One is struck by the smug tone of this document and the relish with which you linger over the most wackó details: "The substance [Entelev, or Cancell] was first envisioned in 1936 by James V. Sheridan, a chemist working at the time for Dow Chemical. According to a 1984 magazine interview with Sheridan, the idea for Entelev came to him in a dream that he believes was inspired by God. . . ." You inform us ad nauseum that "the American Cancer Society does not have evidence that treatment with [Substance X] results in objective benefit in the treatment of cancer in human beings." You convey the impression that the treatment has been thoroughly and objectively tested before it was damned. But is that really true? In his book *The Cancer Industry* Ralph W. Moss documents twenty-eight unproven treatments (among sixty-three on the quack list in the 1970s and 1980) on which "no investigation at all was carried out by the American Cancer Society or any other agency before the method was condemned." In seven cases, he reports, the results of the investigation appeared to be positive. And let's not get into the cases of alternative treatments that, wittingly or not, have been investigated improperly—wrong dosages, wrong timing, wrong patient group, and so on—

resulting in negative results. I'm not claiming that any of these unproven treatments is a cure for cancer, but I have to take some of your pronouncements *con grano salis.*

Of course, I receive a steady stream of clippings from all my friends heralding possible new cures that aren't available because they would cost $500,000 per subject (recombinant DNA techniques) or would involve chopping down endangered species of trees (taxol) or are in an early research stage (Phase I studies) in which only the nearly dead are permissible guinea pigs. I have called up researchers at Sloan-Kettering about some bold new treatment, only to be told, brightly, "Oh yes, we're in animal studies now." The interval between animal studies and a universally available treatment might be ten years, even thirty years—*if* it pans out at all. Cancer patients aren't big on long-range plans; we barely worry about cholesterol or IRAs.

So, American Cancer Society, I have become a persona non grata. I have not yet taken a shuttle bus across the border to Tijuana or anything like that, but I don't mind drinking a tea based on an old Indian recipe now and then, however quaint and foolish that might sound in a press release. My dinner companions are invariably amazed by the sheer quantity of my vitamins and supplements as well as by their strangeness; others are polite enough not to comment on the fact that my hands and feet have turned yellow from beta carotene. It was not always thus. I used to order Big Macs and would rather chat with militant Shi'ites than with raw foods people, macrobiotic people, wheat grass people, Shaklee people, super blue-green algae people, or anyone who makes a lifestyle out of strange food. But now I am eating meals that look as if they were dragged from the ocean floor.

I know that anecdotal evidence—for example, Mrs. Eugenia Burdock, only weeks away from death from lymphoma, takes wacky treatment X and forty years later is alive and well and running her own chinchilla ranch—is not a statistic, but, personally, I'd rather be an anecdote than a statistic. I intend to live! Frankly, I don't expect that vitamin C or shark liver oil or seaweed by itself will save my life, any more than chemotherapy alone will. In my heart I feel that what *will* save my life is the journey from mere survival to a richer, deeper connection to life.

> *Sixty percent of all breast cancer recurrences appear within the first 3 years after initial treatment, 20 percent within the next 2 years, and 20 percent in later years. As a result, you should be examined frequently during the first 5 years after your treatment. . . .*
>
> —"AFTER BREAST CANCER"

And so we have come around the cycle and come back to Halloween, a year and four months since diagnosis. To all appearances I am well and healthy, and my tests show no detectable cancer. In other parts of the world today is *el dia de los muertos*, the day of the dead, when two worlds meet, the seen and the unseen, the living and the dead. In Mexico this is a time to acknowledge the presence of death within life. The Four Horsemen of the Apocalypse ride through the streets; ancient terrors are unleashed—famine, plague, pestilence, death by water, death by fire. In our country we drive over to K-Mart and buy a Ninja Turtle costume and make sure our kids don't eat any unwrapped candy—as if the Four Horsemen had been exterminated from our universe. This year I have curly hair (real—it's really mine!) instead of a turban. I buy myself a cheap witch's costume; my son goes as Louie, of Huey, Dewey, and Louie. It occurs to me that last year, in my turban, I was more authentic, more in line with the spirit of *el dia de los muertos*.

I think it has taken me over a year to truly accept my condition and to understand that it is no more and no less than the human condition. We go around thinking that real life is about adding a rec room to the basement, but this is not real life. Cancer is real life. When you accept cancer, it is as if new systems within the organism automatically open —like the oxygen masks and flotation systems that automatically drop in your lap on a 747 in an emergency. When you walk this earth on borrowed time, each day on the calendar is a beloved friend you know for only a short time. You know that a year is 365 days, twelve months, four seasons, two equinoxes, two solstices, thirteen full moons, thirteen new moons—each of them a celebration. You note all the minutiae of seasons, discovering within a single season, say, fall, some three or four miniseasons, each with its own attendant phenomena. You find that your favorite is the very last stage of fall just before the muted mauves and bare brittle branches of early November, when the whole world is carpeted with yellow leaves and you glimpse distant hills and lights you never saw before. You strike up new relationships with the old pagan holidays—Beltaine, Samhain, Midsummer's Night, St. Agnes's Eve.

I can tell that some of my friends feel sorry for me. They don't understand how I can wake up every morning to circumstances so horrible and get through the day in a more or less cheery manner. Of course, no one would willingly choose cancer. But healthy people can never really know what we cancer patients have. We have a gift beyond measure, the daily bliss of being alive. Forced by our disease to walk through the valley of the shadow of death, like any woman who gives birth, we get to experience the sacredness of life. This first happened to me on my initial visit to my surgeon, when the bad news implied by a mammogram was confirmed by needle biopsy. Before seeing the surgeon I had to spend a hellish hour in the waiting room. Amid the ubiquitous muted beige walls and wall-to-wall carpets, the atmosphere was thick with fear, it seemed to me, and I was too terrified to read. To transform my fear into something else, I tried mentally sending love to the other patients in the room. I especially focused on one incredibly ancient woman slumped in a wheelchair in the corner. She was presumably facing some sort of hideous surgery, and she was all alone, unspeakably alone, it looked to me, having been dumped there by an attendant. Her craggy face, the hollows of her cheeks, the deep solitude of her eyes, seemed to contain all the beauty and pain of the universe. Meditating on her, my heart seemed to open in the midst of hell and fill with an overwhelming love for my fellow creatures. I was, for a brief moment, in what Native Americans call the "sacred hoop," and my fear was gone.

r o s e m a r y   b r a y

first
stirrings

It is five A.M.; it doesn't matter which morning. For the
past several months, there have been dozens of mornings in
which I watch the sun's ascent through slivers of the vene-
tian blinds in my bedroom. My husband lies next to me,
snoring gently; I nudge him into turning on his side to sleep
in silence. City birds are singing in a monotone, and the
newspaper delivery truck has already rumbled up the street
and gone. I shift my unwieldy body from one part of the hot
sheet to another, yawning but unable to sleep; this is the
second night in three that I haven't closed my eyes. I have a
meeting in less than four hours; I'll be there, bleary and
resentful. I turn over again, or try to; this time, the baby
kicks me squarely in the bladder. Time to get up, to release
the ten drops of urine I was sure would be a flood. I keep
telling myself that it won't be long now, that he'll release
me soon, stop crawling around inside me and prodding me
when I sit hunched over in chairs. He'll be in my life forever, but perhaps at a distance I can deal with. Mostly,
though, I curse under my breath every woman who perpetu-
ates the lie of blissful fecundity. It's clear to me through the

haze of sleeplessness that wanting a baby is one thing; wanting to HAVE a baby is quite another.

A decade ago, when my husband and I decided to
marry, I got a host of reactions from friends and acquaintances. To my surprise, many of them were negative. People
warned me of the dangers of losing myself, being taken over
by my husband, being trapped by the institution of marriage
itself. Some of these doomsayers were themselves married
women, issuing their dismaying reports from the front, as
it were. I did speak to a few happy couples, but not many. I
decided to ignore the grim folks, for the most part—it
was not as though Bob and I were strangers to each
other before our wedding day. We would be happy; I would
not lose myself; marriage would be hard, but not impossible.

I was right. I did not lose myself, but found instead more
in me than I knew was there. It was hard, but not impossible; we were happy. So happy, in fact, that having a baby
seemed the logical next step. We were happy enough to
want more of us around. It took time; for a period of months
when I swore I was infertile, I wept at the sight of a child or
the first trickle of blood, angry with myself for being so un-
original. Then we decided on adoption and my pain eased.
We prepared ourselves for the inevitable invasion of privacy
that would allow the agency to check us out. We went to
orientations and did our first interview, which lasted four
hours. Exactly nine days later, I stood in our slightly seedy,
white-tiled bathroom, watching a big, pink plus sign appear
in the window of a home pregnancy test. Bob was in the
living room, watching the climax of an obscure Gregory

Peck movie; I called to him and showed him the test, watched his expression turn from vague frustration to a be-wildered delight.

"Oh, my God," he said, and laughed. We stared at the test resting on the edge of the pedestal sink, then stared at each other. "So, Merry Christmas two days late," I said, and started to cry. It was my last truly happy day for months.

My body and I have never been friends. Plagued with a weight problem since adolescence, awkward enough to have flunked gym in kindergarten, I tend to think of my body primarily as something to anchor my head, the place where the really important stuff is going on. Over the years, I have learned to be more gentle with myself, declaring between us a kind of truce in which I agree not to subject us to further bizarre diets and Spartan programs of torture; my body, in turn, agreed to function without causing me severe limita-tions. To make this deal, I gave up the public approval that comes with thinness and some of the energy that weighing less can bring. I gained, however, possession of my sanity. It seemed like a fair trade to me.

But my pregnancy ended our cease-fire; hormone after hormone stepped into the breach. Fewer than twenty-four hours after I learned the good news, my stomach responded with a dreaded nausea that abated only if I ate or slept. Bland food, the advertised salvation of pregnant women ev-erywhere, made me even queasier. Only Szechuan food and ginger saved me. Even so, the relative license to eat that pregnant women take for granted did me little good. At a time when my doctor expected me to gain weight, I actually lost two pounds one month, as I discovered at a prenatal checkup. For nearly thirty-eight years I had waited not to be hungry. Now the moment was here—and it was the wrong moment.

Yet tests revealed that the baby and I were growing well and doing fine. But my body held even more surprises. One night, after showering, I was idly examining my breasts. Brushing against one nipple with a bare hand, I wondered why I felt damp when I had just finished drying off. I looked down to find small beads of clear fluid at a nipple's edge— my breasts were simply warming up for the work ahead, and I was secreting on schedule. The fear washing over me was startling. It was the fear of the inevitable, the steady progression of events that would lead me to the birth of another human being. That night in my bathroom, I wanted no part of it.

A few weeks later, I sat at my computer working. I felt a flutter, almost a tickle, low in my abdomen. Still concentrating on my task, I vaguely noted to myself that whatever I'd eaten was starting to talk back to me. But when it happened again, I realized it was not food sending me a message, but my son-in-progress. I had always heard that this was a magical moment for pregnant women: the first stirrings of new life, the "quickening" that made an amorphous blob of cells into YOUR son, YOUR daughter. But I didn't feel magical. I felt invaded, occupied by hostile forces. The very first picture I visualized was a scene from *Alien*, in which John Hurt is trying to eat his dinner with the rest of the crew, until he is gnawed to death from within by the hideous monster that exits from his stomach with a bloody snarl.

That flutter was good for an hour of miserable tears, with Bob doing his best to console me. But for days I was beyond consolation. I felt betrayed into nonexistence; this baby I had prayed for and longed for would not be joining my life, it seemed, but overtaking it all together. It was all I thought about, all anyone else thought about who knew me. I was in the grip of primordial fears. I had already begun to disappear. My slide into panic was not aided by many of those who had preceded me into parenthood; their idea of congratulating me consisted primarily of rueful laughter, followed by the knowing comments: "If there's something you really want to do, or somewhere you want to go, you'd better do it now!" or "Just wait! Your life will never be the same." The specter of impending motherhood had done what nearly ten years of marriage had never achieved: brought on a sense of being trapped. Had I discovered too late that this life of mine, which would never be the same, was a life that had made me happier than I thought?

Every twinge, every tickle, every new symptom my body created did nothing for a time except to remind me of my bondage. Even my mind began to fail me; a head that once was filled with opinions and ideas became instead a repository for dreamy scenes of me and the baby in the park, in his room, on the bus, or in the playground, surrounded by admirers of my perfect child, my awareness of the outside world gone forever. And when I was not mourning the imminent death of myself, or my marriage, I focused on the baby's safety, as though my traitorous thoughts might jeopardize his very life. Annoyed as I had been at his first stirrings inside me, I grew anxious every few hours that I could not feel him squirming.

Only the counsel of a few close friends saved me from a complete slide into hysteria. I relied on them, on their contrarious stories of how much they hated every waking moment of their pregnancies, that only the results—their own sweet-faced and self-possessed infants—justified the months of what they agreed was some version of hell. These women rescued me from my early terror of being an unnatural mother already plotting her escape from parenting, lost in the nightmare that I'd never write another word. The comment I cherished most came from my dear friend Renita, a professor and Old Testament scholar whose exquisite daughter, Savannah, was born nine months before my son. She made it her business to tell me to ignore everyone who talked about the end of my life. "Girl, pay these women no mind," she told me. "All these people who tell you what they can't do now that they have children—they weren't doing anything *before* they had kids."

Ultimately, though, it is harder to ignore my changing physical self. In these last days before my child's birth, muscles hurt that I didn't even know I possessed; all the old positions that once lulled me to sleep are useless. Sleep itself, something I could always count on, eludes me frequently. And the pleasures of sleeping next to someone warm have given way to the feeling that there are too many people in bed with me right now, a feeling I've refused to act upon on principle. For now, I am making Bob roll over more, while I try to find just one comfortable spot for a few hours of peace. It's plain that my son and I are already trying to find our way together. The mother-to-be in me imagines that love will cure the largest part of my dilemma. The writer in me considers it all one enormous metaphor. We will see.

pam houston

out of habit,
i start apologizing

I am lying, facedown, on a massage table at the Doral Hotel and Spa in Telluride, Colorado. I am here under false pretenses beyond my control, a guest of the Doral and all its services, because the manager hopes I will write a rave article about the hotel. Because of his generosity, I am having several things done to my body for free that I cannot even pronounce. I've been bathed, oiled, rolfed, fangoed, facialed, shiatsued, reflexologized, stretched, pressed, and dried. More people have seen my naked body in the last three days than in the last three years, and I'm starting to get used to it, my modesty slipping away. I've begun to float from personal service room to personal service room in a fragrant, supple, semiconsciousness. So far I've lost three hotel bathrobes, two sweat shirts, and my watch.

It is unlike me to have so much attention paid to my body, to pamper and indulge this fleshy mass that I have spent my whole life trying to reduce, or reshape, or disguise.

I'm being worked on, this hour, by a technician whose name tag says "Wendy," and she's doing something to me called the Rosen method, a loose combination of body massage and psychotherapy. Considering the fact that every insecurity I have ever harbored has had to do with the shape of my body, the Rosen method seems like the ideal treatment for me.

"You have such strong legs," Wendy says, "but you are using them to hold up the rest of your body, and that's not what they are for."

My legs are strong and beautiful; dancer's legs, my mother's legs: She spent a lifetime developing sinewy, shapely leg muscles, and then gave them, like a promise, to me.

"You are pulling your body up with your shoulders," Wendy says, "pushing and pulling, when you should only be supporting; no wonder everything is so tight."

I try to imagine standing without legs, or staying erect without shoulders, but quickly give up. I am already fantasizing about next hour's foot massage when Wendy says, "Is there some good reason you've convinced the rest of your body that your hips and stomach and pelvis don't even exist?"

When I was younger, I used to believe that if I were really thin I would be happy, and there is a part of me that still believes it's true. For a good part of my life I would have quite literally given anything to be thin . . . a finger, three toes, the sight in one eye. Now I find it only mildly surprising that for the majority of my lifetime I would have traded being ugly, deformed, and thin for being pretty, whole, and fat.

. . .

I am boating the whitewater section of the upper Dolores River at flood stage. With me in my sixteen-foot inflatable raft are three beautiful Texan women who quite literally cannot fathom my strength. We are approaching an obstacle in the river known simply as The Wall, a place where almost the entire volume of water rushes into a huge sandstone monolith, dives under it, skims along its base, and comes out, frothy and white, on the other side.

Sneaking around the wall without hitting it requires lots of anticipation and, at this high river level, almost superhuman strength. A hundred yards downriver from me I see my husband's boat careen closer and closer to the wall, I see one of his passengers disappear under the lip of the boat's front tube, the other two dive behind him into the river's swirl. When his boat makes contact with the sandstone I hear the splintering of wood, see an oar fly high into the air, taste the sudden rush of adrenaline in the back of my mouth.

My husband is the strongest human being I know, but I have the advantage of being second. I pull on the oars harder than I've ever pulled before, completely alert, making every stroke count. A voice that I recognize as mine tells my crew to get down on the floor of the raft, but I am not conscious of making the command. Every synapse in my brain and every muscle in my body is focused on pulling away from that wall. My feet, my thighs, my stomach, my back, my arms, my hands all work together, in a movement that is, I think, very like a wave, to bring the oars upstream against the rushing water. The wall gets closer and closer, and just when I think I am doing no good at all I feel the boat responding, moving backward against the current that's been driving it toward the rock. The nose of the boat barely kisses the wall and one more stroke pulls us safely away.

"Damn," says one of the Texans. "Hot damn."

We go to work rescuing the other boat's passengers.

I am walking down the street in Manhattan, Fifth Avenue in the lower sixties, women with shopping bags on all sides. I realize with some horror that for the last fifteen blocks I have been counting how many women have better and how many women have worse figures than I do. Did I say fifteen blocks? I meant fifteen years.

I am sitting at my parents' dinner table in the summer between my freshman and sophomore year. I have brought the first boy I have ever really cared about home from college, and we are making vaguely interesting small talk while my mother portions out the food.

I have been at college so long I have forgotten the rules by which my family eats dinner. I am not allowed to have bread, dessert, or seconds, ever, and there is an especially tricky rule that has to do with how much money has been spent on dinner and whether or not I am, or am not, supposed to finish everything that's been put on my plate.

My young boyfriend is telling a story I know to be funny

rather unsuccessfully; I'm embarrassed for him, and I absent-mindedly reach for a roll.

"You start eating like that," my father barks at me, "and before too long you'll be as big as a house."

I stare at the spinach coagulating on my plate.

The trick has always been to look only selectively into the mirror. To see the bright eyes, the shining hair, the whispered print of the blouse falling open to reveal soft tanned cleavage, the shapely curve of a taut muscular calf.

My husband manages a restaurant here in town. He employs fifteen twenty-one-year-olds from California. They are all variations on blonde, on tan, on figures drawn to perfection. They call my husband Mick Dundee (after the movie about the human crocodile), which I find particularly revolting; they are the kind of girls that can't talk to a man without touching him. When I come into the restaurant they smile at me politely, curiously, something between wonder and doubt in their eyes. My husband, who is blond and tan, and also built to perfection, says they do this because I am a published author, but I secretly believe they are trying to imagine what he could possibly see in someone with a body like mine.

My thinnest friend Kris says, "I don't know, but it seems to me that if the only thing that's wrong with you is that you think you weigh too much, you actually have it pretty good."

"The only thing," I say to her, calmly, "the only thing?"

I am helicopter skiing in Idaho with a man named John that I, for no good reason at all, feel the need to impress. Six inches of snow have fallen just after midnight, and under those six inches there's a thick sun-ruined crust. The helicopter leaves us on the dark side of the Tetons. The man I am here with was born in the Sun Valley Lodge, he could ski before he was confidently walking. We are neither lovers nor quite yet friends. We find ourselves on top of this mountain together, practically by accident. And yet I need to ski well in front of him, and that need is almost enough to keep me from being scared.

John hops off the cornice and into the pristine howl as if he's stepping off a sidewalk, as if it wasn't almost ninety degrees vertical, as if the sun wasn't hitting it and making it tetchy for avalanche, as if there wasn't that crustiness trying to grab his skis from underneath.

My last thought is, The sooner I go, the less time he'll have to watch me, so I launch myself, trying to find a rhythm, trying to make figure eights out of his perfect turns. The crust beneath the powder makes a terrible noise as it grips and releases, grips and releases, but I keep turning, thinking about weighing and unweighing my body, thinking about keeping my shoulders in the fall line, thinking about the ever-reliable strength in my knees.

I ski without my normal worst-case scenario tape playing

in my head, although here there's more justification for it than usual. I ski way too fast, take too many chances, I become what the ski bums call focused, believing entirely in my body's ability to perform correctly, to absorb the slope's imperfections, to ride out the speed. I feel strangely light and incredibly agile, the turns becoming the downbeat in a song it feels like I could play forever. I ski past John who has stopped to wait for me in a small grove of trees. The tails of my skis send up an arc of powder that coats him, and when I finally stop, ten perfect turns later, his head is thrown back in laughter and he looks like an angel in the snow.

"Let's see if we can make it all the way to dinner," my mother would always say, "without eating anything at all."

My friends Terilynn and thin Kris and I are sitting in a coffee bar talking. I tell them about the girls at Mike's restaurant. Kris tells me I'm crazy, that I have an unrealistic view of my appearance, that those girls would never think such a thing, looking at me. Terilynn, who is imperfectly shaped in several of the same ways I am, is not quite so convinced.

"You're wrong," I tell Kris, "I have a perfectly reasonable idea of my own attractiveness . . . good legs, shiny eyes, a pretty face, nice hair . . . on an attractiveness scale of 1 to 100, I'm in the high seventies, and ten pounds thinner, the mid-eighties."

"So what am I?" Kris says.

Both Terilynn and I put her in the high nineties, with a parenthetical reference to the fact that women, coveting her extreme thinness, might put her slightly higher than men.

We give Terilynn a seventy-two, with a high-eighties' incentive if she continues to lose weight.

From there we get a little crazy, rating everyone from Jodie Foster (91) to Bill Clinton (84) to Gerard Depardieu (89) to Madonna (upon whom we are unable to reconcile, the numbers ranging from 27 to 78).

"This is the nineties, girls," the waitress says when she brings us the check. "We're supposed to be into inner beauty now."

Sometimes I'm afraid the main reason I spend half of my life outdoors is simply because there aren't any mirrors.

I'm sitting on my front porch, blank computer screen in front of me, except two words at the top: The body. I am determined to write something positive, having just turned thirty and having sworn not to spend as much of the second half of my life preoccupied with my physical imperfections as I did the first. A woman walks up the street, bone thin in a running bra, lycra shorts, and a Walkman. I look down at my shapeless flannel nightgown, my fuzzy slippers, my belly, my hips, and turn my computer off for at least another hour. The woman is striding big confident strides up my street, which is the steepest in our mountain town. She looks as if she will keep that pace right up and over the mountain.

. . .

I am hiking to the top of Mount Timpanogos, the highest mountain in my part of Utah, 11,750 feet above sea level, 5,340 feet above the trailhead where four hours ago I parked my car. Hiking Timpanogos is not scary or life threatening, it's just grueling, roughly equivalent to starting on the rim of the Grand Canyon and then walking *up* one vertical mile to the river.

The only time safety on Timpanogos becomes an issue is in a sudden summer thunderstorm, when the shale that makes up the last hour of the climb turns slippery and loose, and lightning strikes the part of the mountain that's above tree line, which for the hiker who gets stranded up there can amount to hours and hours of dodging the heart of the storm.

Today there is only blue sky on my side of the mountain, not so much as a cumulus cloud. Maybe that is why I'm so surprised when I arrive at the summit and see the other half of the sky, horror-film black and crackling with thunder and lightning, sheets of rain like iron curtains walking toward me from a storm center only a few hundred yards away.

The way I see it I have two choices; I can either pick my way between the lightning bolts for a couple of hours and risk a shaley mud slide under combined pressure of the rain and my weight, or I can leap down off the ridge of this mountain and into one of the permanent snowfields that line the mountain's steeper "unclimbable" side. I won't have to stop exactly, just stay on my feet and do a little boot skiing for maybe ten minutes and a couple of thousand feet down to the bottom of the ice field and tree line. If I lose my footing and start rolling, my problems become a little more complex. I tighten down the straps on my day pack, find the shallowest part of the slope above which to get airborne, and count to three.

On two and a half I realize that no matter how hard I try to find one, there is no scenario of liking my body when it is stationary, no scenario that doesn't take place in a moment of life-or-death athleticism, of do-or-die strength.

I am lying on another table, faceup this time, staring at the monkey my gynecologist has pasted to the ceiling to prove he has the sense of humor his schedule doesn't often allow him to show. He is a decent man, direct and gentle, but this is Utah, where men still own women's bodies, so the bills come to my house in some long since departed boyfriend's name.

We have our usual birth control conversation. "What do you get when you cross Dan Quayle with an IUD?" I ask him, and he just shakes his head. I can't help myself. There's something about being in the gynecologist's office that turns me, instantly, into a stand-up comedienne.

This is the big 3-0 visit. A complete physical, my yearly pelvic, and because I have family history, the first mammogram of my life. The doctor broods over something he doesn't like in my folder while the nurse makes me get on the scale. Out of habit, I start apologizing, though the number turns out to be slightly lower than last year.

"There's something here that troubles me," the doctor says. "Just wait here a minute while I go call the lab."

"Where's he think I'm gonna go dressed like this?" I say to the nurse, but my voice cracks apart at the end like a mirror, my humor shot through with brittle fear. It has been less than a month since my best friend died of cancer, less than a year since my mother died of a heart attack, or long-term starvation, or the sheer displeasure of living with the things her aging body did.

No diagnosis yet and already the regret is settling in. I should have loved my body better, should have loved its curves and folds and softness, should have practiced standing with my pelvis the way Wendy told me to. But instead I have ignored it, left the cancer to grow in its dark uninhabited recesses; I think of the drawer that holds my summer T-shirts, where every dark winter the mice move in.

When the nurse leaves the room I pull the hospital gown to one side and look down at myself, the inch of extra flesh on each hip, the way my belly pushes out in a particularly annoying way that makes the occasional bystander ask me if I'm pregnant.

A wave of love for my body that is as unfamiliar as it is terrifying washes over me. I'm afraid at first it is desperation love, the kind I've felt for a man only on the brink of his leaving, but this is more penetrating, all encompassing; a love so sad and deep and complicated I am left, for a change, without words. I can almost feel the cancer spreading now, one cell at a time through the dark parts of me, and I stand alone in front of the mirror, trying to love it away.

The doctor opens the door and smiles, apologetic. "My mistake," he says, appearing not to notice my nakedness. "You're as healthy as an ox."

"How healthy is an ox?" I say, remembering a National

Geographic special about oxen getting bugs up their noses that made them insane, but the doctor is already out the door and with the next patient.

I let my legs go loose and try to stand using only my pelvis. I drop my shoulders as low as they will go and try to think about transferring my body weight (this takes tremendous concentration) to my hips. I take one more long look in the mirror before putting on my clothes.

department of the interior

The mud mother shaped her little ones, the humans, and held them in her lap. She rocked them, those red clay children with their tiny fingers, their smooth faces. She rocked them and swayed. And the wind came to breathe life into them. That first aliveness, that first gust of air inside the clay people and they came to life and the mud mother loved her children and she sang to them, O bodies, O infants, our future, my children, flesh of the earth.

1. DISEMBODYING AMERICA

A few miles from where I live is the buffalo herd. Dark and massive, they are a remnant of a more whole world, of a mighty tribe of animals. Near their fenced refuge is the grave of Buffalo Bill Cody, one of America's killer heroes, whose fame grew out of the horrifying slaughter of the powerful creatures contained in such diminished numbers nearby, and the starvation and near destruction of many tribes of people.

On a recent holiday, a cluster of white Americans stood at the fence gazing at the buffalo, trying to get their attention. It was late spring and the light-brown calves were sitting in tall grasses while their elders grazed around them. Looking at them, I wondered if they felt anger and despair being watched that way by the descendants of their killers. Do their cells, like mine, remember the terror, the changed world and destroyed land?

The people of science would say this question is a projection. It is anthropomorphism, one of those words that change compassion and empathy into pathologies. During the fire in Yellowstone, a park ranger told the people not to feed starving elk. "There is no scientific proof that animals feel pain," he said, over National Public Radio.

This was not an alien form of thinking to me. I've heard it said to cover various forms of suffering. It's only been in the last few years, after all, that newborn babies were determined to feel pain. Before this, surgery was performed on them without anesthesia. The denial of the nervous systems of animals and infants has a historical precedent in the denial of intelligence and soul in Indians and other peoples. In the late 1800s a trial involving Ponca leader Standing Bear was held to determine if he and his band of people were human beings.

As American Indian people in the political body of the U.S. we are overseen by and located under the governmental offices of the Department of the Interior, along with the rest of wilderness, forest, animals, fish. Like them, we are held in low regard.

Tribal people, animals, wilderness, life itself has been powerless against the force of weapons forged first by a violence-loving Europe and then by the American legal system. And I think now that the reason so many of us yet identify with animals is the shared helplessness we've experienced against a death-loving culture and the extreme powers it uses against us and others. It is a culture that fears and destroys what it perceives as wild, including its own inner-ness and physicality.

The wilderness, mentioned in the Bible nearly three hundred times, is almost always referred to as the place of evil, as the devil's place. It is seen as a dangerous realm, the untouched place of demons. It lives at the edge of the civi-lized world, and in the human mapping, it is the place inside humans that behaves according to instinct and inner drive that cannot be controlled by will. Wilderness is what the dominating have tried to push away from themselves, both in the outside world and inside their own bodies. Because of human denial of their own predation and human fears, wolves came to a near end for insisting on their own wild-ness, as did bears and mountain lions. It is the domestic and submissive, those who can be controlled and contained in a human-determined territory, who have most easily survived.

Of course, there were some who preferred the wilds of America. In the nineteenth century, there were those few mountain men who entered the wild willingly and were changed by it. There were also the white women who found their ways into tribal communities and did not wish to re-turn to the white world. Although fictions of the frontier included captivity narratives that claimed white women were abducted, tortured, and raped by tribal men, the truth was that most simply did not wish to return. They had stepped out of a world surrounded by emptiness, by inani-mate matter, and they had entered the living body of land, self, people, the soul of matter in a world where everything was alive and depended on all the rest.

For white Americans in the present time, Indians have come to represent spirit, heart, an earth-based way of living, all things they have felt missing from their lives that have been split off from a larger living. In this way, we fill a need for them. But we do not fit easily into their system of symbols and what that system, even now, wants us to be. This need of theirs goes back to earlier times, to when we were on the receiving end of federal policies of extermination. At this time of hunger and killing, while the true stories of Indian lives were missing, images of Indians were manipulated to present what the image-makers knew white America wanted. While the living bodies of tribal people were destroyed, photographs and paintings romanticized Indian lives. There were the photographs of dying leaders, the posed depictions of people living traditional lives they no longer, in reality, were allowed to live. What comes to my mind first, however, is a portrait photograph of Charles Eastman. Dressed in traditional clothing, he appears to be a chief. What isn't supplied in the portrait is that Eastman, author and medical doctor, a Santee Sioux survivor, was the attending physician at the massacre of Indian people, primarily women and children, at Wounded Knee. The grief inside him must have been enormous. And yet he was portrayed as the brave warrior, the precise image of what the Americans had tried to kill.

And there was Four Bears, a Mandan leader who wanted peace. Four Bears was painted by Catlin in his traditional clothing at the same time that he and his people were dying of the smallpox the painters and photographers helped to spread. Catlin, by the way, was also invited to Osceola's death in order to paint him as he was dying.

As America has become increasingly disembodied, what is killed has appeared as part of their symbol system—in the abstract. Human lives were traded for the image of that life; embodied matter exchanged for an idea of spirit. For settlers and missionaries, this originated with a belief in transcendence and an afterlife in heaven. They wanted to escape the body, to rid the continent of heathens, to civilize and cultivate the land. They wanted a world of spirit that was apart from, and better than, the body. They wanted to rise above bodily needs, desires, and all forms of human pain and being.

In the north, as the fur trade nearly extincted the beaver, the Northwest Company produced currency that carried the images of a beaver and an Indian. One of these bills was the value of a beaver hide. The money became the sign for the value of the living thing, and its worth was not in its life but in its death, carried out in the name of European high fashion.

This was the case for later currency as well, the Indian head, the buffalo nickel, replacements for what was being slaughtered. This disembodiment continues today in various shapes and forms; in a recent commercial a jeep is superimposed over a herd of running buffalo, teddy bears that have taken the place of the real bears, cars—Cherokee, Mustang —named for the very tribes and wild animals that were violated. In the safety of our homes, we can listen to tapes of the disappearing rain forest, whales, and wolves, or watch videos of wilderness, all safely contained inside an appliance, inside our walls.

Ironically, for those who have forgotten to listen to the

earth's voice, there is admiration for all the things and places they have tried to disappear. In a country where spirit has been so pitted against body, it's a form of crude myth-making, of story without meaning, without truth, without understanding. As wilderness and Indians have been seen as a part of the mythic past of white America, the destruction to them has been immense and ongoing; a recent issue of *LIFE*, with a focus on the American West, carried a photograph of Buffalo Bill and several native men from his Wild West show on its final page. In the photograph they are traveling by gondola through Venice. The caption reads: *No, it's not a scene from a spaghetti western. It's 1890, and those guys in warbonnets aren't just typical featherheads from central casting. They're real Indians in a Siouxreal situation—touring Europe with Buffalo Bill's Wild West show. They stopped off to see Venice on their way—and to introduce the Italians to buffalo mozzarella.*

Such ridicule of native people is the same kind of think-ing that allowed for genocide, then carved faces of presi-dents into Sioux holy land, a thinking that has no imagina-tion, no place for respect, empathy, or compassion, no love. What does it say that women and men who had intelli-gence, grace, and bearing, who were powerful leaders, who led strong resistance movements, were forced to be showmen, to be on display, who in order to survive became bodies owned by Buffalo Bill, the very man who had carried out starvation policies against them and was famous for his efficient slaughtering of buffalo.

It's evident that we are still containers for the needs and desires of white America, and yet our bodies themselves still suffer. Even those of us who walked out of that genocide by some cast of fortune struggle with the brokenness of our bodies and hearts, with hungers never fulfilled, with self-destruction in the forms of suicide, alcoholism, and child abuse that is a hatred of what comes from the body. The terror, even now, remains inside us. History is present in our cells that came from ancestral cells, from bodies hated, starved, and killed. It is clear to us that the destruction of the body and the destruction of the land have coincided in our joined American history. And it is our task, and the work of others, to return to and hold dear the beautiful, flawed, embodied spirit alive in its imperfect matter.

2. REANIMATION OF THE WORLD

Culture evolves out of the experience of living with a land. For traditional Indian people, this habitation with land has developed over centuries, in some cases longer than 10,000 years. Deep knowledge of the land has meant survival, in terms of both sustenance and healing. Native people recognize that disease of the body is often caused by imbalance, sometimes originating within the human body and spirit, sometimes in the outside world. Either way, relationship with all the rest of creation is central to healing. Cure begins, and ends, with relationship. The purpose of ceremony is to restore the individual to their place within all the rest. If medicinal herbs are used, the effectiveness of the cure depends on an intimate knowing of the plant, the land around it, the mineral content of the soil, whether there has been lightning in the region, rainfall, and even which animals have passed through the territory of the plant. The healing capacity of plants is strengthened inside human knowledge; the stories of the plant, both mythic and historical, are essential, adding the human dimension to the world of nonhuman nature. It's an intricate science, recon-necting and restoring the human body with earth, cosmos.

There has been a growing understanding among non-Indians of the need for such relationship and connectedness. In the young science of ecology, it is known that every piece of the puzzle of life is necessary. This is a time of what I call the reanimation of the natural world by white men, as they are newly discovering an old understanding, that everything on earth is alive and that the relationship between all these lives makes for the whole living planet. While native people have been ridiculed for these views, James Lovelock has been hailed as a genius for his return to old Indian ways of thinking and knowing, for originating what he has called the Gaia hypothesis.

This is not an entirely new concept to Western culture; Paracelsus, like traditional Indian people, knew that har-mony with the land and universe was the goal of healing, that body and land, such as in the tribal ceremonial sense, are intricately connected.

But by and large, the Western way of knowing has lost track of this understanding of the world, and the body is still associated with a kind of wilderness; there are dangers inside us, it is believed. And the body truly speaks its own tongue. When we go inside ourselves, there is fear, sometimes, and sorrow, a language of pain and need that we wish to avoid. What dancer Martha Graham meant when she spoke of the house of pelvic truth is that the body is a landscape of truth-telling. Our animal selves are more than nails and teeth that remain from before evolution, and that have torn their way through the world. The experience of the wild is inside us, beyond our mental control, and it lies alongside the deep memory of wilderness, and it has rules and laws that do not obey our human will.

More than symbol, more than the bread and wine of Christ, the body is a knowing connection, it is the telling thing, the medium of experience, expression, being, and knowing. Just as the earth is one of the bodies of the universe, we are the bodies of earth, accidental atoms given this form. An ancient and undivided world lies curled inside us with an ancestral memory that remembers our lives in the wilderness. What the body knows and where it takes us is navigated from an inner map not always carried in daily consciousness.

There are other dangers to these inner truths. Psychologist C. A. Meier said that as the wilderness decreases outside us the wilderness inside us will grow. While the word *wilderness* is still used by him in its most negative connotation, in many ways his statement has proved accurate. There was a recent case in New York where boys went "wilding," attacked a woman, raping and beating her, and left her for dead. In their own term, "wilding" is a truth distorted but carried down through American history with its aggression against tribes, its loss of species, its body hatred and fear of the true, untouched by humans wild.

For some, the only connection to this inner world has been violence. It is why so many men have described times of war as times when they felt the most alive. It is through events of war that they are thrown into the powerful world of bodily feeling. This is one of the unfortunate results of our broken connection with self and with land. And it seems, with the ever-increasing violence of our contemporary world, that we are losing the ability to be genuinely touched, both physically and emotionally, and that our lack of connection is destroying our capacity for deep love.

We are in need of an integrity of being that recognizes this disregarded inner world. I mean integrity in the true sense of this word, the sense that addresses a human wholeness and completeness, an entirety of living, with body, land, and the human self in relationship with all the rest, and with a love that remembers itself.

There are sacred dimensions to such love and they allow for viewing the world in all its beauty with gratitude, depth, and the thread of connection. For as we breathe, we are air. We are water. We are earth. We are what is missing from the equation of wholeness.

The body, made of earth's mud and breathed into, is the temple, and we need to learn to worship it as such, to move slowly within it, respecting it, loving it, treating ourselves and all our loved ones with tenderness. And the love for the body and for the earth are the same love.

Crazy Horse, one of the brilliant and compassionate leaders of the Sioux nation who witnessed the death of the animals and loved ones, wore a stone beneath his arm that was given him by an old medicine man named Chips. The stone was his ally. For Indian people, even now, the earth and its inhabitants all have spirit, matter is alive, and the world is an ally. This is necessary to remember as we go about a relearning of the sacred flesh, that we are energized by the stars, by the very fire of life burning within all the containers and kinds of skin, even the skin of water, of stone.

3. ALL MY RELATIONS

It is a sunny, clear day outside, almost hot, and a slight breeze comes through the room from the front door. We sit at the table and talk. As is usual in an Indian household, food preparation began as soon as we arrived and now there is the snap of potatoes frying in the black skillet, the sweet smell of white bread overwhelming even the grease, and the welcome black coffee. A ringer washer stands against the wall of the kitchen, and the counter space is taken up with dishes, pans, and boxes of food.

I am asked if I still read books and I admit that I do. Reading is not "traditional" and education has long been suspect in communities that were broken, in part, by that system, but we laugh at my confession because a television set plays in the next room.

In the living room there are two single beds. People from reservations, travelers needing help, are frequent guests here. The man who will put together the ceremony I have come to request sits on one, dozing. A girl takes him a plate of food. He eats. He is a man I have respected for many years, for his commitment to the people, for his intelligence, for his spiritual and political involvement in concerns vital to Indian people and nations. Next to him sits a girl eating potato chips, and from this room we hear the sounds of the freeway.

After eating and sitting, it is time for me to talk to him, to tell him why we have come here. I have brought him tobacco and he nods and listens as I tell him about the help we need.

I know this telling is the first part of the ceremony, my part in it. It is a story, really, that finds its way into language, and story is at the very crux of healing, at the heart of every ceremony and ritual in the older America.

The ceremony itself includes not just our own prayers and stories of what brought us to it, but includes the unspoken records of history, the mythic past, and all the other lives connected to ours, our family, nations, and all other creatures.

I am sent home to prepare. I tie fifty tobacco ties, green. This I do with Bull Durham tobacco, squares of cotton that are tied with twine and left strung together. These are called prayer ties. I spend the time preparing in silence and alone. Each tie has a prayer in it. I will also need wood for the fire, meat and bread for food.

On the day of the ceremony, we meet in the next town and leave my car in public parking. My daughters and I climb into the backseat of my friend's car. The man who will help us is drumming and singing in front of us. His wife drives and chats. He doesn't speak. He is moving between the worlds, beginning already to step over the boundaries of what we think, in daily and ordinary terms, is real and present. He is already feeling, hearing, knowing what else is there, that which is around us daily but too often unacknowledged, a larger life than our own small ones. We pass billboards and little towns and gas stations. An eagle flies overhead. It is "a good sign," we all agree. We stop to watch it.

We stop again, later, at a convenience store to fill the gas tank and to buy soda. The leader still drums and is silent. He is going into the drum, going into the center, even here as we drive west on the highway, even with our conversations about other people, family.

It is a hot balmy day, and by the time we reach the site where the ceremony is to take place, we are slow and sleepy with the brightness and warmth of the sun. In some tribes, men and women participate in separate sweat lodge ceremonies, but here, men, women, and children all come together to sweat. The children are cooling off in the creek. A woman stirs the fire that lives inside a circle of black rocks, pots beside her, a jar of oil, a kettle, a can of coffee. The leaves of the trees are thick and green.

In the background, the sweat lodge structure stands. Birds are on it. It is still skeletal. A woman and man are beginning to place old rugs and blankets over the bent cottonwood frame. A great fire is already burning and the lava stones that will be the source of heat for the sweat are being fired in it.

A few people sit outside on lawn chairs and cast-off couches that have the stuffing coming out. We sip coffee and talk about the food, about recent events. A man tells us that a friend gave him money for a new car. The creek sounds restful. Another man falls asleep. My young daughter splashes in the water. Heat waves rise up behind us from the fire that is preparing the stones. My tobacco ties are placed inside, on the framework of the lodge.

By late afternoon we are ready, one at a time, to enter the enclosure. The hot lava stones are placed inside. They remind us of earth's red and fiery core, and of the spark inside all life. After the flap, which serves as a door, is closed, water is poured over the stones and the hot steam rises around us. In a sweat lodge ceremony, the entire world is brought inside the enclosure. The soft odor of smoking cedar accompanies this arrival of everything. It is all called in. The animals come from the warm and sunny distances. Water from dark lakes is there. Wind. Young, lithe willow branches bent overhead remember their lives rooted in ground, the sun their leaves took in. They remember that minerals and water rose up their trunks, and that birds nested in their leaves, and that planets turned above their brief, slender lives. The thunder clouds travel in from far regions of earth. Wind arrives from the four directions. It has moved through caves and breathed through our bodies. It is the same air elk have inhaled, air that passed through the lungs of a grizzly bear. The sky is there, with all the stars whose lights we see long after the stars themselves have gone back to nothing. It is a place grown intense and holy. It is a place of immense community and of humbled solitude; we sit together in our aloneness and speak, one at a time, our deepest language of need, hope, loss, and survival. We remember that all things are connected.

Remembering this is the purpose of the ceremony. It is part of a healing and restoration. It is the mending of a broken connection between us and the rest. The participants in a ceremony say the words "All my relations" before and after we pray; those words create a relationship with other people, with animals, with the land. To have health it is necessary to keep all these relations in mind.

The intention of a ceremony is to put a person back together by restructuring the human mind. This reorganization is accomplished by a kind of inner map, a geography of the human spirit and the rest of the world. We make whole our broken-off pieces of self and world. Within ourselves, we bring together the fragments of our lives in a sacred act of renewal, and we reestablish our connections with others. The ceremony is a point of return. It takes us toward the place of balance, our place in the community of all things. It is an event that sets us back upright. But it is not a finished thing. The real ceremony begins where the formal one ends, when we take up a new way, our minds and hearts filled with the vision of earth that holds us within it, in compassionate relationship to and with our world.

We speak. We sing. We swallow water and breathe smoke. By the end of the ceremony, it is as if skin contains land and birds. The places within us have become filled. As inside the enclosure of the lodge, the animals and ancestors move into the human body, into skin and blood. The land merges with us. The stones come to dwell inside the person. Gold rolling hills take up residence, their tall grasses blowing. The red light of canyons is there. The black skies of night that wheel above our heads come to live inside the skull. We who easily grow apart from the world are returned to the great store of life all around us and there is the deep-est sense of being at home here in this intimate kinship. There is no real aloneness. There is solitude and the nurtur-ing silence that is relationship with ourselves, but even then we are part of something larger.

After a sweat lodge ceremony, the enclosure is aban-doned. Quieter now, we prepare to drive home. We pack up the kettles, the coffeepot. The prayer ties are placed in nearby trees. Some of the other people prepare to go to work, go home, or cook a dinner. We drive home. Every-thing returns to ordinary use. A spider weaves a web from one of the cottonwood poles to another. Crows sit inside the framework. It's evening. The crickets are singing. All my relations.

c o n n i e   p o r t e r

beauty and the beast

Sometimes I find myself in a search for origins. Recently I have begun searching for the ultimate origin—how the universe began. In my spare time, I've been reading quantum physics, studying the world of the subatomic, trying to find where *it* all began. The more I read about quarks, muons, bosons, the strong and weak nuclear forces, antiparticles, particle accelerators, the more I have begun to believe in the uncertainty principle.

Heisenberg's principle states that increasing the accuracy of the measurement of one observable quantity increases the uncertainty with which other quantities can be known. The principle applies to the world of subatomic particles, but I've made a quantum leap and have begun applying it to my life.

In my life I have tried to find the moment I first tied my shoes, the day when I truly understood how to hit a backhand, the meal when I first enjoyed the oily richness of avocados, the moment when I fell in love with a man I no longer even know. I don't feel the failure of memory stops me from finding these moments. It's the uncertainty principle. After all, each of us is a universe unto ourselves, an

assemblage of subatomic particles bound by the laws of physics. Our mad scramble to take pictures, scribble in journals,
record our lives on videotape, is not an attempt to preserve
memories, but to fight against something quite elementary
and inescapable. It is an attempt to reduce the uncertainty
in our lives, to be sure about shoes and backhands, avocados
and men, as if one particular instant in time holds some key
to who we are. When I look back at records of moments in
my life, I often do so with wonder. The more I am sure I fell
in love with a man I no longer even know on an overcast
Thursday night in June when we walked the beach, his face
suddenly appearing before mine, a shining moon, as he first
tried to kiss me, the less I am sure about what beach it was,
or what it was I loved about him in the first place.

In my readings about the origin of the universe, I have
my favorite theory—there is no one moment where *it* all
began. Time is finite in the past, but bound by a curved
hemisphere. Trying to find that moment is like trying to find
the point on Earth where *Earth* began, or attempting to find
the origins in our lives. I've come to feel it is truly less
important to know any one moment as a crystalline bubble
of time floating through space with a self-contained meaning than it is to see them all as part of a continuum. What
do all of the moments, certain and uncertain, say about who
we are?

There are two moments in my life, I can happily say, I
have no pictures of, no journal entries about. They both
involve me wresting with a pair of uncooperative jeans. The
first struggle was when I was a sophomore in high school.
The jeans were Levi's, designed over a hundred years ago for

white men. They were cut narrow in the thighs and had absolutely no room for a behind. I had plenty of behind and thighs, but I still wanted them. Levi's were in fashion, and I was at the age where I had discovered that word—Fashion— the prevailing style. Though I only wore a size seven, I had to buy pants four or five inches bigger than my waist size in order to accommodate my figure. The jeans fit like a second skin over my behind and thighs, but the waist was so big, a gap stood out in the back, one that could not be fully cinched by a belt. Whenever I sat in class there was a very real risk of mooning anyone who sat behind me. I had bowed down to the great beast of fashion; little did it matter that my butt was showing.

The second struggle with jeans was when I was a sopho-more in college and the fight was with a pair of Sassoons. Now these were the "disco years." Don't get me wrong; I am not one of those people who think that "Disco Sucks." I enjoyed going out dancing two, three, four nights a week. I don't know if the concept of disco was such a big deal for black people. We've been gathering for sweaty, heart-pound-ing dance sessions where the music is driven by a hypnotic drumbeat for thousands of years. The fashion of those disco years is something I still question. For men, there were mil-lions of yards of polyester spun into gaudy printed shirts and broad-lapeled suits. I see them sometimes when I'm shop-ping the Goodwill or Salvation Army stores. These shirts and suits will survive thermonuclear meltdown, or will at least be around until some fashion maven decides they and leisure suits are once again in style. If you don't believe me, witness the return of bell-bottoms and platform shoes.

Someone is planning for their return. What won't be back from the disco years, I am fairly certain of, are the designer jeans for women. They were meant to be worn tight enough to cut off circulation. You bought them a size or two smaller than your actual size, and stuffed yourself in.

I still remember shopping for a pair with a friend. In order to pull them up, I had to lie down on the floor of the dressing room and have her press on my stomach. When I told her I was in pain, she said, "Oh, Connie, this isn't bad at all. I read about this one woman in New York City. She had her friend *step* on her stomach so she could get into her pants." With those inspiring words, I sucked my stomach in, and I got the jeans to zip. My friend had to hoist me up, stiff-legged and sore. Before I could even look in the mirror, I felt a sensation inching up my stomach. It felt like my skin was bursting open. "Oh, damn, the zipper popped!" my friend yelled. She ran out of the dressing room to get me another pair. Perhaps that should have been a signal for me to stop. But as I looked in the mirror, I thought I looked good, stuffed as I was like a sausage into a casing. My friend returned and we began again, her pushing, me sucking my stomach in, and this time trying to suck in my butt. They zipped! The beast was no match for me. I had defeated it again.

For over a year, I wore the jeans out to dance. I wasn't able to sit in them, or bend, or make any sudden moves, but I didn't have to lie down to get them on. They had loosened up some, about a quarter inch. I had an awful stomachache when I peeled them off at three or four in the morning, and half-inch welts around my waist where the jeans cut into me, but those things did not matter. Now you might say, with the uncertainty principle at work, how can you be sure of any of this? Perhaps the jeans were not Sassoons. Maybe they were Bonjours, or Cacharels. They could have been. I'm certain of the battle with them and with the other jeans in high school because I still have the butt I attempted to squeeze into those pants. It is like some squash left on the vine too long, getting bigger and bigger. Remembering those struggles is not just stopping to gaze at some embarrassing moments in my quest to please the beast. Wasn't I a silly young woman? Most young women are. What I am more interested in those moments for is their place in the continuum. Because they point out to me, the way I am shaped, with the roundest of butts, is not pleasing to the beast now, nor was then, and perhaps it may never be.

I find it quite interesting that in recent years parts of black women have been seen as pleasing by the beast, not on black women, but on white women. Braided hair was seen as beautiful and exotic when Bo Derek wore her hair corn-rowed and beaded in 10. Some even called it the "Bo Derek" look. Michelle Pfeiffer brought our lips into fashion. The "pouty" look I heard it called, lips that were sexy yet a little sullen. Full lips, but not too full, were in for about a year. I saw white women on some talk show having their lips injected with silicone.

I suppose imitation is the sincerest form of flattery. The braids, the lips, having white women put them on is some kind of a compliment to black women. While Bo and Michelle are considered beautiful for having taken a piece here and a piece there, someone like Whoopi Goldberg with her braids and dreads and full lips is not. Some people see her as ugly. But what disturbs me even more is that many people see her as someone to be laughed at not for her comic genius, but because of her looks. A few years back she even starred in a movie entitled *Fatal Beauty*.

As I've been reading about the world of the subatomic, I've come to realize that the view of the universe on that level is limited. One can find the reason why rainbows appear in the sky, why there is gravity, or how planets are formed. But from that vantage point, one cannot see the iridescent rainbows of Oahu, feel the queasy first dip of a monster coaster, see Venus bloom in a purple western sky after a sunset. With all of its power to explain the universe, quantum physics holds little power for me in actually describing it. It is filled with dissection—particles, and those particles with particles. If one were to describe a human being using the world of the subatomic, it might be impossible to recognize what was being described as a living, breathing person. It is true we are a collection of particles subject to the laws of physics. But how could humor, love, beauty, grace, be explained by talking about the activities of electrons, protons, and neutrons? We are living proof that the whole is truly more than the sum of its parts. Because our parts are in the droplets of the rainbow, the steel of the roller-coaster tracks, the clouds that shroud Venus. Sometimes the long view is what is needed, the distance to recognize the whole and see its beauty.

To take the long view of someone like Whoopi and accept her as beautiful is to do what the beast of fashion has never had any intention of doing: be inclusive. The beast relies on a kind of uncertainty principle of its own. It makes money by trying to make us feel unsure about how we look, disassembling us part by part, feature by feature, outfit by outfit, and then selling us what it says are the pieces we need to be whole again, to be the beauty reflected in its eyes. This dissecting is dehumanizing, and when it comes to black women, I think the dehumanization is so complete that it is hard to recognize. It can lead one to feel that someone like Whoopi Goldberg is ugly. One can point to her eclectic style or dress, or some unnameable quality she lacks. One can much more easily label her a "Fatal Beauty" and dismiss her than do the hard job of looking at why she is dismissed. To me, she looks like millions of other black women. I don't know if it is supposed to be her dark skin, or her nappy hair, or her full lips, or maybe even her round behind that lead some to dismiss her.

It is easy to blame the beast, to hate it. Talking about it is like talking about the *media* or the *government*. All three are bloated creatures that have hundreds of years of both racism and sexism to feed on. We can't blame all of society's problems on them. We feed them all, though at times I feel we are sure it is the other way around. *They* make us the way we are, the fashion mavens, the reporters, the politicians. *They* are the ones who have forced attitudes and taxes, ill-fitting clothes and violence onto us.

This past year, two characters have appeared on the Fox network and have become wildly popular, at least among people I know. They are both black female characters played by black male comedians: Wanda, played by Jamie Fox, and Sha-Na-Na (Sha-Nay-Nay), played by Martin Lawrence.

Wanda wears a blond wig, is cross-eyed, has a permanently curled upper lip. Sha-Na-Na wears braids, fake fingernails, and high-top sneakers. The characters have some things in common. Each has a heavily padded, exaggerated behind, about two to three times as large as a real one. Both are dark-skinned women who dress in outlandish clothes, are aggressive with men, forever in search of a sexual partner, and desperate because men find them repulsive. I have a niece who is twelve and who likes to watch both of these characters.

My niece is just beginning her fascination with the beast. She has arrived at the castle and has begun poking through the rooms. She does her nails, handles a curling iron and a steam iron far better than I do, and will not leave the house unless her French roll and finger curls are perfect, her clothes carefully ironed and matched. I must say that at that same age I was a slob. I never thought about doing my nails, and if I could get away without combing my hair, I would do so for days. Even now I go for days with my hair uncombed, and I've never had a manicure. But my niece is quite different. She is at that curious age where her mind is just opening up to a world of new ideas and also is just beginning to shut down. Though she likes Wanda and Sha-Na-Na and finds them funny, she also finds them repulsive. She thinks they are ugly and stupid and that men should reject them; after all, she reasons, they aren't real. You can't walk down the street and meet women like them. They fall into this special category—worthy of being verbally abused and ridiculed because it is worth a good laugh.

I don't know what either comic intended when he created his character. I must admit, the characters are funny, especially Sha-Na-Na, who is a nosy next-door neighbor. Too often it is painful to watch these women. I know a certain amount of comedy depends on exaggeration, on stock characters we can recognize easily. But the amount of exaggeration used for each fits too neatly within too many stereotypes. Neither character is really given a chance. They are cast into desperation, and when they act it out, it is good for a laugh. Their creators make absurd the idea of either woman being seen as a lovable, sexual being. Having any man love them or even desire them is as outlandish as master falling in love with mammy, or any male lead with the "fatal beauty." Lawrence and Fox, in the guise of Sha-Na-Na and Wanda, have assembled women, part by part, stereotype by stereotype, outfit by outfit, and asked us to accept them as whole, as real. My niece is right; these women are not real. But that does not mean I can easily laugh at their mistreatment because I know the source of it. It is a kind of warped internalized view that some of us black people have of ourselves. From that view, what makes us unique is also what makes us ugly, laughable even—lips and noses, hair and butts. All of this can't be laid in the lap of the beast. It is simply feeding off of the racism and sexism inherent in America's history. If not thrown another scrap, it has enough to live on for hundreds of years more. But it is fed with characters like Wanda and Sha-Na-Na whom their creators have literally made the butt of jokes. Unwittingly, Lawrence and Fox perpetuate destructive stereotypes about black women, and do as much harm as any maven conjuring up images of women with store-bought lips.

As natural as it is to look for beginnings, it is to look for endings. For the universe it may be the "big crunch," all the matter being squeezed into a singularity, or time running backward, or maybe there will be no end at all. My time of being ruled by the beast has ended. These days I wear my jeans "relaxed." They're being advertised heavily now for both women and men, "Relaxed Riders." I don't think they are specifically made to accommodate me. I suppose it's more that the baby boomers have grown big butts in their middle age. I have given up the battle, though, not just with the jeans but with the beast as well. I am not certain in what year or day it happened. Was it the day I refused to buy a "popcorn" dress or those "slave sandals," or was it when I turned my nose up at the mere idea of wearing anything that was part of the "Annie Hall" look? Perhaps if I had actually let my friend stand on my stomach to jam me into my jeans, I would be in a different place now. Perhaps the place might be where I no longer had a spleen. Or a place where I waited impatiently every month for the latest issue of *Glamour*, *Vogue*, or *Essence* to tell me what I had to do, what I had to buy in order to stay on the good side of the beast. Time, more than anything, has swept me away from caring about what it has to say. There is something natural about young women beginning the search, doing some disassembling, examining themselves part by part, and then reconstructing themselves. When I was younger, I had no idea who I was, or how to go from who I had been—part tomboy, part nerd —to being a woman. I thought there was truly some magic piece to be found somewhere in the beast's castle, like a pair of jeans, that would make me complete.

In the fairy tale, the beast claims he is a slave to Beauty. He needs her because of the spell cast on him. Beauty finds out about the spell in a dream. The beast's story is quite tired, really. Of course, he was a prince. He is no longer because he had no pity when an old woman, a hag, he calls her, asked him for help. The reason he turned her away— she was too ugly. The old woman turned him into a beast to teach him a lesson. So now he is a slave to Beauty, and treats her well. He even gives her a magic mirror. But alas, he is good to her for a reason. Well, maybe a few reasons. She is a beauty and can free him from his spell by loving him and marrying him. The magic mirror he gives her even helps to save his own life. She falls in love with him and blah, blah, blah. That was the tale, one that a beast should tell in a dream to a beauty as young as tender and as silly as she was. In reality, our beast would have *us* be *its* slave forever, to wander endlessly through its castle, trapped and uncertain of ourselves. Our beast also labors under a spell, cast perhaps by an old woman, or a black woman, or a fat woman, or a flat-chested woman, or a big-breasted woman, or perhaps one with a full behind. You see, the beast has offended so many. I am uncertain that it even knows it needs to be rescued, but I am certain, if it ever does, it will have to free itself. It will have to pick up its magic mirror and, piece by piece by piece, begin to examine itself.

n a o m i   w o l f

keep them
implanted
and ignorant

It never fails to astonish. The very people who gleefully
mislead and harm women for profit will, when put for once
on the defensive, lay claim to the rhetoric of "women's
choice." In the excerpt from the Dow Corning press conference reprinted in *The Wall Street Journal*, January 15, 1992,
the company concludes that "it is important for the woman
to have the right to make [the] choice, to make an intelligent, informed decision."

I couldn't agree more, and only wish Dow Corning's
phrase-making had some corollary in reality. The reason
that millions of women with implants today face the terrible
possibility of disfigurement, chronic pain, and disease is that
they were not deemed worthy of having the facts. The implant industry was not monitoring, the medical profession
was not overseeing, Congress was not regulating, and the
press was not investigating the dawn of the Age of Cosmetic
Surgery, the fastest-growing and least-regulated medical specialty, whose experimental subjects are at least 87 percent
female.

Women should be free to do what they want with their bodies; that is a basic feminist right. But a real choice on implants requires what medical ethicists call "informed consent." Information about breast implants and other cosmetic-surgery procedures is largely inaccessible to women. According to medical ethicists, who follow the Nuremberg Guidelines established after World War II, any procedure performed on a patient without informed consent is a medical experiment.

When investigating breast implants for my book *The Beauty Myth*, I found that even if a woman does full-time funded research for six months, she won't find facts she needs to make a genuinely informed choice. Why? Because they don't exist.

To whom are women supposed to turn for this information? To Dow Corning? Reached by phone yesterday, the firm said it did contribute funding to one study on cancer and breast implants. It compiled reports from doctors' own files. Also yesterday, the firm said it will make public ninety studies and internal memoranda that have been identified by the Food and Drug Administration as part of the basis for a moratorium on implant use. But until this week (January 23, 1992), at least, the firm had not made public results of one large-scale, long-term, independent study following up on implants—checking for rupturing, hardening, reoperation, and cancer detection difficulties. Such a study is an obvious step.

While surgeons claim a rate of "capsular contraction" (when scar tissue forms around the implant) of 2 percent to 10 percent, Gerald McKnight's *The Skin Game*, an exposé of the beauty industry, estimates actual reoperation rates may be as high as 40 percent to 70 percent. Women don't know that the high reoperation rate taken for granted by manufacturers and surgeons has led to a situation in which the industry offers—in Britain at least—implant replacement insurance to surgeons: a new one when the first one ruptures. The industry can assert that "most" women are delighted with the implants." But in this controversy, a core feminist principle would come in handy: When in doubt, ask the women.

Can women turn to the medical establishment? A spokesman for Rep. Ron Wyden (D., Ore.) says "all normal layers of peer review are missing." The American Medical Association has never established a standard screening procedure for patients of cosmetic surgery. (Reached by phone yesterday, the AMA pointed out that it is not a regulatory body.) Since there are no guidelines for what an "operable condition" might be, cosmetic surgeons have been free to tell women who have nursed that their breasts are "atrophied" and in need of implantation. The field is so unregulated that in many states, any nonspecialist M.D. can call himself a cosmetic surgeon and perform implantations. *Self* magazine estimates that profits from breast-implant surgery amount to $374 million a year. In an editorial printed earlier this year, *The Wall Street Journal* asserted that money is the bottom line in bringing out claims against the manufacturer; it's been money, rather, that has kept the dangers quiet all along.

The AMA does not keep death or mutilation rates for women with implants. Experimental procedures are regularly carried out: One doctor, for instance, has started "stacking" implants—putting two in each breast. While the death rate for cosmetic surgery has been estimated by the industry itself as one in 30,000, another industry survey of 100,000 patients puts it at one in 10,000. No one knows for sure.

Can women go to the government? It was not until 1988, a decade into the Implant Era, that a congressional hearing was convened; this fast degenerated into territorial lobbying between the cosmetic and plastic surgeons. Congress saw 1,790 pages of testimony about how women were being deceived and disfigured. What legislation has resulted? None.

Can we turn to the press? The press bears the greatest guilt of all for this crisis. In the 1970s the Federal Trade Commission ruled that cosmetic surgeons could advertise. This led to an advertising-editorial spiral, especially in women's magazines. The bigger the ads the surgeons took out, the more articles touted the benefits of breast surgery. While some articles mentioned some dangers, nearly all placed the onus for safe surgery on the woman, rather than on government or industry. Many journalists simply recycled the press releases sent them by surgeons. The end product of this cash cow? The October 1990 *Cosmopolitan* article called "Plastic Surgery: I Decided to Have It All."

The ad revenue ran over into the mainstream press: Surgeons ran a full-page ad in *The New York Times* with a famous model selling new breasts. In the *Chicago Tribune*'s WomanNews section, surgeons' ads were a source of revenue. The American Society of Plastic and Reconstructive Surgery offers a $500 journalism award complete with two tickets to a gala banquet.

Serious journalists had the resources to pursue this story. This is more than the story of another unregulated industry in boom years. But in a time of backlash against feminism, a growth industry that could send women the message that they were structurally inadequate was not to be scrutinized. Why? Because implants involved women in pursuit of a positive sexual self-image, the issue was not serious.

The pressure on women to have implants is intense. According to *Psychology Today*, women's dissatisfaction with their breasts rose in the 1980s, when breast augmentation became common for fashion models. The unquestioned glamorization of breast implants is about women's role in society, just as the unquestioned removal of women's ovaries in the nineteenth century and the unquestioned clitoral excising of women in Muslim countries are examples of medicine serving ideology.

"Caveat Emptor": "Weigh the benefits against the risks," say the surgeons and the industry. Once again, their condescension to women is appalling. If you are an adult and are treated like one—whether you are buying insurance or opening a business—you get the facts. In negotiating for their own health and safety, women deserve no less.

hanan   al-shaykh

inside a moroccan bath

The steam rises. It ascends like clouds drifting upward from the earth to the sky, brushing the naked bodies as gently as butterflies or eyelashes closing in sleep. But it spoils eye makeup, robs hair of its shine, dissolves the red on lips and cheeks, and erases penciled eyebrows. I'd be glad if it engulfed me completely and turned me into a ghost. I am hesitant, embarrassed, unsure of myself. I want to rush and hide away in a corner, or just leave altogether.

I didn't expect to react like this. When I undressed and entered the baths, the throb of noise and heaving female flesh took me completely by surprise. What's happening to me, the emancipated woman who writes about frustration, passion, lust, ecstasy, and describes thighs and breasts in minute detail? Why am I staring as if I've never seen a woman's body before, overwhelmed by the sight of them all, even those I know, and shyly clasp my arms across my front, clutching my armpits as if I'm desperate to hide my breasts? This means I'm still suffering from the same complex I always had about my body, which I thought was dead and buried once I dared to wear a two-piece bathing suit, fell in love, married, had children, lived in the West.

The steam increases, rising from the tiles, soapy, sweaty, smelling of henna and perfume, bearing the gossip exchanged by the bathers in spite of the shrieking and yelling of the children. The baths are for washing but also for caring for the body on a grand scale. Bodies that are not laid aside after fulfilling their functions in marriage, sex, and childbirth to become merely factories swallowing and excreting food can continue to expect this fate. I see women descending on their bodies like furies, flaying them with loofahs and stones as if they want to exchange their existing skins for new ones. I've never seen a shop in Europe with half the bath products that they have on offer here: country-style soap, cleansing mud the color of petrol, dried rose petals ground to a powder, ghassoul for the hair, artificial loofahs with bristles that look as if they're for washing the dishes or sweeping the floor, natural loofahs, pumice stones, manufactured stones. Bathing and massaging the body is supposed to be the main point of visiting the public baths, even though most houses have their own bathrooms. From what I've seen of these small, cold rooms, they are mainly used for washing the clothes, while here the women are dotted about the vast space singly and in clumps, intent on pulling and pummeling their flesh, pouring water over themselves, rinsing their hair, embracing the steam as it enters every pore, and sitting in silence from time to time. It's as if the desire to be alone with their bodies as they wait for the heat to strike them has killed the wish to talk with the others. So all this activity is for the sake of being alone with the body released from its prison of constricting undergarments, thick outer garments, headcover and shoes, and cleansed from the dust of the streets, the clinging smells of food, and the sweat running under the arms, between the breasts, and down the forehead with the effort of scrubbing tiles in dim rooms, washing children's heads, rubbing chickens with lemon and cumin.

I look at the women sitting, standing, bending, squatting, stretching, some silent, some shouting and laughing. I gaze at their plump, plump bodies, their hanging breasts, the numerous folds of skin on their stomachs, the fat that makes the flesh around their thighs pucker into circles like fans. And there are bodies disfigured by burn marks, scars, surgery, old age. However, it seems to me as I watch them move gracefully around the baths, floating, ethereal, that they are preparing to make love to freedom and will soon be in ecstasy. I stand here totally confused in the heat. I am in Shoufshawen in Morocco with my Moroccan friend, who has begun scrubbing a patch of the tiled floor with her loofah and soap, muttering to herself for forgetting the extra towels to sit on, then raising her voice to a shrill cry to answer back to an old woman who's accused her of stealing her place.

I would like to sit down in the heart of the muggy warmth and close my eyes so that all I can hear is the slop and smack of the water as it rinses bodies clean of the dust of the outside world, but I can't bring myself to. I am still shocked by my discovery that I am not completely at ease with the shape of my body, having thought I'd gone beyond that stage long ago. It doesn't help when the masseuse remarks laughingly to my friend that she will only charge me half price since she is only going to have to massage half a body.

From the time I first began to have a mental picture of my face and figure without needing to look in a mirror, I understood that I was suffering from an incurable illness: the disease of thinness, with its accompanying symptoms of pallor and weakness. No, I didn't discover this for myself. I heard it constantly on the lips of others, adults and children, and saw it in the way they looked at me. They not only made comments and throwaway remarks, confirming what I already knew, but were out to criticize and reproach me. "Why are you so thin?" "Why are you letting yourself fade away?" Some went to great lengths to stress the defect they had been kind enough to draw my attention to, and I was known as the skinny girl, kibbeh on a stick (i.e., my head was the kibbeh and my body the stick), bamboo cane, cornstalk. They would put their thumbs and forefingers round my forearm and if they met (and they always did) there would be roars of laughter and a general feeling of satisfaction that the magic test had worked. When the teacher wanted to describe the backbone in nature study, she made me take off my overall and turn my back so that she could point with her ruler to each vertebra.

Being thin meant that I was branded as sickly and physically weak, and so I was never encouraged in sports periods or picked for teams. Instead they would call out, "Hey, skinny! If they rolled you up in the gym mat no one would notice!" So the idea that I was different from my peers began to preoccupy me and make me keep to myself, unsmiling and with none of a child's spontaneity. I think now that my reluctance to concentrate in class might have been a product of this feeling of terror that overcame me every time I thought I might have to leave my cozy lair and stand up by the board in front of the whole class.

As soon as I was old enough to know what I was doing, I began to take cod liver oil capsules and make my family buy fresh milk, for I had made up my mind to gain weight by any means possible. When my efforts came to nothing I forced myself to get used to my bony shoulders and my protruding collarbone, which formed a necklace each time I raised my shoulders, although I don't suppose anyone was entertained by this but me.

I used to envy the ripe, round cheeks of the other girls, and their chubby arms and legs. I was jealous of the fattest girl in our class, with her many chins, thick forearms, and her huge bottom that shook at the tiniest movement. I envied swellings of any kind: swollen eyes, cheeks inflamed with toothache, thighs that were red and angry following injections. I welcomed anything that would allow me to enjoy an increase in flesh, to prove that I was not a barren wasteland, had a normal body that reacted to illnesses and external influences. I was so envious, and I withdrew from my fellows and drew pictures of myself looking like a balloon on a couple of matchsticks. I was jealous, jealous and turned inward, convincing myself that I was different. I pretended not to enjoy belly dancing like the rest of the girls because it was old-fashioned, and so I sat out at weddings, my jealous eye observing the swaying breasts and buttocks of the girls who were dancing, and the perfect control they had over their waists and stomachs so that their whole bodies writhed and coiled like serpents in venomous harmony. My other eye tried to pretend it wasn't there, terrified that it would meet the eyes of the dancers and they would insist that I join them on the floor, as was the custom, whereupon I would fall into the snares of shame and humiliation. I was quite certain that if I danced and tried to twist and sway I would bend stiffly like a wooden plank and if I squirmed sensuously I would look as if I'd suffered an electric shock.

I kept apart, in mixed gatherings as well as all-female occasions, persuaded that I was different because of my passion for words and stories, and that I was going to be a writer. I used to retire into a corner with pen and paper, and pretend to be writing poetry, off in another world far removed from my companions' ephemeral preoccupations, knowing in advance with absolute conviction that nobody would ever ask me to dance, or marry me, and that I would never have children. My periods didn't come because I was so thin, and the proof was that I was almost fourteen and therefore well past the age when they should have arrived. So as soon as I saw the long-awaited brownish spots in my knickers, I flew to announce it to the women of the house, then rushed to the neighbors to give them the news, or rather to make them acknowledge that I was normal. However, reaching puberty did nothing to alleviate my anxiety about my scrawny shoulders, the nonexistence of my chest and bottom, and my thin wrists and arms. I used to shut my eyes attempting to push away the recurring image of a boy holding me in his arms, because a schoolfriend had said I was like a soup made of bones when she embraced me one day, and after that I had always imagined that as soon as a boy touched me my bones would stick into him so sharply that this would be his abiding image of the encounter.

I created an image of pure fantasy for myself, a girl sitting staring distractedly at the horizon or up into the sky, alone day and night, a girl who had abandoned her body and become a specter, or a spirit, pale and solemn like one of Dracula's victims. I convinced myself that I had been made of different clay from those plump, fleshy girls who won the hearts of boys with humdrum tastes and greedy appetites. God had created me without bumps or curves to flutter gracefully through life like a butterfly. To my surprise, this self-made persona attracted a boy who used to call me the Virgin Mary, or the nun, and who got out of dancing with me by saying he was afraid I'd break or be contaminated. He sent me Khalil Gibran's books and pictures of sunrises and sunsets.

I did nothing to change my image until I saw a poster of Audrey Hepburn that stuck in my mind. I felt she had come to take revenge on Brigitte Bardot for me.

I saw her closing her eyes and yielding to a kiss. I saw her encircled by two strong arms. I saw her, and I saw myself for the first time: long neck, pale skin, dark eyes, black hair and eyebrows. I bought a copy of *Breakfast at Tiffany's* and a pair of dark glasses with round frames, and borrowed a long black cigarette holder. I followed her news on and off screen. Was she in love? Married? Did she have any children? Was she planning to? I went to see all her films two or three times to observe and register everything that passed between her and the hero and try to detect whether he really wanted to kiss her even though she was so thin. Did he hold her fragile body as if she was any other actress, or was he scared that he would break one of her ribs? Would he reach out to feel her breast or deliberately ignore it to avoid causing embarrassment? I gazed at the relevant scenes to learn by heart the position of her arms and the manner of her response, and eventually made the discovery that with her thin body she had exploded preconceived notions of what a woman ought to be like. I remember writing after I'd seen one of her films, "She isn't the woman everyone falls in love with, or a flirt, or a woman with problems. She's a child, personifying innocence. She's untamed love, a fragrant fruit, graceful as a willow. Her face talks, laughs, cries, lives, captivating the hero and the audience and leaving them satisfied."

By imitating Audrey Hepburn and her hairstyle when I was seventeen, I attracted the attention of assorted poets, journalists, and cinema buffs of the opposite sex in my city, Beirut. First I had prepared the ground and redirected their ideas and enthusiasms along a particular course, feeding them with the notion that I belonged to a new breed of women who were attractive in a special, different way, by virtue of being thin and delicate in contrast to the male's brute strength. As this new-style woman was discussed and the connection made between me and her, I began to gain in confidence and self-esteem, although I put myself in a special category, which separated me from conventional femininity. A poet who was responsible for the cultural page of a daily newspaper began contacting me every time he came across a news item relating to Audrey Hepburn or a photo of her. I felt he was flirting with me via her, especially when he got his hands on the first photos of her in a bathing suit. He said she was like a swan or Lolita. Hope grew in me that I would become an object of desire even if it meant copying Audrey Hepburn's style. I pictured that anyone sitting across a table from me would be enchanted by my slender body and my innocent, childlike gestures, until one day I was sitting in a café with the poet just as she would have sat, confused and lost in the bustle and smoke and loneliness. I inhabited a different world from my family. I had been born and brought up in the heart of a noisy city in a house where they preferred the call to prayer and the sound of the Quran to singing and music. The clash between the city, with the clamor of its cinemas and cafés and universities, and my restricted home environment with my family's subdued voices and monotonous daily routine was almost killing me. Uncertain where I stood, I longed to retreat into a corner and write of the sorrow and despair that gripped me whenever I thought about death and loneliness, or about getting away from home and re-creating myself on my own terms. So I cried tears of bewilderment in front of the poet, wondering what it was I wanted. I cried like Audrey Hepburn when she stood in the rain calling her cat: "Cat! Cat!" The poet reached out a hand to me, squeezed my arm, and patted me on the shoulder. I knew he couldn't take me in his arms like the hero when he was trying to ease Audrey Hepburn's loneliness and confusion in the face of the turbulent world. I was reassured by the warmth of his touch even though I was worried that people would notice. I clung to his hand as if it was my temporary life line, a compass that would help me find my way to the ends of the earth. Within me I carried this image of woman as fragile, delicate, and passionate beside man's overwhelming strength. Then the poet spoke hesitantly, full of sympathy and understanding: "I know what your problem is. It's because you're thin. That's what's responsible for all this grief. This uncertainty. You have to put on weight. A few kilos and you'll see, you'll be a different person. I used to have exactly the same problem."

After this episode I was no longer surprised by the way others viewed me, or how their ideas and perceptions regarding my thinness acted upon each other. I attached myself to an imaginary raft and rode the waves, rising and falling but never losing my grip. When I went to Egypt to study I wrote to a journalist friend who had his own arts and gossip page in a magazine, describing my experiences abroad and enclosing a recent photograph, and I was only mildly annoyed when a poem by him appeared in the magazine a few weeks later that included the line "My love's put on about two kilos and I love her almost twice as much." While I was in Egypt an Egyptian student used to follow me around the university saying "You're pretty. I love you. If only you weren't so skinny. Try and put on a bit of weight. You'd be a really beautiful woman. I'll tell you how to make me fall in love with you. If you do as I say you'll become like a big ripe peach. You have to eat macaroni. Blancmange. Rice. Beef marrow." And I wasn't really hurt when they told me that his girlfriend didn't care when she saw him pursuing me because she was sure that he couldn't fall in love with a woman whose arms and legs were practically nonexistent. Meanwhile his mother took pity on me, totally convinced that being away from my family and my country had affected my health and reduced me to this weakened state.

The poet's words, which had robbed me of my confi-

dence and happiness, made me able, eventually, to stick my
tongue out in response to a remark I heard as I walked
proudly past a café: "What a pity! That face and a body like
a sparrow!" They also made me tolerant with the dressmaker
when she suggested putting a double lining in my dress especially at the shoulders and hips. I blocked my ears and remained attached to my imaginary raft, swinging between the
heights and the depths, but never falling off. I calmed down
and took a hold of myself, reminding myself that I hadn't
come to Egypt because I was desperate to find love, but for
the sense of freedom I could enjoy there. I remembered the
mother of one of my friends back in Lebanon. She weighed
over two hundred kilos, and how her eyes had sparkled
when she found out I was going to Cairo! Her hand had
flown to her throat in a thoroughly feminine gesture. "You're
so lucky! Cairo! Only in Cairo do I feel that I'm really
beautiful." Meanwhile her husband, who was a gynecologist,
remarked that I should massage my breasts with olive oil
every day to make them grow.

The steam rises from my body and the bodies around
me. I realize why I am sad. The moment I entered the baths
I saw myself as thin again, imperfect next to the plump
ripeness of the other women. I am filled with sadness for the
years that should have been like Aladdin's lamp or a magic
carpet, transporting me away to discover the color of music
or the heart of an ant, while instead I had been crammed
into a rigid, gloomy mold with only a tiny chink to breathe
through. Now I am demanding of myself, of the steam, of

the women, why I had been denied this kernel of joy and security, this chance to explore, all because of a handful of flesh that wasn't there. I'd felt poverty-stricken and embarrassed hearing people say all the time that I was thin because I hadn't been fed properly. I'd stopped having the heart to look for emotional attachments, and felt inhibited when I moved and spoke. Sometimes I would rush into the café limping, pretending I'd hurt my foot to distract attention from my thin legs, and also just to confuse things. In my attempts to convince myself that I was desirable, I would be drawn into playing games with men, even those I didn't care about at all. For the sake of this absent flesh I had begun hiding my body under yards of material so that I looked like a cabbage with a human head, and inhabiting dark chambers of anxiety, fearful that I would never be able to have children. A neighbor of mine used to encourage her daughters to eat up food they didn't like by saying "Look at Hanan! If you don't eat up, you'll get like her!" And when one of them shouted, "I like Hanan! I want to be like her!" her mother said, to shut her up, "But Hanan will live all by herself. She'll never have children and nobody will ever call her Mama." How could I carry a child? Would the fetus have room, or would it be squashed up against my pelvis? How would it get its nourishment, seeing that the food I ate didn't seem to put any flesh on me?

I feel that the bodies around me, the hills and mountains of flesh observing me, have themselves nailed the conditions of entry over the door to happiness, by setting the standards of strength and beauty and decreeing what is acceptable and desirable. For these women still stick to the rule that says that the male eye is the only mirror where they can see their true reflection.

In the past, mothers, grandmothers, aunts, and neighbors were equipped with microscopic eyes for seeking out and examining future brides for the sons of the family in the public baths. They preferred to make their inspection there because the steam removed penciled eyebrows, made fine hair cling limply to the scalp, revealed whether the woman's body was firm or not. It had to be rounded, even if this meant there was no waist to speak of, have broad hips and a gently curved stomach sloping down to the thighs, uninterrupted by any bony protrusions. A woman's body was for bearing children, providing them with nourishment, giving them all the milk they wanted, and keeping them warm in the folds of its flesh. It was also for feeding and satisfying man's greedy lust. This is why the famous poets of the pre-Islamic era did not sing about thin women. Their poems about love and beauty are always concerned with curvaceous bodies, and even modern literature glorifies solid, voluptuous flesh and connects it with sexual desire.

But do the standards of the past still apply? Have Arab women not been affected by the West, where the revolutions not just against fat but any surplus flesh have resulted in illnesses, the coining of terms like anorexia and bulimia to designate them, and widespread recourse to cosmetic surgery, sometimes with unfortunate or even disastrous results?

Although it's hard to generalize, I think thinness is still considered undesirable in the Arab world, even among young women and adolescents. By this I don't mean they'd choose to be fat these days, but they like a shapely, athletic figure, combining grace and energy with femininity: prominent bust, slender waist, flat stomach, then curving buttocks and nicely rounded but firm bottom and thighs. They have a keen sense of what men find attractive, but at the same time have their own clearly defined criteria of what is desirable in a man: an athletic, well-proportioned body, "someone who fills his clothes," as they say, for a thin man, according to the conventional wisdom, is weak, has low self-esteem, and lacks personality, the exact opposite of what a woman wants in a man.

Inside the bath, the women's eyes never leave me and I am certain they are wondering where I am from. It must be the color of my skin. Am I from Fez, where the women delight in white skin and black hair? From the way they look I guess they approve of my fair skin, apparently still desirable because the dominant skin color in the Arab world is brown. Nevertheless, brown skin features in all the popular songs, but when I remarked on this to my mother, who was lamenting over the way my skin had changed color that summer, she replied, "Don't let these songs fool you. They're purely to reassure brown-skinned women."

It's my white skin that saves me now. It is a mark of femininity and fragility because it contrasts with the darker skin of men. It inspires poetic comparisons like "pearly white," "white as snow," "white as the surface of a jug of milk." But even whiteness has its conditions: There must be a tinge of crimson on the cheeks, otherwise it represents purity, chastity, and coldness.

The looks and whispers are giving way to laughter, or

barely suppressed sniggers. I have the uneasy feeling this time that they are thinking about my thinness in connection with sex, trying to picture me with a man. I'm used to provoking such reactions in other women fatter than me. Several years ago an elderly relation had picked me up and lifted me high in the air, exclaiming "You poor thing! You're as light as a feather! Does your husband squash you flat?" A friend asked me where my bottom had gone, and there are people who commiserate with my husband, saying there's nothing for him to hold on to.

I return their stares, wishing they knew what I am thinking: They will leave here buried under mounds of cloth to protect themselves from the shock of the cool air outside and perhaps also from the wounding glances of men, but when they reach home they will throw it all off and prance and sway before their husbands. Some will dress up in belly dancers' costumes, like a woman I know, or in underwear so clearly designed to be crudely seductive that it ends up with a surreal quality: I once saw a pair of battery-powered panties with a light that flashed on and off at the crotch. I know these women are scared of their husbands being prey to other women and want to keep them at home at any price, so they attract them at the level of lust and purely physical satisfaction, discounting the idea, on behalf of both themselves and their men, that love is also the desire to possess and delight in beauty.

I am boiling hot and move into one of the baths' cool rooms. Suddenly I think of my daughter, who is eighteen, and feel myself returning to normal. I see her slender figure in my mind's eye, and people complimenting her on being so tall and slim. I recall a photo of myself in my adolescence and decide that my thinness wasn't sickly but attractive: I look exactly like my daughter in it, except that I am seven centimeters shorter than her. I laugh involuntarily at the memory of another photo taken around the same time of me with my stomach sticking out. I used to take deep breaths and inflate it so that I looked fatter, even though I knew it gave me a distorted shape.

I retreat into myself. I will try to give this quietness to the one I love. I am perfectly content to be leaving and going back to the European city where I live, where people compliment me on keeping my figure. But I am still weighed down by these old-new feelings, which bring back to me a picture of my friend's father, the gynecologist, stamping on his brakes in the middle of a Beirut street indifferent to the stream of cars behind him, and shouting through the window as if there was no one else for miles around, "Hanan al-Shaykh! So you're married at last! Are your tits any bigger these days?"

janet   burroway

changes

HAIR

I was maybe thirty-five, six. I was in a high bed between enameled walls for one of those operations that needn't be named because it's unspellable. The black nurse arrived with basin, towel, soap, razor, and ready cheer. I moaned, and the muscles of my stomach clenched, maybe with fear, maybe with more minor dreads, remembering the shaving of my pubes when my first son was born, my angry certainty that it was unnecessary—that anger silenced by my ignorance— and the long scratchiness of the hair growing out.

Now the buoyant nurse told me to turn on my side and raise a knee. Oh, I said, relieved, she wasn't going to shave me then?

"Just in back! Oh, lord, love, I'm not going to take your glory!"

She drew the vowel out, voluptuous. I sighed with relief and pride. My glooory. It was so. The hair on my head is fine and straight, the stuff I shave under arms, on shins, is negligible and spiky. But there! Then! A nether Afro, black with red highlights, luxuriant, an ebullient mass. Brushed, it would spring back instantly into ringlets. The American euphemism "beaver" is ignorant, a thick flat metaphor, nothing like. But a "bush," yes, resilient, silky, and sunny; it was a ready growth, warm May sprout, moss and glossy.

I remember the delicate baldness of girlhood, and how as a child I a little fearfully imagined myself in that goatee. Now, the other side of glory, I look at the thinness of my fur and find it somewhat stingy of nature, mean-natured, not necessary, that I have become thus sparse.

Nobody, I take it, minds but me. It is not a death, a serious separation, is not grief. I seem to function better, come to that, than in the glory days. Hormones are keeping my bone marrow dense, knowing better how to choose a lover keeps me at better joy.

More. I'm lucky. By the time she was my age my grandmother wore on her head a half-wig called a transformation; by this age my mother's skull showed blue-white beneath the "poodle" cut crimped to hide it; in his forties my brother was egg-pated above his beard. I've escaped this Pierce-side-of-the-family tendency to baldness, and my barber who styles himself a stylist tells me that there's no sign I'm thinning on top.

Only below, this bush of best youth, this kinky growth, this sable V, this little lawn, this springing grass, this private isle, reminds me that the very hairs are numbered.

What do you say to the losses of age? Oh, well. Oh, well.

TONE

K., who has a younger lover, moans that he's always wanting her on top. Why does she dislike this? I thought we fought through the fifties, the sixties, to gain the right to that position. I thought we wanted access to men who al-

lowed, liked, preferred, requested it. I thought it was a
distinct advantage of the younger lover, the liberated generation. I thought we fought to overturn "missionary"
laws.

No. I know perfectly well what she means. She says,
"Your face is so much better on your back."

This is not very articulate, but it brings that discovery
back with a rush. I was doing something sweet. P. had no
bedroom mirror and I had a spare. This one was big and
clear and old, with a many-times white-painted frame of
heavy Victorian gingerbread. The glass was loose in the
frame and I was going to secure it before taking it to him for
long-term loan—an indefinite, commitment sort of loan. I
drove the little nails around the back of the frame, covered
the join with heavy tape, then turned it over on the carpet
to check the paint for nicks. Straddled hands and knees over
the silvered glass I caught sight of my face. Stopped shocked.
I watched the crawling creature warily. Its skin and chin
pulled forward off the bone, the jowls slid into the hollow of
its cheeks. The bold eyes hid under the shelf of brow, which
furrowed with the grainy pucker of the pull of center earth.
The quality of the skin was that it foreshadowed its disinte-
gration into cells of infinitesimal size. The opposite of taut is
not, apparently, loose, but netlike. The wrinkles I am accustomed to seeing in my face are few and deep—laugh lines,
crow's feet, furrows. These were hairline fissures dividing cell
and cell.

This was not me. I know my bad side from my good, I
know I am capable of posturing for the mirror, I know what I
look like without makeup, I have even imagined my own

skull. But this was not me, not me. I hung over gravity, I regarded myself gravely: I became grave.

Crepe is death's fabric.

All epidermis aspires to the condition of elbow.

Aging is nature's own *verfremdungseffekt*.

Because the idea of "tone" is a metaphor from music, I have co-opted the word "semiquaver" to describe this quality of skin. Dutifully doing the morning exercises that keep my spine from hurting, legs straight over my torso I watch my knees fall toward me, microcosms of erosion, miniatures of buckling earth, tan temblors of the meaning of change. The flesh semiquavers on my knees. I have become rather fond of the sight.

I ran into a very young woman at the vet's. In other times I'd have called her a girl. Her legs were thin and without definition but with adequate fullness of lovely flesh. Her ankles ran straight from her calves into her socks and sneakers. Her skin was flawless Florida tan, butterscotch-pudding smooth. I admired this skin for several seconds before I realized that I did not envy and did not *want* it. I would call its texture callow. A lovely accident of flesh, and, lo, I'll choose my own.

You think I'm lying for rhetoric's sake, but don't underestimate the part of change that happens behind the skin. The beauty of bark, or woodgrain; the sound of "texture": text-sure. I finger my lover's elbows forgivingly. We embrace in the frame of gingerbread. I like his aging. I believe, know, that he likes my flesh buckling, semiquavering, text-sure. I like us liking our aging. We feel, to me, to have traded some quality of mere appearance for superior sight.

I climb on top.

HILL

Aunt J.J., eighty-two, is touring Alaska once again with W., her companion of forty years. W. is the elder but will not say by how much. I keep their itinerary on my calendar because by the time I get back from England they will be packing for Switzerland, and we'll need to catch up. After Switzerland it's the Delta Gamma convention, and then the World Future Conference. They live, when they're at home, in the Ozarks of Branson, MO, and J.J. has lately taken to country western. W. keeps up a correspondence with some hundred and twenty people they've run into on their travels. Mornings they power walk, though they just call it walking. "It's lucky," W. says, "once you have the time, to have the health, the means, and the inclination still to travel."

Meanwhile I talk to my stepmother, G., also eighty-two, in the nursing home in Arizona. First I call the nurse, who wheels G. to her own phone; then I call her phone, which the nurse puts in her hand. G. can walk, but won't; so the circulation has dwindled, and her legs are purple blue. Amputation has been mentioned, though not to her. As soon as she hears my voice she begins to cry. "I just don't know how to cope with these interviews anymore," she says.

"What interview is that, dear?"

"Oh, well, you know your dad is always being interviewed by these magazines, and you never know exactly how much you ought to tell them."

My dad died in 1987. So far as I know he was never interviewed by a magazine. G. straightens the sob out of her voice and sighs. "It seems like I just can't figure it all out. I don't know how to keep everything together."

She knows, and means, that her mind is going, almost

gone—though she articulates very clearly what she wants. She wishes she could dig a long ditch and just lie down in it and not get up. She wishes an angle would come and lift her out of all this mess.

I ask stupidly if she got the book, the sweaters. Does she see the picture of me and P. on her dresser? Does she remember that we came out to visit her a few weeks ago?

"Couldn't you come over just for a few minutes now?"

"I'm in Florida, though. It's two thousand miles."

"Florida!" she says. "Florida!"

G. is in tears again, talking of the angel, whom I see with snow-white wings against a backdrop of Alaskan glacier. "All these people, it's not that they mistreat us"—she is sharp enough to give the staff its due. "But I can't do everything they want, gadding about all over the place. I can't. I wish that angel would come and wrap its wings around me, and just hold me until all this is over."

I share genes with Aunt J.J., not with stepmother G. Mentally I ticket myself for Switzerland, the World Future Conference, thirty years from now. Still, it was G. who, coherent a very few years ago, said to me, "Oh, your fifties are wonderful, wonderful! I never felt better in my life than I did in my fifties. After that it kinda goes downhill."

Do I believe her? I fear I do. I fear. I do. *Over the hill,* what a curiously apt expression after all! The driving and striving slowed, the view superb, you hand off the Sisyphus rock to the person on your left and, if you're lucky enough to have the health, the means, and the inclination, you stroll down the other side of the alp, working with gravity, gravity working with you. But don't relax; your job now is to put on the brakes a little. Power walk. Don't sit in the wheelchair, the wheels will do what wheels are meant to do. The angel is not always there when you need her, and stepdaughters are notoriously off in Florida.

TALE

Everyone has this story, the tale of the Goblin Obgyn, so it will not be necessary to tell it again, right?

No. True stories are only believed with frequent telling. So here is mine, not so long ago and far away:

When I was forty-five my second marriage ended with the end of his fidelity. I had been happy in the marriage, he hadn't gone out looking for an affair, but it had happened, and my trust had not survived. I had already been through divorce once, and this time I handled it, on the whole, pretty well—understanding that it's harder work to leave than to be left, and that it's easier to end a good relationship than a bad one. All the same, after a month or so I began to bleed and didn't stop for three weeks.

I went to my GP, a gentle and personable intern in family practice. I wasn't willing to go back to Dr. B., the ob-gyn I used to see, I explained, because he had wanted to perform a hysterectomy for no better reason than that, in his opinion, I already had children enough. When I'd told Dr. B. I was not willing to fool around with my psyche in that way, he'd assured me that the loss of a uterus wouldn't bother me. (*Esprit d'escalier*: Shall we cut your balls off then?)

Now Dr. G.P. asked what I was doing to get myself through the divorce. I was keeping busy in the evening, I said, by getting cast in a play. I was recarpeting, for renewal in the house. I was lunching with women friends and driving to the coast every other weekend to be with my younger son in his summer stock company. If I felt I was in trouble, I said, I'd go for counseling.

"People pay thousands of dollars," he cheered me by assuring me, "to learn how to cope like that." All the same, for medical caution, he'd like me to see a gynecologist. There was a new one in town, young, he probably wouldn't give me any nonsense.

At the new Dr. M.'s, the nurse administered a hemoglobin test and stashed me in the cubicle. Dr. M. came in all brisk-and-clipboard and began to take a medical history. I told him ("me and my big mouth" is the self-deprecatory phrase that comes to mind; in fact I think after all these years I am remarkably trusting, and that this is a virtue, not a lack)—why I had not gone back to Dr. B.

"B.'s a good man," he said. "If he wanted to take your womb out, I probably will too." I blanched and held my tongue. When Dr. M. got to the advent, in my medical history, of a second dilation and curettage, he said, "Good lord, two D & Cs. I'm certainly going to take your womb out. I'm not going to start manipulating you with hormones now!"

"No," I agreed, dry. "But I don't think there's anything wrong with my womb. I think I'm under stress. I'm going through a divorce."

"I know, you're depressed and anxious."

"No," I said, "I'm not. I may be later, but at the moment I'm very active, a bit hyper. It's my usual coping pattern."

"You're depressed and anxious," he repeated, as the

nurse came in with the test results. "That's funny. Your blood is normal."

"I'm sure it is," I said. "I think this is a normal reaction to stress, and it'll abate of its own accord."

"I'm the doctor," he actually said. "I'm not interested in the total picture, just my specialty, and then we'll slot it *into* the total picture. It's very clear that what you've got here is dysfunctional bleeding, and you'll need a hysterectomy."

Dysfunctional bleeding? Is that a diagnosis? I thought that's the symptom I came in with. Hysterectomy? We cut out my uterus to slot it into the total picture? Is that some form of medical collage? Dr. M., having diagnosed and prescribed, now left me to undress for the pelvic.

I sat for a minute seething. I powerfully did not want to be touched by his immaculate hands. I had a stabbing awareness of the times in my life when I would not have been able to get mad. I thought: Just now it's important for me to feel good about myself. I can't afford the luxury of decorum.

I excused myself to the nurse. "He's made me angry, and I'm not going to have the examination. I'll tell him so myself."

I did so, with surface calm and underrage. The doctor sat rigid in his dignity. I was minutely mollified that he didn't charge me for the blood test.

Two days later I had a call from my ally Dr. G.P. "I got to thinking about you," he said in his pleasant way, "and I thought maybe we ought to set up an appointment with a psychiatrist just to be sure, because, after all, you must be pretty depressed and anxious."

Bewildered, I let him make the appointment, and it was a half hour later that I tumbled to it, how the boys' network works. This had been one of the few times in my life that I acted, clean and immediate, on anger. I wondered, then, about those two D & Cs—were they unnecessary too?—and about the thousands of wombs that were waved away, this way, from women caught more vulnerable than indignant. I wonder now, having learned that flooding is a sign of the climateric, which stress my body was undergoing, and when the medical establishment will turn its attention to such matters.

Luckily, the following Tuesday (my bleeding having stopped by then), I was able to convince the psychiatrist that I was sane in spite of my unseemly attachment to my uterus.

STAIR

Beginning in my teens I used to dream of a house through whose stories I descended carrying a baby in my arms. The staircases would lead to doors that opened into rooms that opened into staircases *ad infinitum*. The baby was damaged in some way, clubfooted, or more often, wearing the medieval-painting face of an old man. I loved this off-spring dearly, and would wake sad at its imperfection.

In my late forties, I dreamed that I had left the baby in the house in Sussex. I went to retrieve it—her?—but the house was full of strangers, tourists somehow, browsing through bric-a-brac for sale on a flagstone terrace above the lawn. The baby was upstairs, but though I could see the stairs I couldn't get to them. Someone said the baby wouldn't know me, and I was abashed, having no evidence it was otherwise.

One reading offered of dreams in general is that both

babies and houses are the self, and I can make sense of that. Young, I felt that I carried my deformed self through the labyrinth of my self; middle-aged, I went to the self I had left behind to find a portion of my self that no longer claimed me.

Another reading offered is that the dream of babies is a dream of ovum, those that can come to fruit and those that remain a thwarted promise in the body. I can make sense of that too, the fearful weight of motherhood and then the poignancy of its loss.

But now I am thinking of the stairs. Between the fear of damaged babies and the regret of no more babies lie thirty-five years of friendship with the woman with whom I have discussed such notions. J. is not my only confidante, but she is the one with whom this particular form of friendship most applies; that we talk the ideas of emotion. We cerebrate about feelings. We are moved by concepts. We analyze impulse. We noeticize sentiment. We fabulate explanation.

And the point is, I never dreamed of friendship. Whatever animal-deep blood-dark feelings rule my dreams, friendship happened gradually in ordinary light. When J. and I met it was at a tedious faculty wives' tea. We got together because of trivial judgment on the local restaurants. We spent the first year over Scrabble, embroidery, TV; and have lived in the same town for only one six-month patch since then. Often we were apart for years without a phone call or a note, then took the conversation up midsentence. We ran into each other in London and then it seemed worth the trouble to meet in Belgium, Sussex, Illinois. When I divorced I went where she was. When I went mad she talked me through. When I was happy I discovered that I was telling her the story of my joy. When she went with her family to India I joined them, and we traveled together through Uttar Pradesh ("Oh," she and I still say in praise of each other's clothes, "it's utter pra-desh!"). When we traveled through the climacteric it occurred to us that we'd better not let a year go by without meeting somewhere, and now we do—sometimes alone, sometimes with our men in tow, in rental cars and rural restaurants, all four of us willing to honor the longevity of our friendship.

It's my luck that J. is a family therapist, with a certain amount of codified knowledge about the stuff I write. I offer her fiction's insights too. Years ago she showed me her "stair graph" of intimate relationship. People approach each other in the form of two facing staircases. At first they're far apart on the topmost tread; each takes a tentative step forward, toward the other. Then each descends into herself/himself, and if it seems worth the risk, the effort, takes another step. As long as they keep going into themselves and coming forward, the relationship gets deeper and closer, and can do so till death, though the stairs will never meet. If either refuses either motion, to plumb the self or face the other, the symmetry is skewed and the relationship will strain or break.

We were talking at the time, it will surprise no one to learn, about male-female relationships, and in particular the skewed-asymmetrical-strained quality of my own. The stair graph is a kind of image I can keep in mind even when I am dealing with bifurcating chaos in the gut; and it signally helped me in the area for which she intended it.

Only lately it occurs to me that J. and I, ourselves, have demonstrated her graph, apart and together, delving into

our selves and bringing forward what we've found; and that
—for all the ova come and gone in our reproductive lives—
we've created something that our subconsciouses did not
warn us would be the stuff of life. Mating and maternity are
in the blood; I have carried babies downstairs and gone upstairs to fetch them both literally and figuratively all the
years of my adulthood. But no one is more clearly family to
me than J.

In India it happened that we arrived at Fateh pu Sikri
on the Feast of Id. I have a snapshot of the two of us, J. and
I, backgrounded by the brilliantly silk-swathed stalls, Mutt
and Jeff for build, bare-armed and sweating in 110 degrees of
Indian July, grinning ourselves toward each other down the
ancient steps, old girls in an invented kinship, one step forward, one step down.

HELL

I wake under a feather duvet in a red cover, slightly jet-
lagged. My stomach is clenched in a sickness of fear, which
slowly reveals itself to be attached to something silly, a
phone call I have to make, a repair to be seen to. My back
aches too, and will never again *not* protest against an overnight airplane seat, so that this connection of travel and
pain is a permanent feature remaining to my life. The fear
sits sick, and spreads. Something about London, the bom-
bardment from every side of ambition and accomplishment,
the failure of socialism, the homeless on the corner, the
posturing of heads of state. My own inadequacy. In a while I
will get up, have coffee, do my exercises, have a nice day.
Not yet.

In my middle forties I went through a period of two

years in which I would wake and rage. The fury was unpredictable in its target. There was always something to attach it to—an imagined slight, a real injustice, an irremediable wound from the past. I resigned myself to the condition as permanent, something I had to endure because it was a part of me, probably the fruits of having repressed my anger for so long. Then I stopped drinking alcohol, started taking hormones, and wasn't angry any more.

Now usually I wake with anticipation, admire the plaster rose on my London ceiling or the real banana tree beyond P.'s Florida sliding door, which seems to give off the scent of the coffee he will bring me in a minute. Early-morning moods are rare, and I no longer believe they will outlast the comics page, let alone the calendar. But on the infrequent occasions when the dark ambushes me it is not as anger, but as dread; it takes me by surprise and hits with force.

I have no way of knowing what changes in my body, psyche, spirit, for gain or loss, have to do with menopause, and which have to do with aging, or both, or how much of each. Jet lag, diet, muscle spasm, hormones—I consult the possibilities blind; I recognize recurrent feelings but I can't really judge what comes from situation, what from chemistry. Why should the black mood represent imbalance anyway, instead of simple insight? How much honesty is there in despair? How much of a figment is my usual busy cheer? Here, dark before dawn, muffled in feathers, how much more truth may I touch than in a day of doing?

A statistical analysis on page four of yesterday's *Guardian* shows that pessimistic people have a more realistic view than optimists, both of probabilities and of their own control over events. Optimists, however, *take* better control, and therefore accomplish more. Ergo, self-deception is functional.

When I was in my twenties, in the fifties, in New York, I bought (from a bargain rack, it must have been, because I was too poor for new hardback books) Katherine Anne Porter's memoir *The Days Before*. The only memory of it I now retain is the pencil-soft portrait on the cover and Porter's observation that we trust hate more than love. Love we think needs to be coaxed and nurtured, carefully maintained. Whereas impulses of contempt have the force of permanent truth. "I love you" is always subject to review. "I hate you" comes from the core.

Mostly, I have taken her observation as admonition. Why should we grant hate such force? Why should we think love so fragile when there's so much evidence of its resilience?

But isn't the answer simply: entropy? Both *eros* and *agape* shatter like a cup knocked on the floor. In some far future when "future" is reversed, the universe contracts, and the past is yet to come, then the cup will jump back on the table and repair itself, hate will need fertilizer pellets, and love will cover the world like kudzu. But I can't imagine such a future, let alone believe in it, and in the meantime affection is fragile, compassion delicate. We are clumsy, ravenous, and short of time.

The image of E. looms as I last saw her, her fierce despair and her cantankerous kindness. We said good-bye on the sill of the Sussex house she was about to lose to taxes, and that was before her paralysis as a writer, before morphine addiction, ten years before she died at ninety-two. My own life may seem to have come round to peace and safety. All the same, the rule is: death.

Abruptly I am off on my death run, worried for my friends, the world. I think X.'s health precarious, and R. lives a gray half-life. Y. may certainly have AIDS. Z. drinks too much, and Q. consumes herself protecting him. How fragile and out of control we are. I would touch wood, but that's too solid. Touch paper, touch leaf, touch cobweb.

I'm surrounded with people (young, but of my own age too) who think the race will muddle through; that sense will solve the population problem, technology restore the rain forests and the ozone layer, goodwill cope with the economy. What evidence supports such hope? Liberal democracy has triumphed and sells itself like laundry soap. Ethnic autonomy turns out to be bloody nationalism. England (England!) is pissing away its universities. Money represents not production but rumors of more money. This is not a recision, says J. It is the end of the world as we've (gluttonously) known it.

Serbia! Sarajevo! We have not given a thought to little Bosnia-Herzegovina for seventy-eight years, except I understand that the *Orient Express* went through, and the rugs were a splendid bargain. Bosnian refugees now are being processed through the Austrian camps through which P. and his family moved after the Second World War. The lice are still there. "Ethnic cleansing" fights for front-page space with the incipient collapse of Michael Jackson's plastic face. What do we learn? Are we worth saving?

Dread floods me like a hot flush. I see this will be one of those days dogged by clumsiness and tender skin. I will be too large, mincing, magnet to objects at the level of my thighs. No, I'll be all right. I'll be better once I've had coffee, done my exercises, made that call.

Not yet.

HEAL

I have no memory of stepping wrong off a boulder in the Chiricahuas. I was looking at the canyon, the climb of trees on the other side, the rim of stones like crumbling columns too tight-packed to fall—and the next thing I knew I was ass to the ground, one hand around a wrench of pain in my left ankle and the other clamping a palmful of flesh to the right knee. I figured the ankle was the more serious but that only an X ray would see how serious. The knee I took a look at, prizing my hand off by centimeters.

Pretty bad. The width of my kneecap, a deep scalloped flap like an upside-down cloud shape, cloud-pale but seeping blood around the edges—and is that bone, that bit? I'm aware not only of hurt and pounding heart but of incipient and protracted nuisance. Poor P. He'll have to look after me. He won't mind but I'll be tense with apology. Our poor vacation, we'll hobble through the rest. Poor me. This is going to take a long time.

Hand clamped to the knee, blood seeping, I don't realize how long I've been there until I hear P. calling.

"Jesus, why didn't you yell?"

I'm embarrassed to tell him I was embarrassed to have hurt myself.

It's children who are supposed to be repositories of awe. I don't think so. I think that children accept the natural miracles, and are dazzled only once they have a rudimentary notion of how things work, by things that appear not to— magic, cartoons, fireworks, "effects" that are some way "special." I know that when I was little and skinned my knee, I took it as no great gift that the wound would sting and bleed. I endured the knowledge that my mother would get the dirt out whether I screamed about it or was brave. I knew it would stanch, and scab, and itch, and knit itself, probably with a little scar.

At fifty-five I watch this process with exploding wonder. It happens at wizard speed. The ankle produces its egg swelling within a couple of hours. I can walk on it next day, well enough to perambulate the border into Mexico, to shop for trinkets including a handsome carved cane. It's clear after all no bone is broken, and over the weeks as the swelling recedes it leaves a ring of delicate blue posies around my heel, which gradually like posies fade. The cut is an angry ruck of skin, which sucks itself back to its bed so hard that bending the knee becomes my major problem. I find I am fighting not the hurt but the healing, stretching against the eagerness of my flesh to knit. The blood fists into a dark scab, goes drab, and begins to lift around the edges. The shallower cut at each side of the kneecap smooths and flattens. Within a month, back in Florida in tepid Gulf saltwater, I lose the scab and emerge from the ocean whole, just a slight double-raised pink bloom on my knee, which looks a little tender, though it isn't.

My question is: Why—when, even after a half-century,

and after its ability to reproduce itself is past, a body not particularly well looked after will demonstrate its enthusiasm for survival in such wise, will speed good about the veins, pump blood and antibodies, set itself to coagulation, osmosis, cleansing, and creation, will mend so thoroughly that mobility and convenience are restored that could not be had from half a ton of technology—why, I say, should I ever have bitterly blamed it for such trifles as I have blamed it for: for having too much flesh in this spot, too little muscle in that, for producing this wrinkle, that sag, that gray hair, or this texture? Dear body! My dear body! It has gone about its incessant business with very little thanks.

I wake from a dream of D. We were having tea in a pleasantly shabby Victorian room, books and papers jumbled everywhere. "What are you going to do next?" I asked, and she said, "Nothing."

"Ah." I was a little disconcerted.

"Yes," she said. "I worked so hard early on that I feel I was cheated of my youth. What would you do, if you were going to make up for a lost youth?"

She seemed to want my answer. "I'd get a good masseur," I said. "I'd have a good hard workout, and then a really deep massage."

"I never thought of that." She paid me a look of keen attention.

"Yes, and then I'd dance. I'd read of course, and so forth. But definitely I'd dance."

Waking, I know that I've been blatantly giving me good

advice in my sleep. I giggle, reach my fingers out in a balletic gesture, meaning to touch P.'s back, but my forearm tumbles off the edge of the single bed, into the void under the red duvet. Oh yes. Another week before I'm back in Florida.

Okay. A week of friends and work. My ceiling rose is very pretty. I wrap myself for comfort, and in the hazy sleep-light I remember another quilt, the blue chintz with the cotton satin border that my grandmother made when I was—six? It was kapok-filled, the stuffing held in place by yarn ties; I remember her plump fingers pulling tight the knots.

There is a photograph of me on that quilt, spread on the spiky brown grass in front of the house on Alvarado Street. I am on my stomach, arms stiff in front of me, pointed toe touching my forehead over my arched back. I am ringletted like Shirley Temple, wearing a blue ruffled satin dance dress with tiny straps.

I remember too the buying of that costume, a miracle out of a rummage sale, one sleepy dawn when there was still such a thing as a vacant lot in downtown Phoenix, and the Women's Society for Christian Service had filled it with church tables covered in white paper and old clothes. I wandered among the rows while my mother sorted castoffs that Black and Mexican women waited in the hot dark to buy, for small change that the church would send to Africa.

I remember discovering the satin slip of a ruffled dress, pulling it out of a jumble of plaid cotton and scratchy wools. I remember my fear that some other mother would buy it before I could convince my own; and the hot quarter mom slipped into my palm, which I handed over to the church lady behind the table; for satin, for ruffles. For a snapshot of a pose on the chintz quilt.

There are also photographs of me in pastel taffeta for the Gene Bumph revue, with silver sparkles on the yoke and a tilted pancake hat held in place by tight elastic; in a variegated fall of silk chiffon-turquoise, azure, emerald—when I danced a piece of seaweed to Ruth St. Denis's octopus; in patent leather tap shoes with glossy bows and silver heels; in a pink tutu; in a red satin bum-skimmer skirt with white band jacket, gold lurex frogs.

How I wanted to dance! And how persistently my body announced itself unfit for such endeavor. Apologizing for the extravagance of my lessons, Mom would laugh, "I've got to do something about her, she's so clumsy!" Nor did this register as a cruelty, for I also thought our mutual desire was hubris. I was the stage child of a stage mother. I sat in the dark recital halls and made Shirley Temple moues.

At home my brother grunted while I practiced acrobatics on the living room rug. Chest rolls, backbends. Amos 'n' Andy played on the radio; Dad sat at once inert and intent, because he loved a good "show." My mother darned. I did headstands with my head on a cushion and my hands positioned for a tripod; I did elbow stands with my soles against the door, while my brother sat on the couch mocking, saying: *Ugh! I can do that too!*

There were toe shoes, little wads of lambswool, pain; and the satin ribbons crossed up my calves frenetically, as if I could will myself into a *prima*. There was a sheer rig in an autumnal theme, in the synthetics that had come in by then, skimpy on my solid prepubescent frame. There was the hateful, garish jester's costume when I became too thick for acrobatics and was cast as the physical equivalent of a straight man in what they dignified with the name "Adagio."

Wrong body, wrong body. I gave up the lessons, finally. I went to the North High basketball dance and stood in a corner in flocked nylon, praying for anybody to ask me onto the floor. I learned to jitterbug, defiant, and took a prize at it with my brother's college roommate. I learned to twist in time to chaperon my first college students. Once, in my thirties, I hired a teacher for a party, for a lark, during the disco phase.

My body, my poor body. When was it I learned to put on a tape and dance for me?

I stretch my ankle into a gingerly *point*, finger the polished scar. I think: Dying, we heal. Over the hill, both body and psyche are still scrambling after order for themselves.

I know this. I learned very late why my love affairs ended in diminishment and recrimination. It's a long story that I can tell in a phrase or two. I always chose men I could not please. I worked very hard to understand this, and finally I understood it. I worked very hard to change, and eventually I changed. Bit by bit my psyche coagulated, scabbed and knit.

Now I bend my knee, caress its fresh bloom. The costumes turn in my mind, cutouts of photographs, afloat. They tumble around me in a slow free fall. They are all there, the bows and the spangles, the chiffons waiting, the satin ruffles; they are putting me back to sleep. My duvet lifts and begins to lose its color. It pales and floats as a cloud would float, unsupported in the middle air. Around me, Chagall-like, Aunt J.J. and W. go power walking on a nimbus. G.'s wheel-chair spins. J. is skipping down a stair, E. is rocking back and forth over her Sussex sill. The world's a long way down.

I learned an interesting fact about detachment. Apparently the reason leaves fall is that as summer ends they suddenly produce a burst of fresh growth. They're so productive that the join at the matrix near the branch is weak. Then even a slight wind will break them off.

J. said that older people find it necessary to detach, and do so in myriad ways. They get deaf, they don't remember. They relive their lives, go quiet, go inward, concentrating on self. Dying and healing in tandem, they go about the natural, necessary business of letting go.

This process is hardly begun in me. I have loving yet to do. But I know what it means, I feel the beginning of it, on my cloud duvet. I have nearly learned that I can't control what happens in the world. I've nearly understood that I don't have to. I have nearly got it, that my friends and I are going to die, and that whether the planet offs itself will be decided without particular reference to me. I can do a little, and I'm responsible for the little I can do. I can give X. a call tomorrow, recycle my trash, for instance. I can value P. and celebrate my scar.

That's all. That's all I can do, and all I am required to do. In the gray half-light of sleep I climb my duvet to dance.

l y n n e   t a e t z s c h

fighting natural

Every six months or so, I get my hair frosted. This has been a conservative, mature softening of my younger radical action of bleaching it silver blond or dyeing it black. Basically, I just always hated my own thin dull dirty blond and since fifteen have been doing *something* to change it. Why shouldn't I want to get rid of the "dirty" in that blond and come clean?

Changing my hair color was never done to make myself more attractive to others. On the contrary, most of the few compliments I've gotten about my hair were during the in-between stages when my natural color was dominant. "It's nice to see your natural color, Lynney," my sister Mary would say. Of course, her hair is naturally platinum blond.

If I don't change my hair color to make myself attractive, why do I do it? I don't wear makeup or much jewelry, prefer comfortable to dress-up clothes and shoes, so why this obsession with my hair? Just a personal quirk?

I wanted to think that until last week when two events collided in my life. One, it was time to get my hair frosted—the last cut had removed most of the previous frosting. Two, I was teaching a class at George Washington University on writing about gender issues. We were reading bell hooks' "Madonna: Plantation Mistress or Soul Sister," in which the term "blond ambition" taunted me:

> We thought it tragically ironic that Madonna would choose as her dance partner [in *Truth or Dare*] a black male with dyed blond hair. Perhaps had he appeared less like a white-identified black male consumed by *blond ambition* he might have upstaged her. Instead he was positioned as a mirror, into which Madonna and her audience could look and see only a reflection of herself and the worship of *whiteness* she embodies—that white supremacist culture wants everyone to embody.*

How could I do this to my class? To the women in it who looked to me for hope of finding other options than succumbing to the Beauty Myth? I was doubly transgressing the causes of gender and racial equality, setting a perfect example of the impossibility of changing our cultural codes even after we have deconstructed them.

For some reason, I completely blocked this information from my consciousness when I went to the hairdresser's. When Mike asked me if I wanted to try a new frosting technique that would look more natural and be less damaging to my hair, I decided against it because I wanted a very

* bell hooks, *Black Looks* (Boston: South End Press, 1992), pp. 162–163.

heavy frosting of the palest, pale blond. "Why?" he asked, explaining that from his point of view a much more conservative approach would look better. "I guess I just always wanted to be a blonde," I answered.

It wasn't until I got home, looked in the mirror, and realized I'd be entering my gender class with *that* hair, that it hit me. Why didn't I listen to Mike? I thought with one part of my brain. With the other—I love it!

When I walked into class the next morning, I imagined everyone staring at me, horrified. Yet it's very likely they didn't even notice. Only one person out of all my students and colleagues said anything. A student in my computer writing class asked, "Is something different about you today?" I said, "Yes, new hair and new glasses." "Oh," she said, "a total new look."

I imagined my colleagues said nothing because they thought it crass of me to come in with this brassy blond hair, and if you can't say anything nice . . .

But then I thought, why should anyone notice what a fifty-one-year-old woman does with her hair? Who cares?!

Do I have to frost my hair? Should I not frost my hair? Does it matter personally or politically? Before I could answer these questions, I had to try to find out more about why I do it. After all, if I am compelled by blond ambition, how can I hope to help young women find the strength to fight dangerous dieting, cosmetic surgery, and other crippling cultural compulsions?

I could explain the new clothes I bought and wear as my

realistic and deliberate adaptation to George Washington University professional standards. These clothes and the conservative jewelry I wear say "I'm a feminist, but not too radical. You can feel comfortable in my presence."

The clothes I bought were high class—tailored silk blouses, long skirts, a classic black cashmere/wool blend coat that would never go out of style according to the saleswoman at Bloomingdale's. The idea was to disguise myself to fit into the "look" of the tenured women in the English Department. Yet with this tasteless blond bleach job, I've instantly and permanently undone the illusion. Perhaps I wanted to come out as the low-class renegade I think I really am?

If I were a tenured creative writing professor I would teach in jeans and T-shirts, which are the only clothes I've ever felt comfortable wearing. My young boy disguise—another image to deconstruct. But I don't have enough clout yet to just be me. I'm a temporary instructor in the writing program and no matter how much my pseudocolleagues try to make me feel at home by inviting me to their meetings, we all know I'm just passing through.

The day I announced to my family that I had a date for Saturday night, my older brothers were incredulous, especially when they heard the guy went to Union College. How could their skinny four-eyed dinky-haired sister attract a boy, no less a college man?

They had a right to be incredulous. I was a sophomore in Irvington High School at that time and could possibly have won the award for Most Unpopular Girl in the class. Certainly that was the opinion of the school guidance counselor who said to me, "You don't have any friends because you think you're smarter than everybody."

When I came home in tears that day, my father took the counselor's side. True to his working-class code, whoever had the authority by job title was right by definition. Didn't my father think about what it meant to extend the comment, "Maybe he's right," to its logical conclusions—that I had no friends, and that I thought I was smarter than everyone else?

Perhaps I did think I was smarter than everyone else in my class. Certainly they gave me no cause to think otherwise. Irvington High School at that time had no reputation for academic rigor. I could get A's easily without bringing home a book. The few bright and talented girls I hung around with in ninth grade had gone boy-crazy by tenth. A few years later when I was in college, I ran into one of them with her baby in a stroller, looking miserable and embarrassed to see me.

Outside of my brains, I had nothing going for me. There was no money for the clothes, haircuts, modeling classes, and contact lenses it would have taken to turn the gawky misfit into a passably attractive teenager. There was no savvy older sister who might have achieved miracles with the few resources at our disposal. I got the hand-me-downs from Cousin Carol, a buxom beauty whose family had done well in the retail jewelry business. Her clothes always sagged on me and there was no one to take them in. Sewing class was the one course I almost did flunk.

So how did I snag a date with that college man?

Our backyard was on the border of the next town, so that my friend Hilde, whose yard bordered ours, went to Union High School. Hilde asked me to join her at one of Union High School's Friday night dances. This was my big chance for a fresh start. No one would know me. I could be a different girl—someone glamorous, confident, fun-loving, and not too bright. If you were too bright, you might not find the boys' jokes so funny or whip up the proper enthusiasm for their superior status as males. I had to squelch my desire to compete with them in order to make space for them to appreciate me as a female. The first step was to scrap my glasses, which served two purposes. It would make me more attractive to boys since I would no longer be four-eyed. And the lack of clear definition in my surroundings would give me more confidence. The blurry haze of poor vision would have an effect similar to that of drunkenness. (As the years went by, I became an expert at methods of achieving blurry hazes.)

I was already putting peroxide on my hair to give it blond highlights. Perhaps the duck's ass haircut popular then that would not stay in place because my hair was too thin and limp had finally grown out. Perhaps the night of the dance my shoulder-length hair hung in gentle waves, the frizzy permed endings behaving themselves for a change. Or did I tie it up in a perky ponytail with two wispy pin-curled circles over my ears?

What was it about me that made Pete Reves ask me for

a dance and then another dance and another? Was it the pink clinging short-sleeved fuzzy sweater that I was too self-conscious to wear to school? Was it my dazzling fake smile? When he broke up with me six months later to go back to his girlfriend, it became clear that it really didn't matter much who I had been as long as it was some girl he could use to make his old girlfriend jealous. While heartbreaking, it was a relief to be able to wear my glasses again and stop pretending to be the girl he wanted me to be.

To get your hair frosted it can take from an hour and a half to all day at the beauty parlor. It's hard to figure what makes up the difference in time, and there is no correlation between time and cost.

First, the operator squeezes your head into a tight plastic cap filled with tiny holes. Then he takes a gadget like a crochet needle, jabs it into a hole, grabs a clump of hair, and pulls it out. This process is repeated all over your head, and must be done thoroughly and evenly for the frosting to come out right. Even the most gentle operators with no sadistic tendencies can't help but jab the needle into your scalp and pull your hair when they drag it through the holes.

Originally the caps were made of rubber, which created even more friction against the hair. The plastic caps used today are an improvement, but there is no way to avoid the pain.

"Am I hurting you?"

"Not too bad," I say. I try not to flinch.

When Mike gets to the hair around my ears, my body

tightens in anticipation. I've had my ears jabbed too many times in the past.

But he is careful and quick. I relax as we move on to the next stage—the chemicals.

Mike mixes a paste of bleach and rubs it thoroughly into all the hair sticking out of the cap. I squeeze my eyes shut in reaction to the fumes.

Next a loose plastic covering is put over the whole mess and I'm told to sit under a dryer. Mike sets an alarm clock to check me after ten minutes. Several checks later, the bleach has finally taken enough color out to achieve a pale blond. I go to a hair-washing station where the bleach is washed out, a conditioner put in, and the loathed cap finally taken off.

This has been a relatively painless and hugely successful frosting for me. It took less than two hours, the color is even, and it is just the shade I asked for. I have endured frostings that took all day, that hurt me so much I cried, that came out in globby patches or missed whole sections of my head, or that were so subtle I couldn't tell I had had my hair frosted at all and had to go have it done again.

The thing about getting a frosting that you never forget is that poking at your scalp. There is nothing like it, at least I thought so until the experience I had sitting on a rock in the Galápagos Islands two summers ago. The birds and animals there are not afraid of people, and a mockingbird landed on my head. I sat very still. All of a sudden, I felt a familiar peck and tug as the bird poked through a hole in my hat with its beak at what must have looked like good nesting material—my hair. The mockingbird, however, was gentler than most hairdressers I've known.

On the plane to Los Angeles, I put in my new contact lenses two hours before landing so I could arrive at the University of Southern California with my disguise complete. If I looked like a pretty blond coed and people treated me like a pretty blond coed, maybe I'd learn how to be one.

Fat chance. For one thing, I still had no clothes sense. When another high school senior asked me if I had bought my college wardrobe yet, I said "Hunh?" When I got to USC I took the meager spending money my parents had scraped up to give me to supplement my scholarship and bought a brand-new Olympia typewriter with it. Plus some art supplies.

You may wonder how I ended up at the University of Southern California. Did I choose this school after thorough research, expert counseling, or the guiding advice of my family? The only college my family knew about was the Newark College of Engineering, which my two older brothers graduated from. The next in line followed and couldn't hack it, wasting a year until he figured out he didn't want to be an engineer anyway.

The advice given to us girls by my father was to become secretaries—a nice clean occupation for women. As for my high school guidance office—well, we were not on good terms after their first piece of advice. No, for me choosing a college was accidental—a happy or unhappy chance—the method I've used to make most of my life decisions.

Instead of daydreaming in class through the day's end reading of announcements, I listened one day and heard about a scholarship being offered to a school in Los Angeles. California—three thousand miles from home—about as far as I could hope to get. I thought I was applying to UCLA, actually, so little did I know about what I was doing.

The three thousand miles were the important thing. And the chance to start fresh, remake myself into a sunny California girl with that California-blond disposition. I was counting on those rays to penetrate the down side of my mood swings, ease out the tensions of my insomniac nights. On the plane I had no regrets, no pang of loneliness or homesickness, only high hopes.

Five weeks into my first semester at the University of Southern California, I looked into the mirror and couldn't recognize myself. I didn't know who I was, but I knew enough to be frightened by this discovery. I told my best friend, a girl even crazier than I. She was so scared she told the dorm housemother on me, and I've never forgiven her for this. When the housemother asked to see me, I of course faked it and tried to convince her I was fine. How mortifying to have this fussy old woman poking into my private life!

The kinds of advice I got from the housemother and the school shrink were to act like a normal coed and do normal coed things. Attend football games. Go out with boys my own age. It seems my California-girl look-a-like attempt had attracted the wrong sort—men in their late twenties who recognized my accommodating gawkiness as an invitation.

I'm fifty-one years old and can't remember a day when I felt at home in my body. The only safe place to be with it is alone because then I can ignore it. Stepping out of my house, even to pick up the newspaper on the front lawn, is always fraught with self-conscious anxiety over how to present myself to prying eyes.

Should I look around with a smile on my face in case a neighbor is out, or look down and pretend I am preoccupied so I won't have to acknowledge them?

It's been a cold nasty rainy winter in DC, so the first warm sunny day this spring brought everyone out of their classrooms and dormitories sprawling onto lawns, benches, steps—cluttering available space. I was horrified as I stepped out of my building into this mass of appraising looks. How would I manage to walk the two blocks to my class? Why had I chosen the outfit I wore? Where should I focus my eyes?

Walking away from my car in a parking lot years ago, attempting my preoccupied look, a man stopped me and said, "Cheer up, things couldn't be that bad." So now I always worry about my preoccupied look, maybe it's too stern or sad or angry. What I should look like on a warm spring day is carefree and happy, smiling. But then I remember an article I read about women who walk with their lips partly open being a sign, an invitation, so I want to be careful not to do that.

And what if I run into someone I know, students from one of my classes, or worse, from last semester and I won't remember their names? It's best not to look anyone in the eye, say hello to no one unless they say hello to you first. Otherwise I could commit the blunder I did last month when I thought a young woman walking in front of me was one of my students and started to talk to her and it wasn't and as my face turned scarlet I tripped on my foot trying to get away.

It's true that sometimes when I walk down a sidewalk and a man is standing where I have to pass in front of him, I cannot figure out how to make my feet move smoothly and start tripping over cracks and debris. Then I remember that these students laughing and talking and eyeing passersby are not looking at me, I am already invisible to them because of my age.

When I was a sophomore in high school I tried out for flagswingers—the least talented contingent of the half-time show. The only criteria for judging at tryouts was your beauty and your smile. The judges were not from our school, so I had a chance to pull the wool over their eyes. I got out that pink sweater, some short shorts, took off my glasses of course. Told myself over and over to stand up straight and stick my chest out, as if I were pretending to be some kind of beauty queen. And I smiled till my jaw hurt.

Everyone was shocked the next day to see my name on the list of girls who had made it. That was a triumph, but a short-lived one. The actual experience of being a flag-swinger, hanging out with girls I had nothing in common with, freezing in our short skirts, bored to death watching the games, made it all too clear to me that I would never be a part of any popular group at high school. To clinch the disaster, I had my hair cut short over the summer and it looked ridiculous under the hat we had to wear. It got harder and harder for me to maintain that smile and kick for all I was worth. I quit flagswingers after one season.

• • •

In spite of my self-consciousness, I do like to stand up on a stage with a microphone and read my fiction, especially when I speak in the voice of an angry young man who says to the audience "Fuck you, assholes." People wonder how I could create this character so far from my own experience, but he *is* my experience. I have internalized the anxiety, the dread, the anger and loathing of these young men from Dostoevsky and Jack Kerouac to Bob Dylan and the Rolling Stones. When Dylan sang, "No, no, no, it ain't me, babe," I was on his side despising the cloying female who dared to stifle his creative freedom.

I was mad and I wanted to be bad. But I was a woman. In my version of bad, I always ended up looking like a whore. Attempting to break out of my depression while an art student at Cooper Union, I tossed the sweatshirts and jeans in favor of a sexy skirt and sweater borrowed from my sister. I painted my fingernails silver and black, applied black mascara three layers thick, lipstick a fire-engine smear, wore every chain and necklace I could find in the house, red stockings—hey, guys, I was doing body art, but it didn't have a name then outside of "slut." My life-drawing teacher was so concerned he gave me a story to read about a brazen young woman who turned from the path of virtue only to end up deserted and destitute, a broken old hag. Only a man could be free and easy and be taken seriously as an artist. I had nowhere to put my rage.

So I took it out on my hair. The worst thing you could do to hair was to bleach it and then immediately perm it while it was brittle and ready to break. I'd do the Clairol act at home and then go to a discount beauty parlor for their afro special. Look, my hair doesn't do afro—it's too fine and thin to hold a tight curl, so a day and a half after I leave the beauty parlor, it starts to hang down like a limp drizzle.

I can't cross over into *any* kind of bad.

But with luck one time the new girl at the discount beauty parlor burns not only my hair, but the back of my neck. I expect to suffer in the beauty parlor, so I never mention that my neck is burning something awful sitting under that dryer waiting for the curl to take. The welts on the back of my neck scare the new girl and she brings the manager over who tells me to come back the next week and they'll redo the whole mess for nothing. Two perms on top of a bleach job equals . . . well, of course it all turned into some wild straw, the ends split off and didn't know which way to curl and the short uneven stubs that were left decided to just stand up straight and face the music. This was destroyed, beaten, badly abused hair. And I loved it.

What I've done most to my hair all my life is torture it. I've bleached it, permed it, burned it, cut it, tied it, and dyed it with a vengeance to disfigure, not enhance my appearance. The Clairol home treatment—whether silver blond or blue-black—has been a kind of purging for me, a tearing out of my old life so that I might look in the mirror and see a new person, find a new life, a way to be in the world that worked this time.

At twenty-seven I arrived at Newark Airport with one suitcase and my nine-month-old baby in my arms. When my father and sister picked me up, they made such a fuss over the baby that no one put my suitcase in the car. It was gone, of course, when my father went back to get it. I had come home once again after a failed attempt at living in California—this time with my husband John who had never found a job in the four years we'd lived in L.A. So there I was with the clothes on my back, my baby, and a fistful of debts.

Everyone felt sorry for me, of course—a young woman alone in the world with her baby. One of my brothers handed me twenty dollars to ease the pain. I immediately went out and bought a box of Clairol silver blond. Perhaps if I could look in the mirror and see someone else, this life wouldn't really be happening to me.

The silver blond often turned pink or purple. After a while the silver would wash out and I'd be left with a raw straw yellow. Finally, the roots would grow in, providing a stark contrast to the bleached part. I never bothered to take care of the roots. That wasn't the point. The point was the glorious transformation when you took off the plastic bag after inhaling fumes for an hour and a half—I always left the solution on longer than the instructions said to—and I never did the test strand, of course. The point was that after you washed out all the smelly gunk and dried your hair, you looked into the mirror for that jolt, that shock, the hope that this change would finally do it.

jenefer shute

life-size

I'm lying here, just occupying space, drifting in and out of a dream, when I hear something clattering and rumbling down the hall. I know what it is; my jaw and stomach muscles tense, but otherwise I remain exactly as I am. Why should I move? The trolley stops outside the door with a faint tinkle of crockery; after a brief knock (giving me no time to respond), she comes in, smiling and pert, brisk and trim in her white tunic and pants. (Trim, but don't think I don't notice the almost-sagging buttocks, the incipient droop of the upper arm.)

As she walks toward me, her blockish, cushiony shoes squeak against the floor, jarring my ears, scraping my brain.

"Hello! Still lying there? It's lunchtime."

I make no response as she puts the tray down next to me and removes some kind of cover from the plate, releasing a sickening, mealy odor.

"Sit up and enjoy your lunch," she says brightly, pushing it closer to the bed. "I'll be back in half an hour to see how you're doing." I say nothing and she leaves (shoes conversing in shrill, rubbering shrieks across the floor).

I'm not planning even to look at this tray, but the smell

is so strong that I turn my head and encounter, at eye level, a brown, oily, pimply thing (chicken! as if I would ever eat that) oozing onto a mound of mashed potato and some big green branches of broccoli. I try, and fail, to imagine eating it, like munching on a tree. Everything is heaped, crowded on the plate, everything touching. There's also a glass of milk, beaded with sweat; a puffy roll plus two pats of butter; a dish of flabby yellow stuff growing a skin (custard? are they kidding?); an apple; a little envelope of salt, one of pepper, one of ketchup. The smell is so overpowering that I know I'm going to have to do something.

Reluctantly I roll over on to my side and tip myself so that my feet hang over the edge of the bed. Then, very slowly, I push upward until I'm sitting, curled, with my head on my lap. I rest like this awhile, trying to breathe, and then, tightening my abdominals, raise myself carefully to my feet.

This prevents fainting.

I have to get this tray out of my sight. The smell is entering me as a hollow nausea, and seeing all that . . . food sends a chilly tingle across my skin. Got to get this thing away! I dump it on the other bed and am about to climb back on mine when I reconsider, go back, and pick off a small piece of the roll, which I put in the drawer of my nightstand: just in case.

Then I roll on the bed, flop my arms wide, wait for everything to stop spinning, and, fixing my eye on the ceiling lightbulb, return its stern, milky stare.

So this is what my world has shrunk to: a ward with two gray metal beds, barred at head and foot, with thin spreads, waffled, that might once have been white. The walls, an institutional cream, are scuffed and scarred: Lying here, I trace and retrace each blister, each blemish, each bruise. The cold floor is tiled in beige and khaki, which might once have been lemon and olive, or even vanilla and lime. Through the high, locked windows—is this perhaps the psycho ward, after all?—limp shades diffuse a sooty light. A metal nightstand with a screeching drawer, a locker in which my clothes are locked from me, and a plastic chair— for visitors I assume (though who would come here, I cannot think)—complete the decor.

Since being admitted two days ago, I've spent most of my time lying on this bed, arms apart, hands splayed, eyes fixed on the blind bulb above me. They want me to get up, put on my robe, perhaps wander down to the dayroom to meet the other inmates. But I won't, of course. I'm just going to lie here, drifting through time, dreams washing over me, retinal dots composing themselves pointillist style into a private flow of images.

But then I notice that I'm holding my breath, almost choking: A chemical whiff in the air has stopped my throat. At first I think this is a new symptom—already I'm afraid of running water, of restaurants, of licking a postage stamp— but then it makes sense. The last time I was in a hospital was when I was nine, for a tonsillectomy: In my throat I feel again the dry, violent pain, like swallowing ground glass. Dark clotted stuff in the mouth, salting the ice cream, tinging the vanilla with tinny strawberry.

Vanilla and strawberry and cream. Think about something else. Think about the tonsils, ripped out like tubers.

• • •

A brisk knock, and then the door opens immediately (why do they never wait for me to answer?). In comes Squeaky, interrupting my dream—the surgeon is caressing my hair, the anesthetic taking its ecstatic hold—but I don't even move my head. Out of the corner of my eye I can see her taking in the situation: the full tray dumped on the other bed, me flat on my back, arms outspread, my pelvic bones protruding pointedly under the gray-green hospital gown. She shakes her head and says in what she probably takes for a calm, reasonable tone: "Josie, you haven't eaten anything, have you? That's very disappointing: you know the rules. You remember what the doctor said."

"I'm not hungry," I say.

"It was too much," I say.

"Anyway, I did eat something," I say. "I ate some of the roll."

"Josie," she says, "you know the rules, you agreed to them yourself. Do you just want to lie here forever? What's the point of that?"

Her measured yet whiny tone is getting to me and I just want her out. Out! Out of my room! Still staring at the ceiling, I say "I don't like chicken." They say I'm sick, but what about them, all of them, who think nothing of chewing on a carcass, sinking their teeth into muscle and gristle and blood? They say I'm sick, but what about them, who feast on corpses?

"Well, you wouldn't fill out a menu card, so the dietician picked out something for you."

A corpse and a tree; a fluid secreted by bovine mammary glands; gobs of congealed grease.

"Later, if you fill out the card, you can get something you like. A nice fruit salad perhaps, with ice cream? Or a tuna sandwich, with a banana, perhaps, and some cookies . . . ?"

Banana and tuna and cream: The very words, as if secret, obscene, are making me ill, my heart starting to hammer, the same hollow sickness poking at the base of my throat. To get her to stop, I say "Leave the card here and I'll think about it."

"Okay. And we have a busy afternoon planned for you. The endocrinologist is going to stop by to ask you some questions, and then we'll need to take you for some blood samples."

Blood again. They're after my blood.

Sure enough, a chirpy little woman (thin, birdlike, but with a turkey's tired wattle) shows up, armed with a rubber mallet. She asks me a few questions about my periods; that's all anyone seems to care about around here.

"I forget. Maybe when I was seventeen."

"So you've had no periods for eight years now?"

"No, they come and go. Sometimes I won't have any for a year or two, then they'll come back for a while, then go away again."

"And how long have they been gone this time?"

"I forget. Maybe a year or so."

Why do they think I should care, anyway? Who, given the choice, would really opt to menstruate, invite the monthly hemorrhage—a reminder that the body is nothing but a bag of blood, liable to seep or spatter at any moment?

Then I discover what the rubber mallet is for. She asks me to sit on the edge of the bed and starts tapping away at my knees, a sharp, clean crack on the bone. Nothing happens, so I give a little kick to help things along. Then she tickles the soles of my feet and tells me my reflexes are impaired because the electrolytes are out of balance and the neurons aren't firing properly or some such jargon.

Fine with me. I don't want any involuntary responses; Soon, in this body, everything will be willed.

So I just look at her blankly and flop back on the bed, because all this sitting up and being hammered is making me light-headed. The minute she leaves, I roll over on to my side and begin my leg lifts, hoping I can complete the full hundred on each side without being interrupted.

I am halfway through the second set when the nurse comes back again, pushing a wheelchair, into which she invites me to climb for some blood tests. (More blood.) I tell her I won't get in the chair, I can walk, thank you—I'm desperate to move: My muscles are turning mushy from lying here. But she insists—says it's "policy"—and wraps a blanket around me when I complain of the cold. So off we go, her shoes conversing squeakily across the tiles.

The assistant who's supposed to take the blood looks startled when she sees me and shakes her head at my arms—my white, well-defined arms, ropy with blue and softly furred. (I hate this hair, this down, which keeps growing all over me, even on my stomach: I have tried bleaching it, but more just keeps growing in, dark, like a pelt.) She comes at me with the needle, jabbing and wiggling; she tries both arms a few times, getting flustered.

"Your veins keep collapsing," she says. "I'm sorry, dear, but I have to keep trying."

It hurts and though I don't look, distancing myself from this piece of meat that's being probed, I start feeling sick, my head suddenly receding from my feet, which in turn have disconnected from my knees. Squeaky, ever vigilant, pushes my head gently down onto my lap, and after a few minutes in this pose, I feel ready to continue.

"Come on, let's get it over with," I say.

More prodding, but eventually she finds a vein, and, while I fix my attention on the far wall, she takes eight tubes of blood: to test potassium, calcium, hemoglobin levels. Sugar too: As if they would find sugar in my blood. Even though I don't watch the blood being sucked out—once I made the mistake of observing the thick, grape-colored stuff rising in the tube, stood up, and passed out—I still feel light-headed, and the shaken blood-sucker makes me lie down and drink some apple juice (130 calories; I take only a sip) before we leave.

My keeper wheels me back and explains, in her professionally patient, reasonable tone (I'd love to hear how she bitches with the other nurses on her coffee break) that, though psychotherapy is part of the treatment plan, "they" have decided that I cannot begin yet because, she says, I am a starving organism and my brain is starving and therefore not working the way it should. I say nothing but it's hard not to sneer: My brain's not working the way it should! On the contrary, it's never been purer and less cluttered, concentrated on essentials instead of distracted by a body clamoring for attention, demanding that its endless appetites be appeased. Stripped down, the brain is closer to the surface, taking in colors, light, sounds, with a fine, vibrating intensity.

One day I will be pure consciousness, traveling unmuffled through the world; one day I will refine myself to the bare wiring, the irreducible circuitry of mind.

She also explains to me, again in what she thinks is a neutral, measured tone, that they're sure I'm going to cooperate, but if not, as a last resort, they might have to consider hyperalimentation. Hyperalimentation: interesting euphemism for force-feeding, for attaching a helpless human body to a tangle of tubes and pumping—what, I wonder?—into its unwilling ducts. Hyperalimentation: Isn't that the word, rather, for the way most people eat?

I never feel hungry and despise those who do, whose lives are governed by the peristaltic pulse. Never have they learned to ignore the gaping maw-mouth: Its slightest twinge sends them running to the trough. From the first mouthful in the morning to the last at night, their lives are one long foraging. In the morning, hunched over their desks, they munch on soft dough; at noon, they herd out en masse, meat-hungry, to feed; midafternoon, in a circadian slump, they crave sugar; arriving home, they root in the refrigerator's roaring heart and eat upright before an open door. And all this before the serious eating begins, the ever-to-be-repeated hours of shopping and chopping and mixing and cooking and serving, only to wolf down the result in seconds and greet it the next morning transformed into shit.

But I've freed myself from this compulsion. When I wake, I'm empty, light, light-headed; I like to stay this way, free and pure, light on my feet, traveling light. For me, food's only interest lies in how little I need, how strong I am, how well I can resist—each time achieving another small victory of the will: one carrot instead of two, half a cracker, no more peas. Each gain makes me stronger, purer, larger in my exercise of power, until eventually I see no reason to eat at all. Like a plant, surely, the body can be trained to subsist on nothing, to take its nourishment from the air.

Miss Pert—I think her name is Suzanne—finally leaves me, with a cheery reminder to fill out the menu card for dinner. The minute she's gone, I take it out and study it carefully, reading it and rereading it, savoring not the names of the food so much as the knowledge I will never eat them. Some disgust me, the very words filling my mouth with a viscid sickness: pork chops, hamburger, cheese omelette, clam chowder. But others I linger over, imagining their colors and textures, feeding on images, secure in the knowledge that images alone can fill me.

I prepare myself an imaginary feast, taking about forty minutes to decide on the menu—banana with peanut butter, fried rice, pecan pie—and to imagine consuming it lasciviously with a spoon. When it's over, I look at the menu card again, knowing that Squeaky-Pert will harass me if I don't mark something. Some of the dishes frighten me, their names alone quickening my pulse: spaghetti and meatballs!

Imagine eating that, a whole, giant plate of it, everything heaped together, oozing oil. My heart is racing now, so I put a check mark next to "mixed salad" on the card and push it away from me, to the far side of the nightstand. I lie back again, trying to relax, wondering how big the salad will be and whether they'll try to make me eat the whole thing. Then panic seizes me: I sit up violently, grab the menu card again, and write in emphatic block letters next to my check mark "NO DRESSING!!" I underline this three times and then lie back, trying to calm my hammering heart.

To collect myself, I start doing leg lifts again, picking up where I was interrupted earlier and deciding I will do an extra fifty on each side in case the nurse, my jailer, makes me eat the whole salad. The bed isn't really firm enough for calisthenics, but I'm afraid to get down on the floor in case someone comes in. I'm going to have to get down there eventually, to do my pushups: Maybe I can say I'm looking for something on the floor. (A contact lens? A cockroach?) They think they can wear me down by this constant intrusion—I'm supposed to be on an hourly watch—but I know I can outlast them all.

One day I will be thin enough. Just the bones, no disfiguring flesh, just the pure, clear shape of me. Bones. That is what we are, after all, what we're made of, and everything else is storage, deposit, waste. Strip it away, use it up, no deposit, no return.

Every morning the same ritual, the same inventory, the same naming of parts before rising, for fear of what I may have become overnight. Jolting out of sleep—what was that dream, that voice offering me strawberries and cream?—the first thing I do is feel my hipbones, piercingly concave, two naked arcs of bone around an emptiness. Next I feel the wrists, encircling each with the opposite hand, checking that they're still frail and pitiful, like the legs of little birds. There's a deep hollow on the inside of each wrist, suspending delicately striated hands, stringy with tendon and bone. On the outside of the wrist, I follow the bone all the way up to the elbow, where it joins another, winglike, in a sharp point.

Moving down to the thighs, first I feel the hollow behind the knee to check that the tendon is still clean and tight, a naked cord. Then I follow the outside of each thigh up toward the hips: no hint of a bulge, no softening anywhere. Next I grab the inner thigh and pinch hard, feeling almost all the way around the muscle there; finally, turning on one side and then the other, I press each buttock, checking that the bones are still sticking through.

Sitting up in bed, a little more anxiously now, I grasp the collar bones, so prominent that they protrude beyond the edges of the shoulders, like a wire coathanger suspending this body, these bones. Beneath them, the rows of ribs, deeply corrugated (and the breasts, which I don't inspect). Then I press the back of my neck and as far down my spine as I can, to make sure the vertebrae are all still there, a row of perfect little buttons: as if they held this body together, as if I could unbutton it and step out any time I wanted to.

· · ·

Dinner is as bad as I was afraid it would be. At precisely six o'clock, Squeaky squeaks in with a big tray, which she puts down next to the bed where I am floating again, on my back, imagining myself somewhere else altogether, cool and perfectly hard in a silk-lined gown. Firmly she says "Josie, I hope you're going to eat your salad tonight, otherwise the medical team will have to make a decision tomorrow about hyperalimentation."

I look in horror at the huge bowl of salad on the tray. *It's possible to slow yourself down by eating too much salad.* "This *is* hyperalimentation," I say: a mound of lettuce with chunks of pale tomato, shards of green pepper, hunks of purplish raw onion, and—they must be nuts if they think I'm going to eat any of this—gobs of cheese and hard-boiled egg, with a bruise-colored line where the white pulls away from the yolk. Even though I didn't ask for it, there's a big, stale-looking roll and butter, an apple, a dish of vanilla ice cream, a glass of milk, and a plastic container of some urine-colored oil labeled "Italian."

"I can't eat if you're watching me," I say, which is true.

"Okay," she says, "I'll be back in half an hour to see how you're doing."

As soon as she leaves, I draw the curtain around my bed: No one must ever see me eat, no one must ever catch me in the act—especially now that my appearance excites so much attention, with people always staring at me, willing me to weaken.

The Trobrianders eat alone, retiring to their own hearths with their portions, turning their backs on one another and eating rapidly for fear of being observed.

With the curtains drawn, my heart slows down a little and I concentrate on controlling this food: If I don't deal with it soon, it will exert a magnetic pull on me, commanding me to eat it, filling my consciousness until the only way I could escape would be to run shrieking into the street.

There is a big paper napkin on the tray, so I scrape exactly half the salad out of the bowl and into the napkin, along with half the roll. I bundle this mess up and start looking for a place to hide it: not easy in this cell. My clothes locker is locked and I don't have the key—of course not: This is going to be one of my little "rewards." (Even my shoes have been locked away, my socks.) Under my pillow would be too risky, because the napkin could leak or break, making a big lettucey mess that would be hard to explain. So the only place I can think of is the drawer of the nightstand next to the other bed, the unoccupied one, the one as flat and empty as I would like mine to be.

Once that little bundle is out of the way, I can relax a bit and start working on what's left. I separate the mound of food into piles: lettuce on one side, tomato on the other, pepper pieces neatly stacked and segregated from the rank, juicy onion. The egg and cheese I pick right off and banish to the bread plate: evil. *Cheese is the hardest food to digest, and it contaminates everything you eat it with.* Then I cut the lettuce, tomato, and pepper into tiny pieces, deciding I won't even pretend to eat the onion because lots of people don't like raw onion: It's legitimate, it's "normal." I cut the half-roll into four sections and decide I will eat only one. Of the ice cream, I will eat exactly two spoonfuls, and the apple I will save for another time. So I put it away in my nightstand drawer along with the piece of roll I picked off the lunch tray: just in case.

Now that these decisions have been made, now that the bad stuff has been removed, now that the food is separated, with white space showing on the plate, now I can start eating: one piece at a time, and at least three minutes (timed on a second hand) between mouthfuls, with the fork laid down precisely in the center of the plate after each bite.

Of course the nurse comes back before I'm done and, without even asking, swishes back the bed curtains, revealing me shamefully hunched over the tray, chewing. I freeze, unable to meet her eyes. She says, gently, "There's really no need to close the curtains, dear, when you're alone."

Sullenly I push the tray away and lie back on the pillow, staring up at the mangy acoustic tile.

"Don't stop," she says. "I'll come back in fifteen minutes or so." She leaves, but it's no good: I can't eat any more; I feel sick and upset, with the undigested salad sitting scratchily, bulkily, inside me. My stomach is beginning to swell: I feel it anxiously, palming the dip between my hipbones, sensing a new curvature, a new tightness there. Panicky, before I know what I have done, I have wolfed down three teaspoons of the now almost entirely melted ice cream.

I put the tray on the other bed and draw the bed curtains around it so I don't have to be reminded of my gluttony; climbing back onto my own bed, I draw those curtains too, wanting to be alone, to hide where no one can find me, can tempt me, can torment my will. I want to find a cave or burrow somewhere where the idea of food becomes an abstraction, and this body, ever clearer and purer, evaporates finally into the dark, leaving only consciousness behind.

When the nurse comes back, I ask her to take me to the bathroom (another of these laws under which I now live: I can't leave the ward unaccompanied). This is partly a diversionary tactic, but partly also because I'm desperate to wash my hands and face: My skin feels oily and slimy, as if the fat in the food is oozing out through my pores. She helps me tie on my hospital-issue robe, with a faded blue design that makes my skin look even more cyanotic than it is. I'm cold but she won't let me put on any more clothes. So we walk slowly to the bathroom and she stands near the door while I go into a cubicle, where I'm not allowed to close the door in case I make myself vomit (which I've never been able to do —though not for want of trying). I can't pee under these conditions, so I give up and comb my hair instead (it's still coming out, in dry hanks), tying it back tightly with an elastic band. Then I scrub my face and hands once, and again, then again, until the nurse says sharply "That's enough now" and we trudge back to the cell.

She bustles about, making a big deal of flinging back the curtains on both beds, plumping up pillows, straightening the limp covers. Then, tilting her head to one side, she contemplates the tray and says, "Well, Josie, you did a good job on your dinner."

Relieved, I climb back on the bed and pick up a *Vogue* that's been lying around—I got away with it! again!—when she says "I'm going to have to take a look around, if you don't mind. It's one of the rules."

If I don't mind! What choice do I have, powerless as a child, forced to lie and scheme simply to exercise the elementary—the alimentary—right to determine what does and doesn't go into my body?

She looked quickly under both beds and behind the curtains, checks the lock on the clothes locker, runs her hand between the end of the mattress and the metal railing at the foot of both beds, and then, of course, opens the nightstand drawer on the far side.

"What's this?" she says, though she knows.

"I was saving it for later," I say. "I couldn't eat it all now, so I was going to have some more later, before bed."

She says nothing but just stands there, shaking her head, holding the imperfectly closed bundle of salad and bread, already soggy in spots. Then she dumps it on the tray and says, "Anything you don't eat, just leave on the tray." She seems about to pick up the tray and go, but then, as an afterthought, comes over to the side of my bed, opens the screeching drawer—is there no place that's mine?—and finds the apple and the piece of roll I took from lunch. "This is hoarding," she says. "You can have anything you want to eat at any time—just ask, but don't hoard."

Angry and humiliated and bereft, I don't answer. I put the *Vogue* over my face so I won't have to see her, wondering what I must look like, lying here flat in a faded robe, my fragile limbs sticking out like a grasshopper's, my skin a dry grayish white, netted with veins, my fingertips and nails blueberry-hued, the crook of each arm a purplish mess

dotted with bloody pinpricks, and on top of this all, superimposed over my face, the vivid face of the *Vogue* cover,
each eyelash alert, each tooth a dazzling, clunky tile like a
Chiclet, the skin a sealed and poreless stretch of pink, and
the ripe, shiny lips curved into a radiant smirk.

carnal
acts

Inviting me to speak at her small liberal arts college during Women's Week, a young woman set me a task: "We would be pleased," she wrote, "if you could talk on how you cope with your MS disability, and also how you discovered your voice as a writer." Oh, Lord, I thought in dismay, how am I going to pull this one off? How can I yoke two such disparate subjects into a coherent presentation, without doing violence to one, or the other, or both, or myself? This is going to take some fancy footwork, and my feet scarcely carry out the basic steps, let alone anything elaborate.

To make matters worse, the assumption underlying each of her questions struck me as suspect. To ask *how* I cope with multiple sclerosis suggests that I *do* cope. Now, "to cope," *Webster's Third* tells me, is "to face or encounter and to find necessary expedients to overcome problems and difficulties." In these terms, I have to confess, I don't feel like much of a coper. I'm likely to deal with my problems and difficulties by squawking and flapping around like that hysterical chicken that was convinced the sky was falling. Never mind that in my case the sky really *is* falling. In response to a clonk on the head, regardless of its origin, one might comport oneself with a grace and courtesy I generally lack.

As for "finding" my voice, the implication is that it was at one time lost or missing. But I don't think it ever was. Ask my mother, who will tell you a little wearily that I was speaking full sentences by the time I was a year old and could never be silenced again. As for its being a writer's voice, it seems to have become one early on. Ask Mother again. At the age of eight I rewrote the Trojan War, she will say, and what Nestor was about to do to Helen at the end doesn't bear discussion in polite company.

Faced with these uncertainties, I took my own teacherly advice, something, I must confess, I don't always do. "If an idea is giving you trouble," I tell my writing students, "put it on the back burner and let it simmer while you do something else. Go to the movies. Reread a stack of old love letters. Sit in your history class and take detailed notes on the Teapot Dome scandal. If you've got your idea in mind, it will go on cooking at some level no matter what else you're doing." "I've had an idea for my documented essay on the back burner," one of my students once scribbled in her journal, "and I think it's just boiled over!"

I can't claim to have reached such a flash point. But in the weeks I've had the themes "disability" and "voice" sitting around in my head, they seem to have converged on their own, without my having to wrench them together and bind them with hoops of tough rhetoric. They *are* related, indeed interdependent, with an intimacy that has for some reason remained, until now, submerged below the surface of my attention. Forced to juxtapose them, I yank them out of the depths, a little startled to discover how they were intertwined down there out of sight. This kind of discovery can unnerve you at first. You feel like a giant hand that, pulling two swimmers out of the water, two separate heads bobbling on the iridescent swells, finds the two bodies below, legs coiled around each other, in an ecstasy of copulation. You don't quite know where to turn your eyes.

Perhaps the place to start illuminating this erotic connection between who I am and how I speak lies in history. I have known that I have multiple sclerosis for about seventeen years now, though the disease probably started long before. The hypothesis is that the disease process, in which the protective covering of the nerves in the brain and spinal cord is eaten away and replaced by scar tissue, "hard patches," is caused by an autoimmune reaction to a slow-acting virus. Research suggests that I was infected by this virus, which no one has ever seen and which therefore, technically, doesn't even "exist," between the ages of four and fifteen. In effect, living with this mysterious mechanism feels like having your present self, and the past selves it embodies, haunted by a capricious and mean-spirited ghost, unseen except for its footprints, which trips you even when you're watching where you're going, knocks glassware out of your hand, squeezes the urine out of your bladder before you reach the bathroom, and weights your whole body with a weariness no amount of rest can relieve. An alien invader must be at work. But of course it's not. It's your own body. That is, it's you.

This, for me, has been the most difficult aspect of adjusting to a chronic incurable degenerative disease: the fact that it has rammed my "self" straight back into the body I had been trained to believe it could, through high-minded acts and aspirations, rise above. The Western tradition of distinguishing the body from the mind and/or the soul is so ancient as to have become part of our collective unconscious, if one is inclined to believe in such a noumenon, or at least to have become an unquestioned element in the social instruction we impose upon infants from birth, in much the same way we inculcate, without reflection, the gender distinctions "female" and "male." I *have* a body, you are likely to say if you talk about embodiment at all; you don't say, I *am* a body. A body is a separate entity possessable by the "I"; the "I" and the body aren't, as the copula would make them, grammatically indistinguishable.

To widen the rift between the self and the body, we treat our bodies as subordinates, inferior in moral status. Open association with them shames us. In fact, we treat our bodies with very much the same distance and ambivalence women have traditionally received from men in our culture. Sometimes this treatment is benevolent, even respectful, but all too often it is tainted by outright sadism. I think of the bodybuilding regimens that have become popular in the last decade or so, with the complicated vacillations they reflect between self-worship and self-degradation: joggers and aerobic dancers and weightlifters all beating their bodies into shape. "No pain, no gain," the saying goes. "Feel the burn." Bodies get treated like wayward women who have to be shown who's boss, even if it means slapping them around a little. I'm not for a moment opposing rugged exercise here. I'm simply questioning the spirit in which it is often undertaken.

Since, as Helene Cixous points out in her essay on

women and writing, "Sorties,"* thought has always worked "through dual, hierarchical oppositions" (p. 64), the mind/ body split cannot possibly be innocent. The utterance of an "I" immediately calls into being its opposite, the "not-I," Western discourse being unequipped to conceive "that which is neither 'I' nor 'not-I,' " "that which is both 'I' and 'not-I,' " or some other permutation that language doesn't permit me to speak. The "not-I" is, by definition, other. And we've never been too fond of the other. We prefer the same. We tend to ascribe to the other those qualities we prefer not to associate with our selves: It is the hidden, the dark, the secret, the shameful. Thus, when the "I" takes possession of the body, it makes the body into an other, direct object of a transitive verb, with all the other's repudiated and potentially dangerous qualities.

At the least, then, the body had best be viewed with suspicion. And a woman's body is particularly suspect, since so much of it is in fact hidden, dark, secret, carried about on the inside where, even with the aid of a speculum, one can never perceive all of it in the plain light of day, a graspable whole. I, for one, have never understood why anyone would want to carry all that delicate stuff around on the outside. It would make you awfully anxious, I should think, put you constantly on the defensive, create a kind of siege mentality that viewed all other beings, even your own kind, as threats to be warded off with spears and guns and atomic missiles. And you'd never get to experience that inward dreaming that comes when your flesh surrounds all your treasures,

* In *The Newly Born Woman*, translated by Betsy Wing (Minneapolis: University of Minnesota Press, 1986).

holding them close, like a sturdy shuttered house. Be my personal skepticism as it may, however, as a cultural woman I bear just as much shame as any woman for my dark, enfolded secrets. Let the word for my external genitals tell the tale: my pudendum, from the Latin infinitive meaning "to be ashamed."

It's bad enough to carry your genitals like a sealed envelope bearing the cipher that, once unlocked, might loose the chaotic flood of female pleasure—*jouissance*, the French call it—upon the world-of-the-same. But I have an additional reason to feel shame for my body, less explicitly connected with its sexuality: It is a crippled body. Thus it is doubly other, not merely by the homosexual standards of patriarchal culture but by the standards of physical desirability erected for every body in our world. Men, who are by definition exonerated from shame in sexual terms (this doesn't mean that an individual man might not experience sexual shame, of course; remember that I'm talking in general about discourse, not folks), may—more likely must—experience bodily shame if they are crippled. I won't presume to speak about the details of their experience, however. I don't know enough. I'll just go on telling what it's like to be a crippled woman, trusting that, since we're fellow creatures who've been living together for some thousands of years now, much of my experience will resonate with theirs.

I was never a beautiful woman, and for that reason I've spent most of my life (together with probably at least 95 percent of the female population of the United States) suffering from the shame of falling short of an unattainable standard. The ideal woman of my generation was . . .

perky, I think you'd say, rather than gorgeous. Blond hair pulled into a bouncing ponytail. Wide blue eyes, a turned-up nose with maybe a scattering of golden freckles across it, a small mouth with full lips over straight white teeth. Her breasts were large but well harnessed high on her chest; her tiny waist flared to hips just wide enough to give the crinolines under her circle skirt a starting outward push. In terms of personality, she was outgoing, even bubbly, not pensive or mysterious. Her milieu was the front fender of a white Corvette convertible, surrounded by teasing crewcuts, dressed in black flats, a sissy blouse, and the letter sweater of the Corvette owner. Needless to say, she never missed a prom.

Ten years or so later, when I first noticed the symptoms that would be diagnosed as MS, I was probably looking my best. Not beautiful still, but the ideal had shifted enough so that my flat chest and narrow hips gave me an elegantly attenuated shape, set off by a thick mass of long, straight, shining hair. I had terrific legs, long and shapely, revealed nearly to the pudendum by the fashionable miniskirts and hot pants I adopted with more enthusiasm than delicacy of taste. Not surprisingly, I suppose, during this time I involved myself in several pretty torrid love affairs.

The beginning of MS wasn't too bad. The first symptom, besides the pernicious fatigue that had begun to devour me, was "foot drop," the inability to raise my left foot at the ankle. As a consequence, I'd started to limp, but I could still wear high heels, and a bit of a limp might seem more intriguing than repulsive. After a few months, when the doctor suggested a cane, a crippled friend gave me quite an elegant wood-and-silver one, which I carried with a fair

amount of panache. The real blow to my self-image came
when I had to get a brace. As braces go, it's not bad: light-
weight plastic molded to my foot and leg, fitting down into
an ordinary shoe and secured around my calf by a Velcro
strap. It reduces my limp and, more important, the danger of
tripping and falling. But it meant the end of high heels. And
it's ugly. Not as ugly as I think it is, I gather, but still pretty
ugly. It signified for me, and perhaps still does, the perma-
nence and irreversibility of my condition. The brace makes
my MS concrete and forces me to wear it on the outside. As
soon as I strapped the brace on, I climbed into trousers and
stayed there (though not in the same trousers, of course).
The idea of going around with my bare brace hanging out
seemed almost as indecent as exposing my breasts. Not until
1984, soon after I won the Western States Book Award for
poetry, did I put on a skirt short enough to reveal my plasti-
cized leg. The connection between winning a writing award
and baring my brace is not merely fortuitous; being affirmed
as a writer really did embolden me. Since then I've grown so
accustomed to wearing skirts that I don't think about my
brace any more than I think about my cane. I've incorporated them, I suppose: made them, in their necessity, insen-
sate but fundamental parts of my body.

Meanwhile, I had to adjust to the most outward and
visible sign of all, a three-wheeled electric scooter called an
Amigo. This lessens my fatigue and increases my range ter-
rifically, but it also shouts out to the world "Here is a woman
who can't stand on her own two feet." At the same time,
paradoxically, it renders me invisible, reducing me to the
height of a seven-year-old, with a child's attendant low

status. "Would she like smoking or nonsmoking?" the gate
agent assigning me a seat asks the friend traveling with me.
In crowds I see nothing but buttocks. I can tell you the
name of every type of designer jeans ever sold. The wearers,
eyes front, trip over me and fall across my handlebars into
my lap. "Hey!" I want to shout to the lofty world. "Down
here! There's a person down here!" But I'm not, by their
standards, quite a person any more.

My self-esteem diminishes further as age and illness strip
from me the features that made me, for a brief while anyway,
a good-looking, even sexy, young woman. No more long,
bounding strides: I shuffle along with the timid gait I remember observing, with pity and impatience, in the little
old ladies at Boston's Symphony Hall on Friday afternoons.
No more lithe, girlish figure: My belly sags from the loss of
muscle tone, which also creates all kinds of intestinal disrup-
tions, hopelessly humiliating in a society in which excretory
functions remain strictly unspeakable. No more sex either, if
society had its way. The sexuality of the disabled so repulses
most people that you can hardly get a doctor, let alone a
member of the general population, to consider the issues it
raises. Cripples simply aren't supposed to Want It, much less
Do It. Fortunately, I've got a husband with a strong libido
and a weak sense of social propriety, or else I'd find myself
perforce practicing a vow of chastity I never cared to take.

Afflicted by the general shame of having a body at all,
and the specific shame of having one weakened and misshapen by disease, I ought not to be able to hold my head up
in public. And yet I've gotten into the habit of holding my
head up in public, sometimes under excruciating circum-

stances. Recently, for instance, I had to give a reading at the University of Arizona. Having smashed three of my front teeth in a fall onto the concrete floor of my screened porch, I was in the process of getting them crowned, and the temporary crowns flew out during dinner right before the reading. What to do? I wanted, of course, to rush home and hide till the dental office opened the next morning. But I couldn't very well break my word at this last moment. So, looking like Hansel and Gretel's witch, and lisping worse than the Wife of Bath, I got up on stage and read. Somehow, over the years, I've learned how to set shame aside and do what I have to do.

Here, I think, is where my "voice" comes in. Because, in spite of my demurral at the beginning, I do in fact cope with my disability at least some of the time. And I do so, I think, by speaking about it, and about the whole experience of being a body, specifically a female body, out loud, in a clear, level tone that drowns out the frantic whispers of my mother, my grandmothers, all the other trainers of wayward childish tongues: "Sssh! Sssh! Nice girls don't talk like that. Don't mention sweat. Don't mention menstrual blood. Don't ask what your grandfather does on his business trips. Don't laugh so loud. You sound like a loon. Keep your voice down. Don't tell. Don't tell. Don't tell." Speaking out loud is an antidote to shame. I want to distinguish clearly here between "shame," as I'm using the word, and "guilt" and "embarrassment," which, though equally painful, are not similarly poisonous. Guilt arises from performing a forbidden act or failing to perform a required one. In either case, the guilty person can, through reparation, erase the offense and start fresh. Embarrassment, less opprobrious though not necessarily less distressing, is generally caused by acting in a socially stupid or awkward way. When I trip and sprawl in public, when I wet myself, when my front teeth fly out, I feel horribly embarrassed, but, like the pain of childbirth, the sensation blurs and dissolves in time. If it didn't, every child would be an only child, and no one would set foot in public after the onset of puberty, when embarrassment erupts like a geyser and bathes one's whole life in its bitter stream. Shame may attach itself to guilt or embarrassment, complicating their resolution, but it is not the same emotion. I feel guilt or embarrassment for something I've done; shame, for who I am. I may stop doing bad or stupid things, but I can't stop being. How then can I help but be ashamed? Of the three conditions, this is the one that cracks and stifles my voice.

I can subvert its power, I've found, by acknowledging who I am, shame and all, and, in doing so, raising what was hidden, dark, secret about my life into the plain light of shared human experience. What we aren't permitted to utter holds us, each isolated from every other, in a kind of solipsistic thrall. Without any way to check our reality against anyone else's, we assume that our fears and shortcomings are ours alone. One of the strangest consequences of publishing a collection of personal essays called *Plaintext* has been the steady trickle of letters and telephone calls saying essentially, in a tone of unmistakable relief, "Oh, me too! Me too!" It's as though the part I thought was solo has turned out to be a chorus. But none of us was singing loud enough for the others to hear.

Singing loud enough demands a particular kind of voice,

I think. And I was wrong to suggest, at the beginning, that I've always had my voice. I have indeed always had *a* voice, but it wasn't *this* voice, the one with which I could call up and transform my hidden self from a naughty girl into a woman talking directly to others like herself. Recently, in the process of writing a new book, a memoir entitled *Remembering the Bone House*, I've had occasion to read some of my early writing, from college, high school, even junior high. It's not an experience I recommend to anyone susceptible to shame. Not that the writing was all that bad. I was surprised at how competent a lot of it was. Here was a writer who already knew precisely how the language worked. But the voice . . . oh, the voice was all wrong: maudlin, rhapsodic, breaking here and there into little shrieks, almost, you might say, hysterical. It was a voice that had shucked off its own body, its own homely life of Cheerios for breakfast and seventy pages of Chaucer to read before the exam on Tuesday and a planter's wart growing painfully on the ball of its foot, and reeled now wraithlike through the air, seeking incarnation only as the heroine who enacts her doomed love for the tall, dark, mysterious stranger. If it didn't get that part, it wouldn't play at all.

Among all these overheated and vaporous imaginings, I must have retained some shred of sense, because I stopped writing prose entirely, except for scholarly papers, for nearly twenty years. I even forgot not exactly that I had written prose, but at least what kind of prose it was. So when I needed to take up the process again, I could start almost fresh, using the vocal range I'd gotten used to in years of asking the waiter in the Greek restaurant for an extra an-

chovy on my salad, congratulating the puppy on making a
puddle outside rather than inside the patio door, pondering
with my daughter the vagaries of female orgasm, saying
good-bye to my husband, and hello, and good-bye, and
hello. This new voice—thoughtful, affectionate, often
amused—was essential because what I needed to write about
when I returned to prose was an attempt I'd made not long
before to kill myself, and suicide simply refuses to be spoken
of authentically in high-flown romantic language. It's too
ugly. Too shameful. Too strictly a bodily event. And, yes, too
funny as well, though people are sometimes shocked to find
humor shoved up against suicide. They don't like the incon-
gruity. But let's face it, life (real life, I mean, not the edited-
for-television version) is a cacophonous affair from start to
finish. I might have wanted to portray my suicidal self as a
languishing maiden, too exquisitely sensitive to sustain life's
wounding pressures on her soul. (I didn't want to, as a matter of fact, but I might have.) The truth remained, regardless
of my desires, that when my husband lugged me into the
emergency room, my hair matted, my face swollen and gray,
my nightgown streaked with blood and urine, I was no frail
and tender spirit. I was a body, and one in a hell of a mess.

I "should" have kept quiet about that experience. I
know the rules of polite discourse. I should have kept my
shame, and the nearly lethal sense of isolation and alienation it brought, to myself. And I might have, except for
something the psychiatrist in the emergency room had told
my husband. "You might as well take her home," he said. "If
she wants to kill herself, she'll do it no matter how many
precautions we take. They always do." *They* always do. I was

one of "them," whoever they were. I was, in this context anyway, not singular, not aberrant, but typical. I think it was this sense of commonality with others I didn't even know, a sense of being returned somehow, in spite of my appalling act, to the human family, that urged me to write that first essay, not merely speaking out but calling out, perhaps. "Here's the way I am," it said. "How about you?" And the answer came, as I've said: "Me too! Me too!"

This has been the kind of work I've continued to do: to scrutinize the details of my own experience and to report what I see, and what I think about what I see, as lucidly and accurately as possible. But because feminine experience has been immemorially devalued and repressed, I continue to find this task terrifying. "Every woman has known the torture of beginning to speak aloud," Cixous writes, "heart beating as if to break, occasionally falling into loss of language, ground and language slipping out from under her, because for woman speaking—even just opening her mouth —in public is something rash, a transgression" (p. 92).

The voice I summon up wants to crack, to whisper, to trail back into silence. "I'm sorry to have nothing more than this to say," it wants to apologize. "I shouldn't be taking up your time. I've never fought in a war, or even in a schoolyard free-for-all. I've never tried to see who could piss farthest up the barn wall. I've never even been to a whorehouse. All the important formative experiences have passed me by. I was raped once. I've borne two children. Milk trickling out of my breasts, blood trickling from between my legs. You don't want to hear about it. Sometimes I'm too scared to leave my house. Not scared *of* anything, just scared:

mouth dry, bowels writhing. When the fear got really bad, they locked me up for six months, but that was years ago. I'm getting old now. Misshapen too. I don't blame you if you can't get it up. No one could possibly desire a body like this. It's not your fault. It's mine. Forgive me. I didn't mean to start crying. I'm sorry . . . sorry . . . sorry . . ."

An easy solace to the anxiety of speaking aloud: this slow subsidence beneath the waves of shame, back into what Cixous calls "this body that has been worse than confiscated, a body replaced with a disturbing stranger, sick or dead, who so often is a bad influence, the cause and place of inhibitions. By censuring the body," she goes on, "breath and speech are censored at the same time" (p. 97). But I am not going back, not going under one more time. To do so would demonstrate a failure of nerve far worse than the depredations of MS have caused. Paradoxically, losing one sort of nerve has given me another. No one is going to take my breath away. No one is going to leave me speechless. To be silent is to comply with the standard of feminine grace. But my crippled body already violates all notions of feminine grace. What more have I got to lose? I've gone beyond shame. I'm shameless, you might say. You know, as in "shameless hussy"? A woman with her bare brace and her tongue hanging out.

I've "found" my voice, then, just where it ought to have been, in the body-warmed breath escaping my lungs and throat. Forced by the exigencies of physical disease to embrace my self in the flesh, I couldn't write bodiless prose. The voice is the creature of the body that produces it. I speak as a crippled woman. At the same time, in the utterance I redeem both "cripple" and "woman" from the shameful silences by which I have often felt surrounded, contained, set apart; I give myself permission to live openly among others, to reach out for them, stroke them with fingers and sighs. No body, no voice; no voice, no body. That's what I know in my bones.

p a t r i c i a   s t e v e n s

stiff upper lip

It was somewhat of a shock to discover a few years ago that men weren't looking any more. If I had been a raving beauty in my youth, it might have been more of a jolt; nevertheless, it is hard to accept that now, when I walk down the street, I am close to being invisible. This realization came to me about the same time that I started avoiding myself in the mirror. I would run a comb through my hair, put on a little mascara and blush, and get out of the bathroom. Otherwise, it was too painful. That rectangular piece of glass over the bathroom sink spoke the truth. It was unavoidable: I was really getting wrinkles. I'd given up the sun a few years earlier, after a dermatologist told me that the fingernail-size pearly patch of skin on my left shoulder was a basal cell carcinoma, but it was too late. I had to pay for all those hours of lying on my back, doing absolutely nothing but baking my face under the thinning ozone.

I've accepted some of my wrinkles. Crow's feet are okay with me; they're laugh lines. The crease between my eyebrows is a bit more troublesome as are the lines across my forehead—all are frown lines—but since we all frown, I've come to accept those too. Besides, I have a mild case of myopia and have reason to squint.

The wrinkles that are absolutely unacceptable, though, are the ones on my upper lip. They're little vertical gullies that run perpendicular to my horizontal lip line, and I'm obsessed with their very existence. They remind me of my Aunt Olga, who's eighty years old and still smoking cigarettes, and who in her sixties wore thick, bright, red-orange lipstick that often traveled several millimeters up the numerous minigorges on her upper lip.

My very own lip wrinkles appeared without warning. I was about to brush a light dusting of coral-pink blush on my tan-free cheeks one day when I looked into the bathroom mirror and saw nothing but my upper lip, nothing but Aunt Olga. They were tiny threads then, barely more than microscopic, but as I moved in closer to the glass they loomed gargantuan, each its own Hell's Canyon. I stood there a long time, in total disbelief that my youth had finally come to an abrupt and unmerciful end.

Back in the sixties when I did all that sunbathing, there were rumors that the sun caused wrinkles, smoking did too, but that hadn't stopped me. Even when I was twenty-three or twenty-four and still getting carded when I walked into a bar, it was impossible to imagine I'd ever reach forty. I had my youth and flaunted it. I proudly wore my uniform—a pair of faded, ripped-off-at-the-upper-thigh-and-frayed jeans, a navy-blue skinny-ribbed tank top, tight, cut in at the shoulders to expose my collar bones, and no bra—and I needed the tan to show it all off.

Maybe I flaunted my youth because it was really the only power I thought I had. It's a white man's world now, but it was even more so then, and even with the B.A. degree there were few options. My first job out of college was in personnel work—at the time, one of the few professions open to women. I despised the corporation (I was an employment interviewer for a large insurance company) and got myself in trouble more than once thinking I might change its priorities, and I hated the work itself—placing hundreds of sparkling, hopeful, young high school grads into boring, dead-end, low-paying positions. But I still had my youth, and I got noticed for it, though not always in the ways I wanted to be noticed.

This was before sexual harassment had a name, and I often laughed at sexist jokes because even though they made me uncomfortable, I was more afraid of being labeled a poor sport or worse yet, humorless, if I didn't. It was also the beginning of the sexual revolution, and I got the two confused. I didn't yet understand the difference between a sexist joke and being sexually repressed. To me, it was all the same undiscovered territory.

A year out of school, I was living in Boston and laughing uncomfortably at jokes about sexed-crazed farmers' daughters and pitying those unfortunate middle-aged women at the insurance company, the ones with the silver strands running through their dark, dull, colorless hair, who were struggling up the corporate ladder, unable to throw off their sexually repressed Catholic upbringings as surely I was doing. Ones like Marlene McGuffy who'd been double jinxed—middle-aged *and* single. She also had cellulite, and sometimes when she dared to wear her sleeveless, beige

linen dress to work, I could even see the beginnings of it in
her dimpled upper arms; and she had wrinkles on her face,
crow's feet and frown lines, and tiny crevices in her upper
lip. Lord have mercy! How could she leave the house looking like that?

Cellulite was something my mother's generation was
cursed with, but I wore miniskirts to work, and it never
occurred to me that there was anything wrong with always
having to dip like a Cossack to retrieve something I'd
dropped on the floor. My hair was thick and shiny, and if I
felt like it I could wear it in two ponytails like Kitten on
Father Knows Best, or I could sleek it back like Audrey Hepburn.

Thinking I was making the best of the power of youth, I
also spent a lot of time lying in the sun. When I was on my
belly, of course, I could read—*Far From the Madding Crowd*
one day and *Valley of the Dolls* the next; but when I was on
my back I did absolutely nothing but bake. What I did with
the power of youth was bake and smoke cigarettes. Often I
baked and smoked at the same time.

I started smoking at sixteen, the summer Beverly Rohrs
and I spent a week alone together at Conneaut Lake in
western Pennsylvania. This was the same week I first got
serious about my tan. Every afternoon, for seven whole days,
Bev and I lay on the beach and puffed away on our Parlia-
ments. Then, about four o'clock, we'd return to our room,
take a shower, put on clean shorts, and head over to the
amusement park to pick up boys.

From seventeen to twenty-one, away at college, I did my baking out on the grassy lawns with a group of other young women. Lying on our beach towels, transistor radios nearby, we'd stay under the rays long enough to get a distinct outline under our two-piece bathing suits. Try as we did, we got very little studying done; it was always too hot and humid and sticky and uncomfortable to concentrate on anything.

Once I was out of college, the tan got a little easier to acquire. My friend Patty and I would get in her VW Bug early on Saturday or Sunday morning (or both) and drive to one of the beaches on the North Shore or head for the Cape and braise our bodies all day long. After we'd set down our canvas bags filled with books, magazines, pop, chips, and cigarettes, we'd spread out our blankets on the dry sand about ten yards from the salty waves of the Atlantic and baste ourselves with a homemade potion of iodine and baby oil.

I wasted hundreds, thousands of hours roasting in the sun, and I hate to admit it, but I felt good in my tan. The browner the better. Besides, I could never wear the tiny ripped-off jeans and the skinny tank top if I had skin as white as Morticia's on the *Addams Family*. Neither could I wear my white sundress, or my pale frosted lipstick. I was living in Boston with a California tan, and when I walked down the street, at least some of the time, I got noticed.

I was well aware, even then, that, tan or not, women over forty did not get the same attention. I felt sorry for them. I never dreamed I could get that old, and if by some remote chance I did, I'd of course be happily married to a perfect man who thought I was the most gorgeous woman in the world. I'd also be financially secure and still wearing the cut-off jeans.

Hard as it is to believe, I've not only made it to forty, I've crossed the line to where I'm closer to fifty. Waiters of both genders now refer to me as "Ma'am." Miniskirts are back in fashion, though I can't imagine why anyone would want to wear them. I still wear jeans, but only the ones that go past the ankle, and the perfect husband turned out to be not so perfect. After two pregnancies and two years of nursing babies, the thin tank tops have long gone to the Goodwill and the bra goes on, every day. When I go out in the sun, my sunscreen goes with me. I apply a creamy layer over my face, over my wrinkles, and believe it or not, I go out of the house looking like that!

Still, it was not an easy transition. As my upper lip wrinkles gradually deepened, I became more and more fixated on them. I would sometimes stand in front of the mirror, checking to see how my upper lip appeared at various distances. That way I could determine how far away I'd have to stand from someone to avoid having that person see the wrinkles. I'd practice smiling—a weird, unnatural-looking smile whose sole purpose was to stretch the skin on my upper lip enough to make the gullies disappear. Whenever I was outside, especially in the sunlight, I dreaded running into anyone I knew.

Something else happened too. When I looked at a middle-aged woman, I saw nothing but her skin, and I could not help but make comparisons. At my twenty-fifth high school reunion, I ran into Janet Murgi, a former friend from as far back as the third grade. Oh happy day! She'd been living in Florida for fifteen years and the skin on her face was akin to one of the California Raisins. On the other hand, when I got a close-up of Jane Welsh and saw to my total disbelief that she hadn't aged a day over thirty, I bemoaned my wrinkled fate. My karma was coming back to me: Oh why oh why had I wasted all those years just lying in the sun? Just think what I might have accomplished with all that time I spent lying on a beach, at the side of a swimming pool, on an aluminum-framed chaise lounge in the backyard.

A couple of years ago, I asked Dr. L., the dermatologist who'd burned away my basal cell carcinoma, for a tube of Retin-A. I wanted a miracle, and I greedily spread it over my face. Within days I had a severe reaction. My skin turned rough, red, and flaky, and I looked as though I'd been hanging my head on a stick over a campfire. I even broke out— more acne in a week than I'd ever seen as a teenager. Dr. L. changed the prescription to .025 percent tretinoin (the miracle ingredient), and I smeared that on too. I waited. Nothing seemed to be happening. The change would be subtle, Dr. L. said. Be patient, I told myself.

It was subtle. My skin calmed down and began to feel a little smoother, a little less sun-aged looking, everywhere except on my upper lip. As fate would have it, my lip wrinkles seemed to multiply.

I ruled out a chemical face peel. I'd seen less than a minute of a face peel in progress on a TV documentary, and it made me so queasy I had to flip the channel. The patient had been anesthetized and was lying on her back completely unaware that the plastic surgeon was using an oversized pair of tweezers to peel back the skin on her forehead in one big thick chunk starting at her hairline. It looked unreal, as if it were one of those tightly fitting rubberized masks the characters on *Mission Impossible* used to wear, yet it made my stomach flip over.

Collagen injections, I decided; I would have the canyons filled in. Dr. L. said she didn't do things like that (a great percentage of her booming practice was burning off cancers and precancers), but she suggested a doctor at the university. I called. It was a long process, I was told—I'd have to be tested for an allergic reaction—and it wouldn't be cheap. Then too, the injections were good only for from six to eighteen months before it had to be done all over again. I made the appointment anyway.

When the day came, I found myself sitting in a crowded waiting room on the fifth floor of a large midwestern university teaching hospital. I was there a long time. I got through two *People* magazines before I was even ushered into an examining room. There, without any magazine at all, I waited another thirty minutes. Finally, a resident appeared, a young, slightly-built Asian man with a thick accent. I explained what I wanted. "I used to fry in the sun," I said. I was sure he didn't understand.

"Yes," he said. He was a very serious individual.

"And smoke," I added. "This is the result." I pointed to my upper lip.

He bent over, got close, and, through his frameless

glasses, peered at it. I held my breath and thought about how I'd once vowed never to be the patient of a male doctor again.

"Collagen," I said, breathing once more. "I want you to put it in my wrinkles."

"Oh yes," he said. Straightening up, he stepped back but was still staring at my lip. "Well," he said. "Dr. S. will be in shortly to see you."

"So you think you can do that?" I asked.

"Oh yes," he said, and disappeared through the door.

I was alone again, and with no reading material I had to resort to using the backs of the deposit slips in my checkbook to make a list of all the movies I wanted to see. Thirty minutes and fourteen movie titles later, the doctor came in. He stuck out his hand. "I'm Dr. S." He wasn't afraid to grip a woman's hand, I noticed, and took that as a good sign. He was in his mid- to late thirties, had very pale wrinkle-free skin (I was sure he'd never, ever left home without his sunblock), but there were the faint marks of a probable teenage acne on both sides of his face—the reason, I figured, he'd gone into dermatology.

After he apologized for keeping me waiting so long, I repeated what I'd told the resident, that I wanted collagen. Bending over me like his predecessor had done, Dr. S. kneaded and stretched the skin on my upper lip. "Not too deep," he said.

"They're ravines," I said through his fingers. "It's all I can see." When he took his fingers off my face, I started rambling. "I know that in the scheme of things having your lip wrinkles taken care of isn't very high on the scale of world problems, like there are people starving right now, but . . ." I was apologizing all over the place. "I'm getting paid back for all those years of smoking and lying in the sun." I tried to laugh.

He smiled a little. "We might do an acid peel," he said, stretching out my skin again.

"I saw one on TV and it made me sick."

"We don't do those here," Dr. S. told me. "You're talking about a deep peel. We don't go that deep here."

"Shirley MacLaine had lip wrinkles," I said. "She had them in *Terms of Endearment,* but by *Postcards From the Edge,* they'd disappeared."

Dr. S. smiled broadly now. "This isn't L.A."

"I don't want to do anything stupid," I said.

"I don't do stupid things," said Dr. S.

Was that a stupid thing to say? I wondered.

"Have you tried Retin-A?"

"Yes. It works, but not on my lip. I'm going to be one of those old women who has the little tributaries of red lipstick running up toward her nose." I told him about Aunt Olga.

Dr. S. laughed. He said if I made another appointment he would do an acid peel on just my upper lip. Then he noticed the deep frown line between my eyebrows and started fingering and stretching that.

"That's not the one that bothers me," I said quickly. "That's not the one I'm obsessed with." He nodded as though he understood. I could feel sweat under my armpits.

I returned a month later. This time I got a female resident. She explained that Dr. S. would rub the acid on my upper lip, that it would burn, they would pack it with ice, and I would go home and wait for the skin to turn bright red and peel off.

Dr. S. came in. He told me the same thing the resident had just told me. "I don't want to do anything stupid," I said again. "I saw a woman on *Larry King Live* who'd gone in to have the cellulite sucked out of her thigh, and her thigh caved in."

When Dr. S. grinned I began to realize just how foolish I felt sitting in a room with a male doctor, who was at least ten years younger than me, talking to him about cellulite and wrinkles. "Now instead of a fat thigh, she's got a crater in her leg," I said.

Dr. S. started kneading my upper lip like he'd done on the first visit.

"Could I have scarring?" I asked. I would be taking a risk, and instead of wrinkles, I could end up with a blob of lumpy pulp.

"It's possible, but extremely rare," he said. I thought about the TV pictures of the woman with the caved-in thigh. "I can tell you that I'm conservative," he added.

"How many of these have you done before?" I asked.

"On the whole face, we do farmers all the time," he said. "On just the lip? One."

"What did the woman with the lip think?" I wanted to know.

"She liked it," Dr. S. said proudly.

I imagined having the lip of a twenty-year-old. "All right, let's do it," I said, assuring myself that corn and pig farmers would never do anything stupid.

While the resident got the container of acid out of a

cabinet at the side of the room, Dr. S. told me that he would do me all the way up to the nose so there wouldn't be any obvious boundary lines.

The mention of boundary lines frightened me a little, but by this time I already was lying back on the examining table with Dr. S. standing over me. The resident was on the other side holding the acid vat, and Dr. S. dipped a long, fat Q-tip into it and started rubbing it hard over the right side of my upper lip. It burned and tears ran out of the corners of my eyes, but I didn't flinch. After all, I was choosing this. It wasn't the same as going to the dentist and having a tooth drilled.

With one side done, I got the ice pack, and Dr. S. rubbed the acid hard over the left side. Then, with the tears still running a little, came another ice pack. They kept the ice on for a few minutes, until I said it didn't sting any more. Dr. S. was smiling. "You've got a milk mustache," he said, peering down at me.

"A milk mustache." They hadn't warned me. I sat up and was handed a mirror. "Oh God!" My entire upper lip, end to end, lip line to nose, looked like it had been brushed with white elementary-school paste. "When will this go away?" I was stunned.

"Oh, in a couple of hours," Dr. S. said matter-of-factly.

"How am I going to leave here? I need a paper bag to put over my head."

Dr. S. and the resident were both laughing.

"At least a magazine to hold in front of my face."

The resident went out to the waiting room and stole me the latest edition of *Time*. I held it under my nose and crept my way down the hall. As I walked through the waiting room, a couple of people looked up, but I quickly assured myself that I'd look like more of a jerk with a milk-white mustache than I did holding a *Time* magazine in front of my face. I made it to the parking building and my car, and the woman who took my money tried hard to pretend I looked perfectly normal.

I got home. The milky white faded to pink. It was tingly and I kept going to the mirror to check on it. When my sons got home from school, I told them why my upper lip was pink. My older son looked helplessly up to the ceiling and said, "Why did you do that?" My younger son hardly glanced my way but said, "You look like a fool, Mom," then went off in search of junk food.

Nothing happened. I must have a tough upper lip. Well, something happened in that it did turn red like a sunburn and it peeled off in little flakes, but when I went back for a follow-up a week later, both Dr. S. and the resident were amazed that my lip wrinkles were still there, gullied as ever. "I thought it was a pretty deep rub," they both said at separate times.

"Well, wait and see," Dr. S. said. "There's a slight swelling. When it heals completely, you might see a change. If not, you can come back in a month or two and have it done again." Then he proceeded to tell me that *he* wouldn't do it again because *he* was moving to Florida. Where there was an endless supply of lip wrinkles, I thought.

My upper lip did heal completely but still nothing at all had happened. In fact, the lines may have gotten a bit worse. But I didn't go back. Though the wrinkles hadn't faded, my obsession with my upper lip miraculously had. I also had a bill for $200, and I took that as a sign that my lip wrinkles were meant to be a part of me. I struck up the courage to tell a couple of friends what I'd done, and they (politely or not) told me they'd never noticed I had any lip wrinkles.

I decided to wear my negative history, all those hours waiting in the sun. What I'd been waiting for, I'm still not sure. Did I really think I'd find a good man that way? Looking back, I think I was waiting for something, someone to tell me what to do with myself; I had no idea how to live my life. I was a young woman with unwrinkled skin, a flat stomach, and dimple-free thighs, but I thought that's all I had going for me. I had boyfriends who weren't going to turn into husbands, a job I hated but didn't know how to get out of and still support myself, and the only power I felt was the power of having a young body. Maybe by the mere fact that the men had to look, some of their power had to be given over to me.

Do I have regrets? Sometimes, yes. It would be nice to have my smooth skin back, but more than that I could use the hours. This is my tenth year as a single parent, I decided rather late in life that I wanted to do some writing, and I have to earn a living, so what I always need is time. Even if I wanted to, there aren't any hours left in my day to give over to lying in the sun, to waiting for something to happen. I've also come to realize that I don't have hours to waste fussing over my wrinkles when it's likely there will be many more to come.

And yet, I'm not saying it's easy. I live in a university town where the average age of the residents is about twenty, and I sometimes have a false sense that the world is entirely made up of youth. Even when I know how many aging baby boomers there are now, it's still hard to be around all those young people, particularly the young women who still have their line-free skin and their cellulite-free thighs, the women who are looked at when I've become invisible. They're gorgeous. They have long, thick hair and in the summer they wear denim miniskirts the same size as the bags they sling over their shoulders. If they want to, they can flaunt their youth.

They've also had the advantage of the Women's Movement so if they choose to, they can be engineers, forest rangers, or dentists. At the same time, I see that some things haven't changed at all. On the first sunny spring day where the temperature rises above 60 degrees, I see these young women at the park or in the side yards of their sorority houses, lying in rows on their blankets like hot dogs lined up on a grill. They lie for hours like this, thinking they have nothing else to do, and many times I've had the urge to walk up to a row of them and nudge them all at the shoulders and say, "You're wasting time! And look what happens while you're wasting time? You get wrinkles. See! So quit waiting around. Get off your blanket and make your life happen." And then for an encore I'd slide my shirt a bit off my shoulder and show them the scar where the skin cancer was.

But I never do it. I know they'd just look at me as though I were their mother (which I could very easily be), and then, as soon as I left, they'd roll their eyes at each other and wonder how I could ever dream of leaving my house looking like that.

judith   ortiz   cofer

the story of
my body

Migration is the story of my body.

—VICTOR HERNANDEZ CRUZ

1. SKIN

I was born a white girl in Puerto Rico, but became a
brown girl when I came to live in the United States. My
Puerto Rican relatives called me tall; at the American
school, some of my rougher classmates called me "skinny-
bones" and "the shrimp," because I was the smallest member
of my classes all through grammar school until high school,
when the midget Gladys was given the honorary post of
front-row center for class pictures and scorekeeper, bench
warmer in P.E. I reached my full stature of five feet even in
sixth grade.

I started out life as a pretty baby and learned to be a
pretty girl from a pretty mother. Then at ten years of age I
suffered one of the worst cases of chicken pox I have ever
heard of. My entire body, including the inside of my ears
and in between my toes, was covered with pustules that, in a
fit of panic at my appearance, I scratched off of my face,
leaving permanent scars. A cruel school nurse told me I

would always have them—tiny cuts that looked as if a mad cat had plunged its claws deep into my skin. I grew my hair long and hid behind it for the first years of my adolescence. This was when I learned to be invisible.

2. COLOR

In the animal world it indicates danger: The most color-ful creatures are often the most poisonous. Color is also a way to attract and seduce a mate. In the human world color triggers many more complex and often deadly reactions. As a Puerto Rican girl born of "white" parents, I spent the first years of my life hearing people refer to me as *blanca*, white. My mother insisted that I protect myself from the intense island sun because I was more prone to sunburn than some of my darker, *triqeno* playmates. People were always com-menting within my hearing about how my black hair con-trasted so nicely with my "pale" skin. I did not think of the color of my skin consciously, except when I heard the adults talking about complexion. It seems to me that the subject is much more common in the conversation of mixed-race peo-ples than in mainstream U.S. society, where it is a touchy and sometimes even embarrassing topic to discuss, except in a political context. In Puerto Rico I heard many conversa-tions about skin color. A pregnant woman could say "I hope my baby doesn't turn out *prieto* (slang for dark or black) like my husband's grandmother, although she was a good-look-ing *negra* in her time." I am a combination of both, being olive-skinned—lighter than my mother yet darker than my fair-skinned father. In America, I am a person of color, obvi-ously a Latina. On the island I have been called everything from a *paloma blanca*, after the song (by a black suitor), to *la gringa*.

My first experience of color prejudice occurred in a supermarket in Paterson, New Jersey. It was Christmastime and I was eight or nine years old. There was a display of toys in the store where I went two or three times a day to buy things for my mother who never made lists but sent for milk, cigarettes, a can of this or that, as she remembered from hour to hour. I enjoyed being trusted with money and walking half a city block to the new, modern grocery store. It was owned by three good-looking Italian brothers. I liked the younger one with the crew-cut blond hair. The two older ones watched me and the other Puerto Rican kids as if they thought we were going to steal something. The oldest one would sometimes even try to hurry me with my purchases, although part of my pleasure in these expeditions came from looking at everything in the well-stocked aisles. I was also teaching myself to read English by sounding out the labels in packages: L&M cigarettes, Borden's homogenized milk, Red Devil potted ham, Nestlé's chocolate mix, Quaker oats, and Bustelo coffee, Wonder bread, Colgate toothpaste, Ivory soap, and Goya (makers of products used in Puerto Rican dishes) everything—these are some of the brand names that taught me nouns. Several times this man had come up to me wearing his bloodstained butcher's apron and, towering over me, had asked in a harsh voice whether there was something he could help me find. On the way out I would glance at the younger brother who ran one of the registers and he would often smile and wink at me.

It was the mean brother who first referred to me as

"colored." It was a few days before Christmas and my parents had already told my brother and me that since we were
in *los estados* now, we would get our presents on December
twenty-fifth instead of *Los Reyes, Three Kings Day*, when
gifts are exchanged in Puerto Rico. We were to give them a
wish list that they would take to Santa Claus, who apparently lived in the Macy's store downtown—at least that's
where we had caught a glimpse of him when we went shopping. Since my parents were timid about entering the fancy
store, we did not approach the huge man in the red suit. I
was not interested in sitting on a stranger's lap anyway. But I
did covet Susie, the talking schoolteacher doll that was displayed in the center aisle of the Italian brothers' supermarket. She talked when you pulled a string on her back. Susie
had a limited repertoire of three sentences: I think she could
say: "Hello, I'm Susie Schoolteacher; two plus two is four,"
and one other thing I cannot remember. The day the older
brother chased me away, I was reaching to touch Susie's
blond curls. I had been told many times, as most children
have, not to touch anything in a store that I was not buying.
But I had been looking at Susie for weeks. In my mind, she
was my doll. After all, I had put her on my Christmas wish
list. The moment is frozen in my mind as if there were a
photograph of it on file. It was not a turning point, a disaster, or an earthshaking revelation. It was simply the first
time I considered—if naively—the meaning of skin color in
human relations.

I reached to touch Susie's hair. It seems to me that I had
to get on tiptoe since the toys were stacked on a table and
she sat like a princess on top of the fancy box she came in.

Then I heard the booming "Hey, kid, what do you think you're doing!" spoken very loudly from the meat counter. I felt caught although I knew I was not doing anything criminal. I remember not looking at the man, but standing there feeling humiliated because I knew everyone in the store must have heard him yell at me. I felt him approach and when I knew he was behind me, I turned around to face the bloody butcher's apron. His large chest was at my eye level. He blocked my way. I started to run out of the place, but even as I reached the door I heard him shout after me: "Don't come in here unless you gonna buy something. You PR kids put your dirty hands on stuff. You always look dirty. But maybe dirty brown is your natural color." I heard him laugh and someone else too in the back. Outside in the sunlight I looked at my hands. My nails needed a little cleaning as they always did since I liked to paint with watercolors, but I took a bath every night. I thought the man was dirtier than I was in his stained apron. He was also always sweaty—it showed in big yellow circles under his shirt sleeves. I sat on the front steps of the apartment building where we lived and looked closely at my hands, which showed the only skin I could see, since it was bitter cold and I was wearing my quilted play coat, dungarees, and a knitted navy cap of my father's. I was not pink like my friend Charlene and her sister Kathy who had blue eyes and light-brown hair. My skin is the color of the coffee my grandmother made, which was half milk, *leche con café* rather than *café con leche*. My mother is the opposite mix. She has a lot of café in her color. I could not understand how my skin looked like dirt to the supermarket man.

I went in and washed my hands thoroughly with soap and hot water, and, borrowing my mother's nail file, I cleaned the crusted watercolors from underneath my nails. I was pleased with the results. My skin was the same color as before, but I knew I was clean. Clean enough to run my fingers through Susie's fine gold hair when she came home to me.

3. SIZE

My mother is barely four feet eleven inches in height, which is average for women in her family. When I grew to five feet by age twelve, she was amazed and began to use the word tall to describe me, as in: "Since you are tall, this dress will look good on you." As with the color of my skin, I didn't consciously think about my height or size until other people made an issue of it. It is around the preadolescent years that in America the games children play for fun become fierce competitions where everyone is out to "prove" they are better than others. It was in the playground and sports fields that my size-related problems began. No matter how familiar the story is, every child who is the last chosen for a team knows the torment of waiting to be called up. At the Paterson, New Jersey, public schools that I attended, the volleyball or softball game was the metaphor for the battlefield of life to the inner city kids—the black kids vs. the Puerto Rican kids, the whites vs. the blacks vs. the Puerto Rican kids; and I was 4F, skinny, short, bespectacled, and apparently impervious to the blood thirst that drove many of my classmates to play ball as if their lives depended on it. Perhaps they did. I would rather be reading a book than sweating, grunting, and running the risk of pain and injury. I simply did not see the point in competitive sports. My main form of exercise then was walking to the library, many city blocks away from my barrio.

Still, I wanted to be wanted. I wanted to be chosen for the teams. Physical education was compulsory, a class where you were actually given a grade. On my mainly all-A report card, the C for compassion I always received from the P.E. teachers shamed me the same as a bad grade in a real class. Invariably, my father would say: "How can you make a low grade *for playing games?*" He did not understand. Even if I had managed to make a hit (it never happened), or get the ball over that ridiculously high net, I already had a reputation as a "shrimp," a hopeless nonathlete. It was an area where the girls who didn't like me for one reason or another —mainly because I did better than they on academic subjects—could lord it over me; the playing field was the place where even the smallest girl could make me feel powerless and inferior. I instinctively understood the politics even then; how the *not* choosing me until the teacher forced one of the team captains to call my name was a coup of sorts— there you little show-off, tomorrow you can beat us in spelling and geography, but this afternoon you are the loser. Or perhaps those were only my own bitter thoughts as I sat or stood in the sidelines while the big girls were grabbed like fish and I, the little brown tadpole, was ignored until Teacher looked over in my general direction and shouted, "Call Ortiz," or worse, "Somebody's *got* to take her."

No wonder I read Wonder Woman comics and had Legion of Super Heroes daydreams. Although I wanted to think of myself as "intellectual," my body was demanding that I notice it. I saw the little swelling around my once-flat nipples; the fine hairs growing in secret places; but my knees were still bigger than my thighs and I always wore long or half-sleeve blouses to hide my bony upper arms. I wanted flesh on my bones—a thick layer of it. I saw a new product advertised on TV. Wate-On. They showed skinny men and women before and after taking the stuff, and it was a transformation like the 97-pound weakling turned into Charles Atlas ads that I saw on the back cover of my comic books. The Wate-On was very expensive. I tried to explain my need for it in Spanish to my mother, but it didn't translate very well, even to my ears—and she said with a tone of finality, eat more of my good food and you'll get fat—anybody can get fat. Right. Except me. I was going to have to join a circus someday as "Skinny Bones," the woman without flesh.

Wonder Woman was stacked. She had a cleavage framed by the spread wings of a golden eagle and a muscular body that has become fashionable with women only recently. But since I wanted a body that would serve me in P.E., hers was my ideal. The breasts were an indulgence I allowed myself. Perhaps the daydreams of bigger girls were more glamorous, since our ambitions are filtered through our needs, but I wanted first a powerful body. I daydreamed of leaping up above the gray landscape of the city to where the sky was clear and blue, and in anger and self-pity I fantasized about scooping my enemies up by their hair from the playing fields and dumping them on a barren asteroid. I would put the P.E. teachers each on their own rock in space too where they would be the loneliest people in the universe since I knew they had no "inner resources," no imagination, and in outer space, there would be no air for them to fill their deflated volleyballs with. In my mind all P.E. teachers have blended into one large spiky-haired woman with a whistle on a string around her neck and a volleyball under one arm. My Wonder Woman fantasies of revenge were a source of comfort to me in my early career as a shrimp.

I was saved from more years of P.E. torment by the fact that in my sophomore year of high school I transferred to a school where the midget, Gladys, was the focal point of interest for the people who must rank according to size. Because her height was considered a handicap, there was an unspoken rule about mentioning size around Gladys, but of course there was no need to say anything. Gladys knew her place: front-row center in class photographs. I gladly moved to the left or to the right of her, as far as I could without leaving the picture completely.

4. LOOKS

Many photographs were taken of me as a baby by my mother to send to my father who was stationed overseas during the first two years of my life. With the army in Panama when I was born, he later joined the navy and traveled often on tours of duty. I was a healthy, pretty baby. Recently I read that people are drawn to big-eyed round-faced creatures, like puppies, kittens, and certain other mammals and marsupials, koalas for example, and, of course, infants. I was all eyes, since my head and body, even as I grew older, remained thin and small-boned. As a young child I got a lot of attention from my relatives and many other people we met in our barrio. My mother's beauty may have had something to do with how much attention we got from strangers in stores and on the street. I can imagine it. In the pictures I have seen of us together, she is a stunning young woman by Latino standards: long, curly black hair and round curves in a compact frame. From her I learned how to move, smile, and talk like an attractive woman. I remember going into a bodega for our groceries and being given candy by the proprietor as a reward for being *bonita,* pretty.

I can see in the photographs and I also remember that I was dressed in the pretty clothes, the stiff, frilly dresses, with layers of crinolines underneath, the glossy patent leather shoes, and, on special occasions, the skull-hugging little hats and the white gloves that were popular in the late fifties and early sixties. My mother was proud of my looks, although I was a bit too thin. She could dress me up like a doll and take me by the hand to visit relatives, or go to the Spanish mass at the Catholic church, and show me off. How was I to know that she and the others who called me pretty were representatives of an aesthetic that would not apply when I went out into the mainstream world of school?

In my Paterson, New Jersey, public schools there were still quite a few white children, although the demographics of the city were changing rapidly. The original waves of Italian and Irish immigrants, silk-mill workers and laborers in the cloth industries, had been "assimilated." Their children were now the middle-class parents of my peers. Many of them moved their children to the Catholic schools that proliferated enough to have leagues of basketball teams. The names I recall hearing still ring in my ears: Don Bosco High

vs. St. Mary's High, St. Joseph's vs. St. John's. Later I too
would be transferred to the safer environment of a Catholic
school. But I started school at Public School Number 11. I
came there from Puerto Rico, thinking myself a pretty girl,
and found that the hierarchy for popularity was as follows:
pretty white girl, pretty Jewish girl, pretty Puerto Rican girl,
pretty black girl. Drop the last two categories; teachers were
too busy to have more than one favorite per class, and it was
simply understood that if there was a big part in the school
play, or any competition where the main qualification was
"presentability" (such as escorting a school visitor to or from
the principal's office), the classroom's public address speaker
would be requesting the pretty and/or nice-looking white
boy or girl. By the time I was in the sixth grade, I was
sometimes called by the principal to represent my class because I dressed neatly (I knew this from a progress report
sent to my mother, which I translated for her), and because
all the "presentable" white girls had moved to the Catholic
schools (I later surmised this part). But I was still not one of
the popular girls with the boys. I remember one incident
where I stepped out into the playground in my baggy gym
shorts and one Puerto Rican boy said to the other: "What
do you think?" The other one answered: "Her face is okay,
but look at the toothpick legs." The next best thing to a
compliment I got was when my favorite male teacher, while
handing out the class pictures, commented that with my
long neck and delicate features I resembled the movie star
Audrey Hepburn. But the Puerto Rican boys had learned to
respond to a fuller figure: long necks and a perfect little nose
were not what they looked for in a girl. That is when I
decided I was a "brain." I did not settle into the role easily. I

was nearly devastated by what the chicken-pox episode had done to my self-image. But I looked into the mirror less often after I was told that I would always have scars on my face, and I hid behind my long black hair and my books.

After the problems at the public school got to the point where even nonconfrontational little me got beaten up several times, my parents enrolled me at St. Joseph's High School. I was then a minority of one among the Italian and Irish kids. But I found several good friends there—other girls who took their studies seriously. We did our homework together and talked about the Jackies. The Jackies were two popular girls, one blonde and the other red-haired, who had women's bodies. Their curves showed even in the blue jumper uniforms with straps that we all wore. The blond Jackie would often let one of the straps fall off her shoulder, and although she, like all of us, wore a white blouse underneath, all the boys stared at her arm. My friends and I talked about this and practiced letting our straps fall off our shoulders. But it wasn't the same without breasts or hips.

My final two and a half years of high school were spent in Augusta, Georgia, where my parents moved our family in search of a more peaceful environment. There we became part of a little community of our army-connected relatives and friends. School was yet another matter. I was enrolled in a huge school of nearly two thousand students that had just that year been forced to integrate. There were two black girls and there was me. I did extremely well academically. As to my social life, it was, for the most part, uneventful—yet it is in my memory blighted by one incident. In my junior year, I became wildly infatuated with a pretty white boy. I'll call him Ted. Oh, he was pretty: yellow hair that fell over his forehead, a smile to die for, and he was a great dancer. I watched him at Teen Town, the youth center at the base where all the military brats gathered on Saturday nights. My father had retired from the military and we had all our base privileges—one other reason we had moved to Augusta. Ted looked like an angel to me. I worked on him for a year before he asked me out. This meant maneuvering to be within the periphery of his vision at every possible occasion. I took the long way to my classes in school just to pass by his locker, I went to football games that I detested, and I danced (I too was a good dancer) in front of him at Teen Town—this took some fancy footwork since it involved subtly moving my partner toward the right spot on the dance floor. When Ted finally approached me, "A Million to One" was playing on the jukebox, and when he took me into his arms, the odds suddenly turned in my favor. He asked me to go to a school dance the following Saturday. I said yes, breathlessly, I said yes but there were obstacles to surmount at home. My father did not allow me to date casually. I was allowed to go to major events like a prom or a concert with a boy who had been properly screened. There was such a boy in my life, a neighbor who wanted to be a Baptist missionary and was practicing his anthropological skills on my family. If I was desperate to go somewhere and needed a date, I'd resort to Gary. This is the type of religious nut that Gary was: When the school bus did not show up one day, he put his hands over his face and prayed to Christ to get us a way to get to school. Within ten minutes a mother in a station wagon on her way to town stopped to ask why we weren't in school. Gary informed her that the Lord had sent her just in time to get us there for roll call. He assumed that I was impressed. Gary was even good-looking in a bland sort of way, but he kissed me with his lips tightly pressed together. I think Gary probably ended up marrying a native woman from wherever he may have gone to preach the Gospel according to Paul. She probably believes that all white men pray to God for transportation and kiss with their mouths closed. But it was Ted's mouth, his whole beautiful self that concerned me in those days. I knew my father would say no to our date, but I planned to run away from home if necessary. I told my mother how important this date was. I cajoled and pleaded with her from Sunday to Wednesday. She listened to my arguments, and must have heard the note of desperation in my voice. She said very gently to me: "You better be ready for disappointment." I did not ask what she meant. I did not want her fears for me to taint my happiness. I asked her to tell my father about my date. Thursday at breakfast my father looked at me across the table with his eyebrows together. My mother looked at him with her mouth set in a straight line. I looked down at my bowl of cereal. Nobody said anything. Friday I tried on every dress in my closet. Ted would be picking me up at six on Saturday: dinner and then the sock hop at school. Friday night I was in my room doing my nails or something else in preparation for Saturday (I know I groomed myself nonstop all week) when the telephone rang. I ran to get it. It was Ted. His voice sounded funny when he said my name, so funny that I felt compelled to ask: "Is something wrong?" Ted blurted it all out without a preamble. His father had asked who he was going out with. Ted had told him my name. "Ortiz? That's Spanish, isn't it?" the father had asked.

Ted had told him yes, then shown him my picture in the yearbook. Ted's father had shaken his head. No. Ted would not be taking me out. Ted's father had known Puerto Ricans in the army. He had lived in New York City while studying architecture and had seen how the *spics* lived. Like rats. Ted repeated his father's words to me as if I should understand *his predicament* when I heard why he was breaking our date. I don't remember what I said before hanging up. I do recall the darkness of my room that sleepless night, and the heaviness of my blanket in which I wrapped myself like a shroud. And I remember my parents' respect for my pain and their gentleness toward me that weekend. My mother did not say "I warned you," and I was grateful for her understanding silence.

In college, I suddenly became an "exotic" woman to the men who had survived the popularity wars in high school, who were now practicing to be worldly: They had to act liberal in their politics, in their lifestyles, and in the women they went out with. I dated heavily for a while, then married young. I had discovered that I needed stability more than social life. I had brains for sure, and some talent in writing. These facts were a constant in my life. My skin color, my size, and my appearance were variables—things that were judged according to my current self-image, the aesthetic values of the times, the places I was in, and the people I met. My studies, later my writing, the respect of people who saw me as an individual person they cared about, these were the criteria for my sense of self-worth that I would concentrate on in my adult life.

margaret atwood is the author of more than twenty books, including poetry, fiction, and nonfiction. Her most recent books are *The Handmaid's Tale*, *Cat's Eye*, and *The Robber Bride*.

rosemary bray is the author of the forthcoming *Unafraid of the Dark*, a political memoir.

janet burroway is a novelist, poet, and playwright. Her novels include *The Buzzards*, a Pulitzer Prize nominee, *Raw Silk*, and *Cutting Stone*. She is the MacKenzie Professor of English Literature and Writing at Florida State University.

judith ortiz cofer is a poet, novelist, and essayist, the author of *The Latin Deli*, *Silent Dancing*, and *The Line of the Sun*. She is a professor of literature and writing at the University of Georgia.

patricia foster won the 1993 PEN/Jerard Fund Award and the 1993 Mary Roberts Rinehart Award for nonfiction. She is the editor of a forthcoming anthology, *The Sister Plot*. She teaches in the M.F.A. program at Goddard College.

lucy grealy is the author of a forthcoming memoir.

doris grumbach is a novelist and memoirist. Her most recent novels include *The Magician's Girl* and *Chamber Music*. *Extra Innings* is a sequel to her memoir, *Coming into the End Zone*.

kathryn harrison is a novelist whose books include *Thicker Than Water* and *Exposure*.

linda hogan is a novelist, poet, and essayist. Her most recent works are *Mean Spirit* and *Savings*.

judith hooper, the author of *The Three Pound Universe*, is writing a book about breast cancer.

pam houston is the author of *Cowboys Are My Weakness*. She is currently at work on a novel.

nancy mairs is an essayist and poet. Her most recent books include *Ordinary Time* and *Carnal Acts*.

connie porter is a novelist and author of children's books. Her most recent novel is *All-Bright Court*.

hanan al-shaykh is a novelist. Her most recent novels include *Women of Sand and Myrrh* and *Zahra*.

jenefer shute, a Boston writer, is the author of *Life-Size*.

p a t r i c i a   s t e v e n s, a Michener Fellow and Nelson Algren Award winner, is currently at work on a novel.

l y n n e   t a e t z s c h is a writer and painter who teaches at George Washington University. She's currently at work on a book of essays.

s a l l i e   t i s d a l e is a contributing editor to *Harper's*. She is the author of *Stepping Westward* and the forthcoming *Talk Dirty to Me*.

j o y c e   w i n e r has published fiction in various literary magazines. The mother of a young son, she is currently at work on a book, *A Conditional Woman: A Meditation on Infertility*.

n a o m i   w o l f, the author of *The Beauty Myth*, is completing a book on female desire.